Catching the Ebb

Catching the Ebb

Drift-fishing for a Life in Cook Inlet

BERT BENDER

Drawings by Tony Angell

OREGON STATE UNIVERSITY PRESS
Corvallis

Library of Congress Cataloging-in-Publication Data
Bender, Bert.
  Catching the ebb : drift-fishing for a life in Cook Inlet / Bert Bender ;
illustrations by Tony Angell.
       p. cm.
  ISBN-13: 978-0-87071-296-8 (alk. paper)
  1. Gillnetting--Alaska--Cook Inlet--Anecdotes. 2. Bender, Bert. I.
Title.
  SH344.6.G5B46 2008
  639.209164'34--dc22

                            2008020947

Oregon State University Press
121 The Valley Library
Corvallis OR 97331-4501
541-737-3166 • fax 541-737-3170
http://oregonstate.edu/dept/press

For Todd and Judith

and all the Benders and Strouds

Contents

List of Drawings by Tony Angell

Acknowledgments

Thanks to the many fellow fishermen I had the pleasure of working with and learning from in my years on Cook Inlet. First among them are my former partner, Dick Gunlogson, my two deck hands, John Chalmers and Mike Chalmers, and the several friends to whom my narrative refers by their first names only—true sea-brothers, I feel. I am equally grateful to a number of fellow voyagers into the world of books—Roger Murray, Glen Love, Ron Carlson, Haskell Springer, Lee Werth, Robert Cockcroft, Robert Foulke, and Elizabeth Schultz. Thanks also to the late Lee Makovich and his son, Nick Makovich, for their help in tracking down *Anna A*; to Andrew Wellner for his helpful research in the files of the *Kodiak Daily Mirror*; to Bill Sullivan for his help in verifying names and other data pertaining to the chapter, "The Cannery"; to Barbara Sweetland Smith for helping to sharpen my sense of the early Russian presence in Cook Inlet; to Mark Willette, research biologist for the Alaska Department of Fish and Game, for his thoughts on the future of Cook Inlet sockeye; and to Philip Tennant and Jim Reid of Doublemono Limited, for permission to use the lines quoted here from The Waterboys' song "Fisherman's Blues." Further thanks to my three former colleagues at Arizona State University, Professors Lidia Haberman, Pier Baldini, and Timothy Wong, for their help with foreign languages; to my nephew and one-time deck hand, Ted Bender, for the charts printed here; to the *Alaska Fisherman's Journal*, where my chapter "Sign of Wind" first appeared; and to Mary Braun, Jo Alexander, and Tom Booth of Oregon State University Press for helping bring my project to light.

Finally, two people deserve more thanks than I can convey in words: Tony Angell, friend of over fifty years and collaborator on my three previous books, for the memorable drawings that grace this volume; and especially Judith Darknall, my wife and untiring companion in our lives' adventure, for her brilliant editorial suggestions and support in this and earlier projects.

Part I: The Life and the Waters

Chigmit Mountains
Redoubt Volcano
Iliamna Volcano
Chisik Island
Kalgin Island
Kenai
Kenai River
Kasilof River
Anc
Pt Possession
Turnagain Arm

COOK INLET

Ninilchik
Anchor Point
Homer
Kachemak Bay
Seldovia
Kenai Peninsula
Sewar
Resurrection Bay

153°
150°

MAP BY TED BENDER, 'ISHMAEL' DECK HAND 1991

SCALE
25 MILES

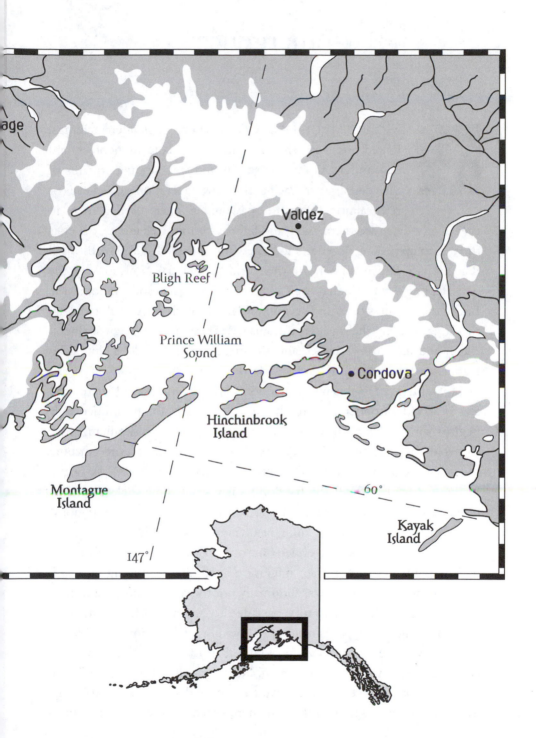

Emergence

 A TREMBLE OF LIFE. Constellations of slender inchlings, limpid and light-shy, astir in their cradle of pebbles and dark water. Along lake shores and surrounding streams of the coastal north Pacific, this new generation of sockeye (or red) salmon. After the spawning mothers nestled them in their redds, defended them, died, and fell back into the elements, the eggs thrived on up-welling water and took new form. Lopsided alevin absorbed the yolk sacs suspended beneath them and became fry. Now, in May, the delicate, bug-eyed wrigglers are still heavier than water and cannot swim. But in the darkness of night they migrate up through the gravel, twisting, thrusting, beating their way to the surface. They sip in the new element. Again and again they surface and sip in the air. Each fills a tiny swim bladder and then—buoyant at last—darts ahead.

Biologists refer to this phenomenon as "the emergence." I share their awe of it and I wonder at its reach. Newly emerged, the fry immediately begin their long voracious quest to eat and grow and, simultaneously, to avoid the multitude of predators that await them at every turning in their improbable careers. The spring zooplankton bloom has begun in the nursery lakes, but the fry don't eat just anything. Selecting their prey, they catch and feast on their first copepods, while dodging rainbow trout, other fish, and many kinds of diving birds. The lucky ones grow within the nursery lake for either one or two years. Then, again in the dark of night, they begin their migration as smolts, swimming en masse downstream, along the banks, and finally out to sea. Awaiting them there and throughout their migratory passages across the north Pacific is an ever-changing variety of smaller fish—young cod, shrimp, squid—on which they will feed, as well as untold numbers of larger fish, diving birds, and mammals keyed to feed on them. Near the end of their ocean life, in either two or three years, their drive to hunt and eat is displaced by the irresistible urge to spawn. But even then, especially then, other hunters

Emergence

gather to intercept them. Seals and sea lions and whales await them in the coastal waterways, and if they survive that long, brown bear, wolves, and glaucous-winged gulls snatch them from the shallow streams. Also awaiting them, but more terribly, are human beings. Well adapted over our many thousands of years to join in this bloody feast, fishermen like myself have devised countless ways to hunt and catch them on their way. My own device was the gill net, deployed from a drift boat in Cook Inlet as the gleaming schools returned, leaping toward their passionate end. I am amazed by my great fortune to have been drawn into their sphere and swept along in this current of life for thirty years.

Yes, the gill net is a brutal device, though in the coastal salmon fishery of North America it poses no threat to other species. And, yes, the thought of any commercial fishing in the twenty-first century arouses our fears for the endangered seas. But, thanks to the marine biologists and management programs that have existed for many years in Alaska, the wild sockeye has not been and will probably not be driven to extinction by the commercial fishery. Most fishermen know quite well that we must be restrained. We accept the necessary regulation, even as we often curse Fish and Game. And, yes, the rapid advances in fishing technology in recent decades—from the more and more powerful engines to more deadly nets and more sophisticated electronics—all these have removed us from the simpler and more rewarding fishing life of the past. But it is still a great life. Any fisherman will tell you that you never feel more alive than when you're "out there." On the water we feel the throb of life and take our place in the ecological web, including the ways we compete and cooperate with each other.

The emergence, and the ensuing stream of life: everything the salmon feed upon as fry, smolts, and adults, and everything that feeds upon them. What great fortune to be a diving bird in the nursery lake, a sea lion, an orca, a bear in the spawning stream, or a fisherman offshore. The sockeye's track: from the nursery lake out into the wild ocean and across the latitudes, back into the coastal waterways, into the spawning beds, and beyond— even into the trees. Because they are fertilized by well-fed bears, trees near streams with spawning salmon are more robust than those located elsewhere. And from the trees, where then? Perhaps into the wider web of life and the atmosphere we breathe.

The Thing

FISHING IS A BLOODY BUSINESS. Yet nothing I know is more exciting than to see bunches of fish hit your net, the more the better. Swimming near the surface, salmon hit the wall of net that hangs from the cork line, each driving its head into a single mesh that slips behind the gills. In their momentum and alarm they leap out of the water on the other side of the net in explosive bursts of white spray. Seeing a single hit on a slow day will bring you to life. You and your deck hand leap to your feet shouting, "Yeah! There! Good hit out by the buoy!" Sometimes you'll see several hits at once, and if this happens just when you're setting the net, the shot of adrenaline might make you throttle up. You're on the fish! And you want to get the net in front of them before they swim by. If you're really lucky the net will "light up all along the line," and you know you might get five hundred or a thousand in a single drift. Your deck hand whistles and jumps up and down on the deck. If the fish keep coming, you know there might be *too many*, and you make quick calculations about what to do. Better start reeling it in right away. It'll take a long time to get it aboard—maybe two or three hours. Or you think, No, leave it in the water. You gotta get 'em when you can. Just let go of the net and run the boat along the cork line from end to end. Clip on some big buoys that might keep it afloat. You *love* seeing all these hits but you don't want to sink your net, see the cork line begin to dip below the surface and then go straight down with more fish than you can pull back to the surface. You might have to cut off your net and let it all go.

If a fish is big and lucky it might hit the net hard enough to break a mesh and keep on going. More likely, it struggles and splashes three or four times, but you have it by the gills and it finally lies gasping in the water or simply drowns. When you bring in the net to pick the fish, some are still alive and fall free from the net only to flop around on the deck until they die or until you send them down the chute into the hold.

Others are still alive and struggling in the web. You grab them one at a time, holding the head with one hand and with the other ripping the tangled mesh back over the gills until the fish pops free and falls to the deck. Blood runs from the mangled gills. It gasps and quivers for a moment longer and then lies still.

Picking a big set for all you're worth, keeping your eye on the rest of the net to see if it's balling up or being sucked into a rip, you can't keep up with the fish. Before you stop picking for long enough to pitch them into the hold, you might be wading in them up to the middle of your calves, stepping on them and trying to keep your footing. It's a bloody mess. You have to rip off a lower jaw to get a fish free, or sometimes worse. And if this goes on and on for a few hours you might try to find relief in some kind of grim humor. Once, when my deck hand John and I had been picking a heavy set for a couple of hours, I noticed one or two fish eyes washing around on the deck between our feet. A common sight. John was pressing on as hard as he could, trying to pick a fish that was tangled in the web. "John," I said, "keep an eye on the deck." He looked down, maybe thinking a scupper was plugged, then got it and said "Shit!"

Sometimes in an effort to confront and deal with their part in this murderous business, fishermen refer to themselves as "fish-killers." A hard-bitten, "yeah, I know it's a fucking bloody mess, but I'm good at it and I like it." I've thought about why it took me so long to see all those beautiful, dying fish as anything more than a good catch, a better payday. I had washed off lots of gurry and knew damned well that I was running a kind of slaughterhouse. But I just couldn't think about their agonizing deaths—strangling and bleeding in the cutting web until they drowned. It wasn't until my friend Mike once imitated a strangling fish that I began to realize it. He grasped at his throat, made a playful, pop-eyed grimace, and choked. As a child I had witnessed and withdrawn from this part of the primal scene. Once, at about age five, I was leaning over the railing on our front porch and was shocked to see a cat ripping the guts out of a mouse. But then, not many years after that, I was living with my grandpa and grandma and they gave me a Daisy BB gun. Grandpa was a hunter, and he also had a birdhouse for a wonderful family of martins that returned on the same day each spring. I was a hunter, too, and I took great pride

Ravens and Prey

and pleasure in shooting birds that competed with the martins—mainly sparrows but definitely not any of the "song birds" that Grandpa loved. He was pleased and proud when I "got one," and he taught me to put a notch on the stock of my BB gun for every one that I killed. I can't forget all those notches.

It's too easy to think of this force in us as just a male trait. Some of the deadliest gill-netters I know are women, like Snooks or Frankie, and I'll never forget how my grandma killed the chickens that she plucked and fried for Sunday dinner. She'd take one by the head and give it a powerful twisting throw, as though pitching a fastball in an underarm motion, until the body flew off kicking and spouting blood. That scene is etched in my memory, but so are the fried-chicken dinners. Farmers are also inured to this work, of course, but most of us prefer to have someone else kill the meat we eat, if we eat meat, and to pick it up from the supermarket. A nice chop all cleanly wrapped in plastic with as little blood showing as possible, and certainly no hair or feathers. And we're quite good at covering it all with a religious veil of some kind. You know, fish isn't really meat, or we ritualize the slaughter—kosher or halal. One time when I was visiting Mt. Athos, Greece, during Lent, most of the monasteries offered only bread and olives, perhaps with a little rice or halvah. But one served up a delicious octopus stew, and when my brother and I asked, quite appreciatively, why we could enjoy this dish during Lent, a monk told us that octopus had no blood and was neither meat nor fish.

I am drawn to writers who are troubled by this thing, our need to kill and eat. Most of the great writers won't touch it. Benjamin Franklin felt the rub and explains in his autobiography how he dealt with it. He had once been "a great Lover of Fish" especially when it "came hot out of the Frying Pan" and "smelt admirably well," but then recoiled from all the blood and resolved to eat no "animal Food." He persisted as a vegetarian until the day he was becalmed on a sailing vessel out of Boston. When the sailors began fishing for cod, Franklin took offense and considered "the taking of every Fish as a kind of unprovok'd Murder." Then, noticing that each of the butchered fish had eaten smaller fish, he thought, "if you eat one another, I don't see why we mayn't eat you." He dined "very heartily" and quips in telling the story that it is "so convenient a thing . . . to be a *reasonable Creature.*"

After the Age of Reason, the new geology and the thought of Nature's being "red in tooth and claw" shook Lord Tennyson's faith. And Herman Melville, bloodied by his work as a whaler, was even more troubled by what he called the sharkishness of life. Yet, like his character Ishmael, he accepted it as part of his unknowable God. Thinking of sharks, sperm whales, and man, Ishmael asks, "who is not a cannibal?" and he embraces his friend, the cannibal Queequeg. Even though Ishmael is taken aback by seeing the character Stubb feast on a whale steak, he directs his moral outrage at the "enlightened gormand, who nailest geese to the ground and feastest on their bloated livers." Queequeg, too, accepts the bloody reality, remarking only that "de god wat made shark must be one dam Ingin." But Ahab will destroy himself by defying this awful God. Just when he seems ready to relent in his pursuit of the white whale, Ahab looks toward the "smiling sky" and cries out, "Look! see yon Albicore! Who put it into him to chase and fang that flying-fish?" During these same years, Thoreau admitted to having "a strange thrill of savage delight" at Walden Pond when he thought of killing and eating a woodchuck raw. But he could resist the impulse by thinking it "a reproach that man is a carnivorous animal," and by consoling himself with his belief in spiritual evolution: "embryo man" will pass "through the hunter stage."

After Darwin noted how the human's canine teeth are "perfectly efficient instruments for mastication," writers began to pay more attention to them. You might sneer at the idea that we are descended from apes, Darwin wrote, but he who does so unconsciously reveals his true descent, retracting "his 'snarling muscles' so as to expose" his canines "ready for action, like a dog prepared to fight." In his poem "The Thing," Theodore Roethke sees a flock of birds chase, kill, and eat a smaller, helpless one. Then, turning to consider the delicacies so nicely arranged on his own picnic plate, he feels his stomach turn. I admire Steinbeck's starker realism in *The Log from the Sea of Cortez*, where he challenges our "dread" in thinking of "our species as a species" and affirms his own part in the "life water," where "everything ate everything else with a furious exuberance."

He wants not only to study and classify the Mexican Sierra, but also to "see the fish alive and swimming, feel it plunge against the lines. Drag it threshing over the rail, and even finally eat it."

But I most appreciate Hemingway's life-long and more troubled determination to examine our place in the war of nature, as Darwin called it. He makes us watch closely as Nick baits his hook with a grasshopper in "Big Two-Hearted River": "Nick took him by the head and held him while he threaded the slim hook under his chin, down through his thorax and into the last segments of his abdomen. The grasshopper took hold of the hook with his front feet, spitting tobacco juice on it." In *The Old Man and the Sea* Hemingway tells how Santiago must force himself to eat his "brother" fish: "Perhaps I should not have been a fisherman, he thought. But that was the thing I was born for. I must surely remember to eat the tuna after it gets light." He commands himself, "Eat the Bonito now." And he consoles himself by recalling that the "*dentuso* [the shark] lives on the fish as you do" and that "everything kills everything else in some way." Thinking that "the punishment of hunger . . . is everything," Santiago reflects the sensitivity that few readers detect beneath Hemingway's hard-boiled exterior. And Hemingway won't let us off the hook. In *True at First Light* he writes that "those who never catch fish . . . who will stop their cars if there are locusts on the road, and have never eaten even meat broth should not condemn those who kill to eat. . . . Who knows what the carrot feels, or the small young radish?"

The best way to deal with this troubling reality as a fisherman is simply not to think about it, a tactic employed by many Hemingway characters through drink, though with little success. Still, I appreciate both the fishermen and the writers who can*not* not think about it, and who, at the same time, catch lots of fish. Maybe the best we can do—and I think this is what Hemingway was coming to—is to emulate the Native American's esteem for the excellent hunter-fisherman and, simultaneously, his reverence for the life he takes. This, while acknowledging that the vital drive to hunt, kill, and eat is alive in each of us. It is an undeniable element in whatever we can do now to accept our place in the ecological web of life and take responsibility for helping to shape a sustainable economy. There is some virtue, I think, in admitting our own role in "Nature red in tooth and claw," without imagining, as Tennyson and Thoreau did, that the human spirit lies outside of nature; and in accepting Darwin's lead as the founder of ecological thought.

I'm sure I wouldn't have fished for thirty seasons if it weren't for the thrill you feel in the hunt. We probably all experience something like this excitement in any number of ways—bird watching, "hunting" with a camera, hunting for bargains, or even tracking down a bit of information in academic research. Humanity is rooted in our history of hunting and gathering. But I know of nothing like the feelings you have in the hunt for salmon. Keyed up, you scan the surface of the water, looking for a jumper, for a streak in the water that might be the edge of a forming rip, for birds feeding on the surface. Any sign of life. You do this for hours. And when you see a sign in the distance or hear a call on the radio from someone who is on the fish, you make the run, sometimes a very long run, in a state of excitement that would alarm someone who'd just come along for the ride. You're a little wild. You might snap an order to your deckhand, or someone might get in your way as you hurry from the wheel in the house to the wheel on the bridge. You're not exactly the calm, gentle person you would like to be. And you get even more excited as you set your net and begin to see hits. When you've finally picked the net on such a day, after fighting for hours to bring the fish aboard, get them out of the net and into the hold, you're splattered with gurry and fish scales. Your back and shoulders ache and your hands are swollen from tearing at the web, but you've got a fine load and you know what the gill-netter was talking about in Peter Matthiessen's *Men's Lives*. "It's a great life if you don't weaken, ain't that right?"

Even in this wild state, and during the peak of the run, when you see fish jumping all around the boat, and glimpse bunches of them speeding ahead through the waves, you are awed by this great pulse of ocean life. You feel blessed or just fortunate to be part of it, to be caught up in it and swept along. You might want to thank something or just give an inward howl or some kind of song, as the bird does after catching and eating the flying insect. You put your net in the water and partake. It's immediate. You don't have to seek permission or try to sell yourself or your fish. Someone will want your fish. They are clean, fresh, beautiful, delicious.

You don't have to screw someone else to get what you deserve, and you "deserve" the fish you get because you went after them and got lucky. They came out of the ocean. And especially if you sell them to a cash buyer on the grounds, the money is good. Hemingway got a taste of this in the 1930s when he was fishing out of Havana. In "On the Blue Water" he described the thrill he got from catching a big marlin and then selling it at the market: he wrote that his pay, "a long roll of heavy silver dollars wrapped in newspaper . . . is very satisfactory money. It really feels like money."

Still, even though it's good to be alive and to take an active part in the bloody reality, you sometimes wince if you're caught off guard and get a glimpse of the way it is. Once, walking along the waterfront in Seldovia, I was delighted to see some ravens dancing in the air. There they were, just across the road at the edge of some black spruce, flapping playfully and dipping in the air. Drawn to the scene, I crossed the road for a closer look and then saw the fledgling bird that was trying to escape, fluttering toward safety till the ravens struck. It was only the old story of life feeding on life, but it gave me pause. These teeth and talons, these beaks and claws. Before that I had glimpsed something of my own red work through the eyes of my son. During his first short summer on the boat he had great fun helping to pitch the squirming fish into the hold. But one day a year or two later, when we were picking a heavy set and wading in the bloody mess before we could get them into the hold, he was sickened by the gore. He has never since eaten fish. I understand.

At some point about halfway through my career, it helped me deal with my role in it all by throwing back the first and last live fish I caught each season. Was I only trying to chalk up some good karma? Was I paying tribute to the life force? It made me feel better. And I once experienced a sense of my intermingled identity with the fish. This wasn't something like the distaste Henry Adams felt at the end of the nineteenth century in recognizing his identity as a vertebrate descended from the ganoid fish. I felt intimately related to a tiny black fish that swam with me in the Gulf of California. I had swum out and then noticed this little fish, not more than an inch long, swimming right next to me. Of course it didn't know me or love me but it wanted to swim close to me. It probably found some advantage in staying close to me, as a pilot fish does with the shark. It wasn't frightened of me, and I wasn't frightened of it, the way I would have been if it were a jellyfish. If I swam away, it stayed close to me. I didn't want to go ashore, and sometimes, swimming away and losing sight of it for a moment, I felt a small sense of loss. Then, seeing it swim near my body again, I greeted it with a sense of joy. "There you are, little fellow. I thought you were gone. I was a little lonely." I would have retched to think of harming or eating my little companion.

What? A fisherman so tender-hearted about a tiny fish, and then going all wild-eyed to see hits in his net? I'm afraid so, and these conflicted feelings are different from those we feel in contemplating our threat to the species we hunt. It helps to know that good management has kept the Cook Inlet sockeye from being endangered. But if they were endangered I could take no pleasure in catching and then releasing them. Although I understand and encourage my good friends' passion for catch-and-release trout fishing, I'd rather not hook the endangered ones at all. Yet I can live with the thought of catch and *eat*. I subscribe to Wolf Larsen's philosophy that "life is a mess"; "the big eat the little that they may continue to move." This view of life evokes grim laughter when you contemplate your own place in the violent order, as Jack London's Martin Eden does before he drowns himself. When "a bonita struck at his white body . . . he laughed aloud. It had taken a piece out, and the sting of it reminded him of why he was there." Are we here only to take our turns in perpetuating the mess of life? Maybe so, but it's exhilarating to be alive and take part in it all. "It's a great life if you don't weaken."

After a good hard day on the Inlet he was glad to head for the harbor. He turned the boat toward the river and chose a fish to clean. It didn't matter which kind. A nice silver, or even a dog or humpy would be fine, but he selected a red. Its beautiful blue-green back showed that it was fresh in from the ocean. Opening it, he lifted out the firm lobes of white milt, tossed them to the hovering gulls, then ran his finger along the backbone to flush the black kidneys free. He rinsed the red fillets and set them aside. Back in the cabin, he popped some potatoes into the oven and sat down at the wheel. When the potatoes were almost done, he squeezed some lemon juice onto the fish and slid it into the oven. There was still a long run ahead, but the aroma from the oven soon helped keep him on course. The white fat now bubbled through, and he smiled when the backbone pulled easily away. Settling in at the helm with one hand on the wheel and the other balancing the plate on his knee, he partook of the amazing red life.

Back in the harbor the next day, he rested, cleaned up the boat and wrapped the cut on his right thumb with a fresh band-aid. Picking fish the day before, he'd caught it in the web. Now friends from other boats were gathered to bake a couple of fish over an open fire on the beach. They drank, laughed, and told stories of how it had been. As soon as the white fat oozed to the surface and you could pull the backbone free, he took a juicy piece and ate it, licking his fingers and thumb. A little blood had seeped through the band-aid. He reached for another piece of the delicate red flesh. He put it into his mouth and again licked his fingers and thumb, lovingly.

Cook Inlet

WHEN CAPTAIN COOK EXPLORED Cook Inlet in 1778 his party interacted with Dena'ina Athabaskan people whose ancestors had lived there for five hundred to a thousand years. Before the Dena'ina arrived, Eskimos known as the Kachemak people had occupied the area. Although Russians would not settle in the area until they arrived at Seldovia in 1885, Cook found that the Dena'ina possessed a few Russian items (probably obtained through contact with the Alutiq people of Kodiak). He did not learn the Dena'ina name for the Inlet, "Tikahtnu" (big water), nor did he name it himself. He referred to it only as an "inlet" or "river." The Englishman Lord Sandwich named it Cook's River, and at about the time it was becoming known to most of the European world as Cook Inlet, the earliest Russians were calling it "Kenaskaya" (Kenai Bay). Big Water is best. Tikahtnu.

Although I won't credit Cook with discovering the Inlet, I revere him, so much that I made my way to the British Library in March of 2003 in order to hold and read the journal of his third voyage to the Pacific Ocean. Actually, I read closely only the entries for the eleven days from May 26, 1778, when his ships *Resolution* and *Discovery* entered the Inlet, to June 8, when they left it, on their way west and then north to Bristol Bay and the Bering Sea. I knew that Cook wrote the journal entries for those dates some months after he had left the Inlet, and wished that a holograph log had survived. I also knew that I'd find little more here than I'd already seen in J. C. Beaglehole's *The Journals of Captain James Cook on his Voyages of Discovery*. But, having spent over thirty summers gill-netting for salmon on Cook Inlet, and knowing well many of the places and phenomena that he noted, I wanted to touch this volume written in his own hand. Besides, the university where I then taught was helping pay the bill: my compensation for teaching several extra classes was a small research fund that I was finally permitted to spend in this way. I didn't tell the university that it also supported my visit to Parliament Square for an anti-war rally (two days later the USA launched operation "Shock and Awe" in Iraq), and another to Westminister Abbey, where I paid my respects to certain figures in Poet's Corner and stood before Darwin's tomb.

The light went on at my assigned space in the Manuscripts Reading Room, indicating that Cook's journal was waiting for me at the desk. There it was, all leather-bound and aged and I was free to take it to my desk! And as the Journal is relatively recent by the British Library's standards—only about 225 years old—I was not required to wear gloves in examining it. Still, I handled it as though it might fall apart in my hands, admiring Cook's clear script. Imagine him at work in his quarters aboard *Resolution*, penning this somewhere in the Pacific Ocean. Cautiously I turned the pages toward the entries for late May of 1778. There, in the entry dated "TUESDAY 26*th*," Cook noted that they were north of the Barren Islands. To the Northwest he had sighted and named Mt. St. Augustine (a conical volcanic island in lower Cook Inlet) and noted that "in a NNE direction the sight was unlimited by everything but the horizon." Also on that day he concluded from observing the mountains to his west and north (the Chigmit Mountains) that this was "part of a great Continent" and that "we should find no [Northwest] passage by this inlet." Yet he resolved to persevere toward the open horizon in the northeast, "more to satisfy other people than to confirm my own opinion." He tacked to the east, briefly entering Port Chatham on the tip of the Kenai Peninsula, and then moved back toward the center of the Inlet. He wanted to sail north, but he began to experience the Inlet's navigational delights. Finding "the wind at North [to be] a very strong gale with rain and thick hazey weather," he tacked to the west.

The wind abated by the next morning and he was soon able to take advantage of the prevailing southerly winds that took him past the entrance to Kachemak Bay (which he did not see) to the vicinity of Anchor Point. There, on the morning of the 28th he lost his southerly breeze and, "observing the Ship to drive to the Southward, in order to stop her dropped a Kedge anchor with an 8 inch hawser bent to it." In this first serious encounter with the Inlet's tides, *Resolution's* crew were bringing the ship ahead on the kedge when the hawser broke near the ship end. This was a significant loss, and they spent most of the day trying to retrieve the valuable hawser and anchor. Cook's log contains "a touch of irritation" for this date. They had put out two boats "to creep for the kedge" and had hooked it on the first try, but, as Cook wrote, they "lost or spit it before it was got up to the boat and no one in the boats thought of letting go a grapling to mark, so that it never could be hooked again." This is the first recorded incident of a captain in a bit of a sweat while contending with the Inlet's hazards, voicing his exasperation with the crew. And it appears that Cook's subsequent bouts with the Inlet's powerful tides over the next several days underscored the great value of the lost anchor. On his way out of the Inlet on June 5th, he returned to Anchor Point in a futile final effort to retrieve it. Even with today's precise navigational equipment, it would be quite a trick to fish for a lost anchor in those waters, and no one would try it except at dead slack tide. We don't know the stage of the tide when Cook attempted it, but I can imagine them arguing about just where to make their drag—a few miles off shore in a wide, amorphous stretch of water with no prominent landmarks to guide them. I love knowing that the anchor is still there.

Cook noted that in this area "there was a strong tide seting to the Southward out of the Inlet, it was the Ebb, & ran between three and four knots an hour." From this point on up the Inlet his method was to anchor during the ebb and then drive up with the flood, even when light winds opposed them. Further up the Inlet he recorded tides running five knots, noted outside the mouth of Turnagain Arm (so named because they had turned again in their search for the Northwest Passage) that the "Water fell upon a perpendicular, while we lay at anchor 20 feet," and on leaving the Inlet he wrote that "the Tide . . . is considerable in this River and contributes very much to facilitate the navigation thereof" (the *South-East Alaska Pilot* indicates tides of up to 8 knots at certain places in the Inlet). Cook also noted while in the area of Anchor Point that "there was a good deal of Sea Weed and some drift wood driving out with the tide," and further up the Inlet he described "very thick and Muddy water, large trees and all manner of dirt and rubbish floating up and down with the tide." This is as close as he comes to describing the rip tides that run more or less up and down the Inlet, drawing in driftwood and other debris in great swaths. The rips also draw in schools of salmon that have lured many a gill-netter into costly entanglements with debris and other gill nets. You can be drifting at the edge of the rip and suddenly find your net being sucked into the churning center before you can get it aboard. The largest of these rips is known to gill-netters as the middle rip, which separates a branch of the cold Alaska Coastal Current that sweeps in from the Gulf of Alaska and up the eastern half of the Inlet from another stream of water that flows down the west side of the Inlet. This latter, western, stream is formed of warmer, fresh water that flows into the northern Inlet.

When Cook made his way above the Kenai River (which he does not mention), he saw what Beaglehole calls an "Alaskan Hellespont," the East and West Forelands. Here the points "contracted the Channel to the breadth of four leagues, through which ran a prodigious tide: it looked frightfull to us who could not till wheather the agitation of the Water was occasioned by the strength of the stream or the breaking of the waves against rocks or sands." Here, too, salmon are often funneled by the currents late in July, bringing gill-netters into proximity with other navigational hazards that were not present in Cook's day—the several off-shore oil-drilling platforms that begin just north of the Forelands. Sweeping on a big flood toward one of these high monsters with too much of your net out might be as frightful as the white water that Cook described. And when Cook approached this same area again, on his way out of the Inlet, he experienced another of the Inlet's hazards—one of the many sandbars that are exposed only at low water. Making his way down the Inlet on the ebb, he drove *Resolution* aground on what seems to have been Middle Ground Shoal. And here again we can imagine Cook's exasperation, with his ship "stuck fast" in waters where "prodigous" tides, "frightfull" breakers, and high winds could easily bring his third voyage to the Pacific Ocean to a crashing end. In his journal entry, snugly recorded some days or weeks later, Cook again expresses a captain's exasperation in such crises: "by the inattention and neglect of the Man at the lead, the Ship struck and stuck fast on a bank that lies nearly in the Middle of the River." Luckily for both the captain and the man at the lead, this must have happened close to slack water and in calm weather. Then, like many a fortunate gill-netter over the last century, Cook experienced great relief when "the flood tide made" and "the Ship floated off without receiving the least damage or giving us the least trouble."

On way up the Inlet, Cook weighed samples of water in order to test its salinity, noting how it freshened on the ebbs. Still, he sent parties further ahead into both Knik and Turnagain Arms to confirm his belief that the Inlet gave no Northwest Passage to the Atlantic. Finally, he sent an armed party ashore at Point Possession, near the entrance to Turnagain Arm, with directions "to display the flag, take possession of the Country and River in his Majesty's name and to bury in the ground a bottle containing two pieces of English coin (dated 1772) and a paper on which was inscribed the Ships names date, etc."

The landing party, led by Lieutenant James King, was greeted by another group of Natives (they had encountered several others along the way) who were at first alarmed to see the armed English, but eventually approached with offerings of an animal skin and some fresh salmon. The English hoisted the flag and drank a toast of "good English Porter," even sharing the drink with three of the Indians who "were fond of the liquor," as the surprised King wrote in his journal. The Indians accepted the empty bottles, but were frightened off when the English began to search the area for specimen plants and such. When the English returned from their brief search, the Indians approached again and traded two of their dogs for a pair of belt buckles. One dog got away and the other bit its new owner. The man immediately shot the dog through the head, in part to impress the Indians with the power of the English weaponry. You shouldn't injure the Indians themselves, King wrote, but rather take "away the life of some Animal; for they are so very little inclin'd to reason upon effect, that simply showing them the force of your ball by fyring at any inanimate thing makes but little impression." The Indians ran away in fear and the English returned to their ships with the dead dog. As another member of the party (Lieutenant Edward Riou) wrote, some of the Indians' dogs were "fat and Young," and the one in question "was shot Immediately thro' the Head, willing to mangle the more Useless part, as they were intended to be eat." Captain Charles Clerke wrote that the Indians "had abundance of Dogs, of the Fox-nose Species, some of which our Lords bought to regale upon, as a fresh Meal, and a very good one it is."

Making their way up and down the Inlet, Cook and his men observed other phenomena that are familiar to gill-netters today. At anchor about six miles off the eastern shore in the vicinity of Clam Gulch and looking to the northwest he saw "some low land that we judged to be an island lying under the western Shore." Trying then to make his way up the Inlet he again encountered "a very strong gale at NNE nearly right down the Inlet" and therefore "stretched over to the Western shore" hoping to find a sheltered anchorage below the island. Countless modern gill-netters have hoped for the same kind of shelter either at the south or north ends of Kalgin Island. The north end provides good protection from southerly winds, but there is little relief from any winds at the south end. Many have approached the south end of Kalgin Island and turned away as Cook did when he found that *Resolution* was "falling suddenly into 12 fathom water from upwards of 40 and seeing the appearance of a Shoal ahead spitting out from the low land." And when Cook returned to this area as they worked their way back down the Inlet on June 3rd, always anchoring on the flood and riding the ebb, the sky cleared for the first time since they had entered the Inlet. He caught sight of Mt. Redoubt and perhaps the more southerly Mt. Iliamna. Cook's description of the smoking Redoubt still holds true: "the Volcano is on [the north] side of the hill next the River and not far from the Summit; it is not considerable emitting a white smoke but no fire which made some think it was no more than a white thick cloud. . . . But this besides being too small for one of those clouds, remained as it were fixed in the same spot for the whole time the Mountain was clear." In more recent and spectacular eruptions Redoubt and other volcanoes in this range (St. Augustine and Mt. Spurr) have spewed huge clouds of abrasive ash, causing jetliners to steer clear and gill-netters to pack extra filters for their engines.

My favorite entry in Cook's journal is for June 3rd, when they were headed back down the Inlet, in the vicinity of Drift River, between the West Foreland and the north end of Kalgin Island. Recording that "a good many of the Indians attended upon us all the Morning," Cook wrote he found their company "very exceptable, as they brought with them a large quantity of very fine Salmon which they exchanged for such trifles as we had to give them: the most of it was Split ready for drying." Very fine salmon, indeed—king salmon, perhaps, from a run that still peaks in early June. Or perhaps Cook was treated to some sockeye, with their distinctive deep red flesh, from the early run into the Kenai River. Of course the Indians knew the value of these fish, but Cook's remark impresses me. He was quite familiar with the Atlantic salmon that abounded in English waters and recognized excellent fish when he saw it. I wonder what he'd think of the so-called Atlantic salmon that flood the world market today—the farm-raised fish concocted of growth stimulants, heavy doses of antibiotics, and food dyes in order to catch the naive consumer's eye for economy and color. I imagine Cook tasting the mushy flesh, spitting it out in disgust, and demanding another of the Indians' fine dogs instead.

Of course Cook didn't make his way to Cook Inlet just to enjoy its excellent salmon. But less than a hundred years later Joshua Slocum did. He sailed all the way from Australia to Cook Inlet, where he made good on a venture to catch and salt a load of sockeye for his market in San Francisco. This was one of Slocum's most memorable adventures before he made history by sailing alone around the world aboard his sloop *Spray* between 1895 and 1898. Slocum is justly admired for that feat, and for his earlier years as a sea captain during the last years of sail. But he is rarely credited for having been one of the most enterprising fishermen of the late nineteenth century. He grew up in Nova Scotia, where his father owned a brig and engaged in the salted-cod trade to Haiti. The young Slocum went to sea as a merchant seaman and soon rounded Cape Horn as a mate on British sailing vessels. He temporarily left the merchant marine for the more adventurous and independent life as a drift gill-netter for salmon. He made his way to Astoria, at the mouth of the Columbia River, where he designed and built his own boat—a lovely and efficient twenty-five-foot double-ended vessel that became the standard gill-netter in the early Columbia River fishery and was later modified as the slightly larger sailing vessel that was used in the Bristol Bay salmon fishery. After putting in a successful season on the Columbia, he logged further experience on sailing vessels, shipping lumber and grain in the Pacific Northwest before taking command of the bark *Washington* at age twenty-seven. His first voyage on *Washington* was from San Francisco to Sydney.

From Sydney he sailed on to Cook Inlet, building a number of small gill-netters on the crossing and arriving at the mouth of the Kasilof River in the late spring of 1871. The first American to enter Cook Inlet after the Seward Purchase, Slocum anchored *Washington* at Cape Kasilof, set up a saltry, and then drew on his experience on the Columbia River to establish the first commercial gill-net fishery on Cook Inlet. But before he could load the salted sockeye and sail for his market in San Francisco, the bark dragged anchor and was driven ashore. Like Cook, it seems, Slocum encountered one of the Inlet's northerly winds, from which Cape Kasilof provides no protection. But he responded to this disaster by crafting a "canoe" like the one he would later use to survive a similar predicament in1888, after losing another vessel, the bark *Aquidneck,* in Paranagua Bay, Brazil. This time he sailed down the Inlet to Kodiak, where he chartered a Russian vessel and returned to Kasilof for his cargo. After all that he still turned an impressive profit for *Washington*'s owners by sailing his catch back to San Francisco. In what was apparently his final fishing venture, around 1875, Slocum acquired the schooner *Pato* in Manila. From there he sailed to the Sea of Okhotsk, caught and salted a load of cod, and ran it on to his market in Portland, Oregon.

When Slocum set up his gill-netting and salting operation at the Kasilof River in 1871, there was already a small salmon saltry in operation on the Kenai River, and others soon followed on both the rivers. In 1882 the Alaska Packing Company of San Francisco opened the first salmon cannery on Cook Inlet, at Kasilof, and the Northern Packing Company opened the first cannery on the Kenai River in 1888. By this time the large canning companies had done away with the drift boats and won legislation permitting them to own and license fish traps, which remained in general use for many years. Only after GIs returning from World War Two began a revival of the setnet and driftnet fisheries, despite opposition from the cannery owners, and after Alaska became a state in 1959, were fish traps banned. By the late 1970s the canning industry lost its economic basis, giving way to freezer operations that capitalized on the lucrative market for fresh-frozen salmon in Japan. But that, too, yielded to economic pressure from the farm-raised salmon industry. In 1998 the production of farm-raised salmon around the world surpassed that of wild salmon, and in

Margaret's Grave

the fall of that year Columbia Wards Fisheries (by then called Wards Cove) closed the old plant that had operated on the Kenai for over eighty years. Still there, the old saltry-cannery-freezer plant now operates in the tourist industry as a lodge with shops and a restaurant.

At many places around the mouths of the Kenai and the Kasilof rivers, as well as at the village of Ninilchik and the ports at Homer and Seldovia, you can find remnants of the early canneries: rusted fragments of antiquated machinery, half-rotted pilings, a partly collapsed retort in which canned salmon was cooked. Along the highway from Kenai to Homer an occasional old drift boat collapses into a mud flat, fireweed poking up through its broken planks, while others with sagging keels remain propped up with rusted-out fuel drums. Some of these brave little vessels were so crudely built that you wonder how seaworthy they could have been. Yet many have outlasted their once-proud owners, some whose scattered ashes lie subsumed in the Inlet's glacial silt. Related to these relics are Captain Cook's lost kedge somewhere off Anchor Point and the still-disintegrating remnants of Joshua Slocum's *Washington* around Cape Kasilof. And just inside the mouth of the Kasilof lie the buried remains of my first boat, *Margaret*. Lost in the late 1970s to the economic storm of an ever more competitive fishery, she was abandoned there by her last owner. Over a period of three or four years I watched as she settled into the sand and finally disappeared—but not before I visited her one last time. After snapping a photo of her with Mt. Redoubt towering in the distance, I somewhat guiltily took fragments from her planks and ribs. I sent one to my old partner, Dick, and one has its place here on my desk. Although these relics still retain their faint scent of old-growth Port Orford cedar, they'll soon lose their shape in Dick's memory and mine. But *Margaret* has long since become a more durable part of the Inlet world.

The Wake

AS I TRY TO ACCOUNT for how I got here, how I became the sort of person who would venture into both commercial fishing and academia, and how I came to write this book, I imagine being on the boat. It's flat calm with no land in sight. I'm on the flying bridge and look over my shoulder. The wake churns violently right behind the boat, soon settles, meanders, then diminishes into a faint and invisible track.

Looking back, I always see my grandpa on my mother's side, Grandpa Stroud. He was Charles Stroud, born in 1880 somewhere in southern Missouri or Oklahoma to a Cherokee woman from what he called "the Indian nation," and a man of Scottish and English descent. In an old photograph he stands with a crew of loggers next to a wagon loaded with huge logs. Grandpa is a tall young man with high cheekbones and he leans against the wagon. By the time he married my grandma, he had become a railroad man. I remember him from his last years as a conductor on the little Frisco railroad line (the Saint Louis and San Francisco Railroad). He and the family lived in the little town of Chaffee, Missouri, which was perfectly situated for his run from Memphis to Saint Louis. An imposing figure in his conductor's uniform at six feet and two hundred pounds, he would stand by the train, take the watch from his vest pocket, and command, "All aboard!" When he signaled the engineer the steam engine would puff, the wheels would shudder and jerk with a screech of steel grinding on steel, and the train would pull steadily ahead. Grandpa would put his watch back into his vest pocket, walk and then begin to jog alongside the moving train, catch hold of a handle, and swing aboard. I would wave and stand in awe as Grandpa's train disappeared down the track. When I accompanied him on short runs, Grandpa took me forward to meet the engineer, and I walked with him through the passenger cars as he took tickets. I bathed in the glow of his congenial authority, for the passengers and black porters all seemed to know and admire "Charlie."

As a boy I was vaguely aware of the dark side of life in this little southern town, where no black people have lived for nearly a hundred years. I heard the story that the last black person to spend a night in Chaffee was lynched. This would have been around 1910, shortly before the Strouds moved there. The Strouds were divided in the Civil War, some fighting for the South and some for the Union, and my roots there seem to implicate me in the ongoing American tragedy that resurfaces as I write this—in the Emmet Till autopsy and the new trial of the Mississippi Klansman for the murder of three civil rights workers in 1964. I know that Grandpa shared the predominant racist views of his time and place, and I am embarrassed to recall how innocently I partook in the family's traditional way of ending a meal. Grandpa would see the one remaining piece of fried chicken, a last biscuit or dab of mashed potatoes and gravy, and remark that food left on the plates would bring a cloudy day. When no one took the last bits, he'd finally say, "Well, I'll just eat it m'self, then." And turning to Grandma, he'd almost always say, "Mama, that sure was a good meal. Few white folks and no niggers at all can have a dinner like that."

I believe that Grandpa's good nature would have led him to more enlightened views. He was a wise, loving, and playful man who took me on his knee, gave me sips from his hot toddies, and held me in countless bear hugs that showed me how to breathe. He taught me how to skip, and also how to hunt. I long ago lost interest in that way of being in the outdoors, but I trace my love of the hunt in commercial fishing to what I learned from him. Although he never told me anything about the ocean or showed any interest in the watery world of the nearby Mississippi River, I did acquire a distinct early impression of the ocean world in my grandparents' kitchen. During the year when my brother and I lived with our grandparents, the four of us would gather each night around the radio in their kitchen to hear the news broadcast by Walter Winchell. We listened mainly for news of the war, because two of their sons were stationed in the Pacific with the U.S. Navy, and Winchell's staccato introduction always transported me. "Good evening, Mr. and Mrs. North and South America, and all the ships at sea. Let's go to press." All the ships at sea.

The family home was an early prefabricated house sold by Sears and Roebuck. Its dark, damp cellar made a good place to play if you could keep away from the maze of spider webs that filled the space between the low cement walls and the underfloor of the house. Shelves along the tops of those walls contained rows of mason jars full of Grandma's canned goods, and it was an adventure to retrieve a jar of peaches or green beans without touching the spider webs. The coal furnace was also down there, as was Grandma's old wringer washing machine and a makeshift shower. Standing on the wood grate as I showered, I'd keep a watch out for daddy longlegs and other spiders. Once, when a neighbor boy and I were playing in the coal bin, Grandpa came down for his shower. He was modest enough to keep his back turned. Yet we could not keep our eyes from him there in his misty shower and caught sight of his great sac, hanging far down on a ropy thread, halfway to his knees.

My grandparents' oldest son, my Uncle Bert, also figures in this story. I was named after him, and he helped draw our family to the Pacific Northwest. He and his family lived in Seattle, and when my dad's work as a welder at an oil refinery in Casper, Wyoming, came to an end in the early fifties, my uncle suggested that he might find work in Seattle's shipyards. To help us make the move, he and my aunt offered us their home for a few years, while my uncle worked as an electrician in Ketchikan and then Fairbanks. When I was looking for my first teaching job in 1962 and chanced to see an opening in Anchorage, I asked for my uncle's advice, and he nudged me in that direction.

Because we had lived in separate parts of the country while I was growing up, I never had the opportunity to share in my uncle's love of the outdoors. I never went camping or fishing with him. He was an avid hunter and killed moose, caribou, and mountain sheep during his years in Alaska. When I was preparing to drive up the Al-Can highway on my first trip to Alaska, he gave me one of his old coats and an old army rifle, a Springfield .30-06. I killed a moose with it on the Kenai Peninsula that year, packing it out with my hunting partners in two trips over a six-mile trail. We all needed the meat and divided it equally. When I began my fishing career the following summer, my partner Dick and I followed the advice of other fishermen and took the old Springfield with us aboard our little gill-netter *Margaret*: we might need a rifle to scare seals away from our net. As it turned out, we never needed it, and stepping down off the boat one day when we were unloading at the end of the season, I slipped and dropped the Springfield into the Kenai River. I worried at the time about how to tell Uncle Bert. Within a few years, though, I became so affected by the bloodshed in the Viet Nam war that I never hunted again. I now enjoy thinking of the old Springfield lying deeper and deeper beneath the Kenai's glacial silt. My uncle plays a further role in this story, for the impression he made upon me when he died in the Gulf of Alaska in 1976.

My dad also helped shape my course toward a fishing career, but not because he was an outdoorsman, certainly not because he loved the water. Although he came to love trout fishing in streams, he was nervous and uncomfortable even in a small boat on a lake. His special gift was to show me by example the dignity of hard, blue-collar work. He didn't finish high school, and during the Depression worked, when work was available, in the International Shoe factory in Cape Girardeau, Missouri. At the beginning of World War Two he learned to weld and continued in that work until he retired. He took pride in his work and was a loyal union man, though he also hated the corruption he often witnessed within the union. When we lived in Casper, Wyoming, after the war, he often had to work outdoors in terrible conditions. His work clothes would be peppered with holes burnt through by the welding sparks, and in his early years especially he suffered from flashes, burns to his eyes received when he lifted his welding hood momentarily and chanced to look at a fellow worker's weld. In the shipyards on Seattle's Lake Union he worked long hours in cold damp crawl spaces below the waterline and breathed in the thick smoke from his welds. Cleaning up at home, he would try to remove the grime by snuffing warm salt water into his nostrils.

One summer in Casper, when there was no work at the refinery, he made a deal with our landlord to paint the house for two months' rent. We were especially pinched because my mother was in the hospital undergoing serious back surgery. I was inside the house when I heard a crash and rushed outside to find him in a broken heap in the driveway. He had fallen from the ladder, dislocating his shoulders and shattering bones in an elbow and in both wrists and arms. A long but successful operation left him in casts for several months, and then he endured the humiliation of having to be fed and assisted in everything he did. My mom, brother, and I took turns in feeding him, or helping him in the bath or on the toilet. After many months of therapy he finally recovered the use of both hands and eventually resumed his work as a welder. Again he was often required to work long hours, but he was happy to get the time-and-a-half that the union contract guaranteed for overtime. Still, his wrists and arms continued to ache until he died. I was with him when he died in a nursing home at age eighty-four, though I couldn't tell if he knew I was there. His hands were blue and he struggled for hours, his chest heaving and heaving until he gave a prolonged series of slow gasps. When the nurse said that it was over at last, I noted that it was 5:30 p.m. It was just like my dad to work a little past quitting time.

My mother also worked hard, and to the end of her life felt the injustice of having been denied a chance to go to college. My grandma and grandpa sent two of her brothers to college, but in those years when American women had just recently won the right to vote, her place was thought to be in the home. Years later, what I knew of my mother's disappointment contributed greatly to my developing interest in American women writers from the late nineteenth and early twentieth centuries. But my mother's part in shaping my life stemmed mostly from her unconditional love, an incalculable force in buoying my self-confidence. She also initiated my love of music and reading, listening to opera on the radio and regularly accompanying me and my brother to the public library in Casper. Without her imagination, determination, and financial support, neither my brother nor I would have gone to college. When my mother called me and my brother to her bedside after she had decided to remove the life support that only a ventilator could provide against her terminal emphysema, her last words to us were, "Family! Family! Family!"

After my mother died in 1984 and during the last ten years of my fishing career, I missed my regular visits with her in Seattle, but still flew through there on my way to and from Alaska and my home in Phoenix. Sometimes, as the plane approached the airport in Seattle, it would fly over Bellevue and I could see the neighborhood and even the house where she had lived. Down there, in her garden, among the roses and rhododendrons, I imagined–somewhere there must be lingering traces of her life. A gray hair, perhaps, or a tattered bit of yarn from her sweater still caught on a twisted branch or thorn.

My brother Charles played a minor role in leading me toward the commercial fishery, but a crucial role in helping me find my way toward my other life as an academic. When we moved to Casper after the war, he was my main companion in developing a love of the outdoors as a sport fisherman. He once impressed me by setting off alone on a fourteen-mile hike one winter, when he needed to pass that requirement on his way to becoming an Eagle Scout. It was a cold, snowy day and he had to make the hike, build a fire, and cook himself a meal. By late in the day the snow had developed into a blizzard and my mom and dad and I drove outside of town to look for him along Garden Creek. We found him on the final leg of his hike, cold as hell, but he refused to get in the car and finished the hike on his own. He was only twelve years old at the time, but a very big brother indeed, in my eyes.

As his little brother I needed to distinguish myself from him and chose to compete in arenas other than the classroom. His academic reputation hounded me in grade school and junior high, where teachers would wonder how I could be the brother of the boy who had done so well in their classes. I found my place in athletics where I eventually did well enough to bolster my own self-confidence. As we grew older and our sibling rivalry moderated, especially when he went away on a scholarship to Harvard, I began to pick up on his example and on his suggestions for books I should read, such as *Catcher in the Rye*.

Nevertheless, when I went on to the University of Washington, I continued to identify myself mainly as an athlete and ended in graduating with the lowest possible grade average. Then making my way to basic training for ROTC infantry officers at Fort Benning, Georgia, I first entered a number of indoor track meets in the east. Having won second place in the shot put at the Milrose Games in New York, I headed on to Boston for another meet and for a week's visit with my brother at Harvard. While he attended class I worked out at the Harvard field house, and there I met another shot putter who astonished me by inviting me to attend some of his lectures. For the first time I began to understand what my brother had been suggesting to me for years, about the exciting intellectual life at

Harvard. That a fellow jock could be so turned on by classroom lectures! That the lectures *were* so stimulating! All this helped me appreciate the life my brother had made for himself. And three years later he deepened that growing appreciation immeasurably, by inviting me to accompany him and his new wife on part of their year's adventures abroad. By this time I had finished my time in the army, taught for a year at a junior high school in Anchorage, and begun my fishing career on Cook Inlet, in partnership with my friend Dick, on our boat *Margaret*. My brother had won a Sheldon fellowship, providing funds for a year's travel, and he made the most of it by plotting out visits to the most important museums and centers of antiquity. Being with him on part of his fellowship year, especially in Egypt and Greece, where we spent a week together visiting the monasteries at Mt. Athos, gave me a sense of cultural history that I had not acquired in my own college education.

That experience cemented my determination to return to college as a late-blooming English major with an eye toward graduate school. My summer earnings as a fisherman helped finance this project, but in the third year of our partnership I began to realize that I'd be better off fishing my own boat. Dick also needed to increase his earnings and so bought my half of *Margaret*. That provided the down payment for my own boat, and a low-interest loan from the National Marine Fisheries Service swung the rest. I named the boat *Sounion*, after a place I had visited with my brother, Cape Sounion, in Greece. My new boat was no longer than *Margaret*, but, unlike *Margaret*, it had a chain-driven reel for pulling in the net, which allowed me to fish it alone. Fishing it for seven years, I gained self-confidence in the fishery and financed my remaining years in graduate school. Also, when Alaska began its limited entry program in 1973, my seven years of owning and fishing *Sounion*, along with my three years as partner on *Margaret*, established a history in the fishery that entitled me to one of the new permits. Limiting the number of boats that could fish the Inlet, the new program helped keep the bourgeoning fishery from destroying itself. From then on anyone wanting to enter the fishery had to buy an existing permit from someone who wanted to sell out.

During the ensuing years the price of salmon crept up and with it the value of limited-entry permits. There were fewer vessels on the grounds, but the Alaska Department of Fish and Game had also restricted the amount of time we could fish. Thus, in order to remain competitive, fishermen began to invest in bigger and faster boats. Outdated boats like *Margaret* began to disappear, and wooden boats, in general, began to give way to more efficient vessels made of aluminum or fiberglass and powered by larger and larger gasoline and diesel engines. With these and other advances in fishing technology, the simple fishing life I'd enjoyed in the 1960s was slipping into the past. Although, like the old sailors after the advent of steam, I came to romanticize that life in retrospect, I welcomed many of the changes in the gill-net fishery. Wanting to keep up with the competition, I found a larger, more efficient aluminum boat that I named *Scrivener* (after Melville's Bartleby), and eventually built an even larger and more powerful boat, *Ishmael*. With a bigger, faster boat, and more and more sophisticated electronics, you could remain in the game. You could catch more fish, and with more power, the new comforts, and added safety, you wouldn't *want* to go back to the old days. Far from beating on like so many boats "against the current, borne back ceaselessly into the past," as Fitzgerald writes in *The Great Gatsby*, we Cook Inlet gill-netters had the throttle wide open and knew we were headed for a strange future.

When I finally completed graduate school in 1971 and began to look for a teaching position, I found that the national market for college teachers had suddenly dried up. I could arrange for only a single interview, and it for just a one-year appointment at Arizona State University. I thought it odd that the interview would be held at the Disneyland Hotel in Anaheim (in conjunction with a conference for English teachers), but I was in luck. In the introductory smalltalk before the interview, I happened to mention that the previous evening I had attended the Los Angeles *Times* indoor track meet, and the interviewer lit up. He, too, had been a track and field athlete in college, and we hit it off. A week later he offered me the job and hinted that the one-year appointment might be renewed. Of course I accepted it, but shortly after I arrived to begin work there that fall, I began to sense something like the sterility of academic life that had bothered me in graduate school.Some of my professors at UC Irvine had been unable to conceal their slight distaste in hearing that I spent my summers as a commercial fisherman.

I began to realize that the Disneyland interview had opened the way into the Disney world of higher education at Arizona State. The genial man who had interviewed and hired me was the new department chairman. He was a good old boy from Texas and had produced no substantial scholarly work of his own, yet he didn't hesitate to begin firing five other assistant professors whom he had hired along with me. We probationary assistant professors were housed three to an office and soon realized that we were competing for what might be just one permanent position. Presumably, the single criterion would be one's publications, but most of my unfortunate colleagues had exceeded the publishing records that our new chair and many of the senior faculty had established in the early years of their own careers. It was a buyer's market, though, and it was easy for the department to find new faculty anxious to fill the ranks. Although I managed to publish enough to survive those first years, another problem arose during the year when I came up for tenure. The tenure committee had long known that I left the university each summer for the grubby, blue-collar work of commercial fishing, but it now appeared that some had objected to my being away at all. Because my yearly contract was for only the nine-month academic calendar, I was free to spend my summers as I wished. But when I made this case to the senior member of the committee, while also pointing out that my summer's work had not prevented me from exceeding the requirement for publications, his response made me recall the Disneyland song and realize that the academic world can be a very small world, after all. With a characteristic whine, my senior colleague said, "Well, not that *I* feel this way, but some members of the committee don't think it's fair for you to be able to go away each summer and enjoy that added income."

I did get tenure and the fishing continued to be good. Now, though, instead of helping me survive in graduate school, my summer earnings supplemented my low salary as a junior professor and sometimes even doubled it. And I was grateful, not only for the added income that provided a more comfortable lifestyle, but for the balance the dual careers gave to my life. I found great fulfillment in reading, writing about, and being able to teach great works of literature, but the sterility of academic life and politics made my summers on the Inlet more and more appealing. Each fall I'd begin to escape by thinking of gear I needed for the next season or planning projects on the boat. If I chanced to visit Seattle or other port cities during the academic year, perhaps while attending literary conferences, I'd haunt the waterfront, breathe in the salt air, and hang out in marine-hardware stores in search of brass fittings or special tools that I couldn't do without. I could read a paper on Melville or Joshua Slocum at a conference in Toronto or San Diego and spend much of my time looking at boats or gear. And when I returned to my fishing life on Cook Inlet each summer I relished both the simpler reality of that life and my camaraderie with fellow fishermen. Even so, by the end of each fishing season, I knew that I'd have a hard time satisfying myself with the fishing life alone, especially if that meant winter fishing in Alaska. I was always quite happy to return to my life at the university. Even back in the ideal world of books, though, some things in academic life rankled. When you submitted your academic work you were subject to the deadly ambiguities of academic evaluation, but at the end of a day's fishing you could count and weigh your fish. You could calculate your pay in hard dollars. If the price of fish fluctuated with the market, that reality was easier to accept than the state legislature's regular efforts to trash the university's budget, or the dean's way of distributing funds to administrators rather than to classroom teachers. Although your fishing friends could be even more competitive than academics, the fish tickets told who had the best day, and you always knew that even your most competitive friend would cut loose from his own net and rush to help you in a crisis.

But gradual changes in the Cook Inlet wild salmon fishery ate away at the simpler life we had known in the sixties and early seventies. I joined in the rush, partly to keep abreast of the competition within the fishery, and partly in response to tax laws that pushed many of us into investing more and more in bigger and better equipment. Though I continued to enjoy the column in the *Alaska Fisherman's Journal* called "In Search of the Simple Life," I also loved the character Speedy's refrain in Peter Matthiessen's great novel about the Caribbean turtle fishery, *Far Tortuga*—"You in de

modern time, mon: sailin boat a thing of de past. . . . Modern time, mon."
So, after fishing the aluminum boat *Scrivener* for several years, I decided to
build a larger and faster one. I managed to do this by applying for a year's
sabbatical leave and by devoting the first half of that leave to producing
the academic work that I had promised to do. Then, having paid my
academic dues, I, my wife, Roberta, and our two-year-old son, Todd,
moved temporarily to Port Townsend, Washington, where I built a new
boat during the winter of 1978. Still very much inspired by *Moby-Dick*,
the subject of my sabbatical project, I named the boat *Ishmael*, shocking
my dad, a Missouri Synod Lutheran who knew Ishmael only as the biblical
"wild man" and outcast.

   We gill-netters got fat when the new Japanese market for frozen salmon
drove up the price of fish and, in the ongoing technological arms race, we
spent a lot of our money on more powerful engines, new developments in
electronic gear, or the cost of hiring spotter planes to put us on the fish.
More and more there was a premium on speed, and individual fishermen
seldom ventured far from the fleet to hunt for the fish on their own. One
cost of the more high-powered and competitive fishery that developed
over the years was that the time you spent on a set, drifting on the tide
with your net out, became more intense. Gone were the more relaxed days
when you could set out your net, turn off the engine, and drift on the tide,
quietly as though under sail. Tuned in now to radar, fishfinders, lorans,
and communication networks that kept fishermen keyed up in their search
for any sign of fish, the fleet became a more deadly force.

   Fishing communities that had centered around life at the canneries began
to disperse. With their bigger, more powerful boats, fishermen became
more independent. They no longer needed to rely on help or services from
the canneries' tenders that had formerly patrolled the grounds, receiving
fish or taking disabled gill-netters in tow. Many fishermen no longer
lived at the canneries but more or less commuted from their permanent
homes in Kenai, Soldotna, or Kasilof; or some who came up from the
lower forty-eight each summer found rooms in town. The fishing periods
themselves became more intensely competitive, and, with our faster boats
and with more complicated regulatory practices by Fish and Game, we
found fewer opportunities to go on clam-digging expeditions or gather

for beach barbecues in places like Snug Harbor. Meanwhile the population on the Kenai Peninsula grew and the canneries ceased to be remote, self-contained communities. Many of the cannery workers on the Kenai River now lived permanently in the area rather than in the cannery bunkhouses; and others who had hitch-hiked or driven up the Al-Can camped as transients in nearby woods for the few weeks' work they might be lucky enough to get during the peak of the season.

The fishing life still worked for me, though, and in 1980 I absolutely needed the fishing income when my nine-years' marriage ended in divorce. Although that marriage ended unhappily, it had produced our beautiful son. In the divorce agreement, I got to keep my fishing boat and permit while Roberta kept the other property that we had accumulated in the marriage. The fishing income helped provide child support for Todd and eventually funds for his college education. My subsequent happy marriage to Judith has now lasted more than twenty-five years. In the meantime, I built on the academic work I had done during my first sabbatical year and in 1988 published *Sea-Brothers: The Tradition of American Sea Fiction from* Moby-Dick *to the Present*. That book included a study of Darwin's influence on American sea fiction, and that led me into more extensive research on Darwin's influence on American literature, in general—work that eventually produced the first two books on this neglected subject.

During our summers in Kenai, Judith, Todd, and I lived in a trailer that we parked on the cannery grounds, right on the bank of the Kenai River. On very high tides the water came within a few feet of the trailer, from where I kept my eye on *Ishmael*, anchored in the channel a few hundred feet away. We had a ringside seat to the spectacle of passing beluga, the constant antics of seagulls and terns, bald eagles patrolling the river banks, and the traffic of fishing boats. We watched for the occasional jumpers that signaled the beginning of the run's upriver migration to the spawning grounds. And as their numbers swelled on the flood tides of late July, we watched with nervous awe, amazed by the great pulsation but also afraid that Fish and Game might wait too long to let us fish again.

On July 2, 1987, we got a glimpse of the future. Judith, Todd, my deck hand Mike, and I left Kenai at high water a little before noon, headed south and across the Inlet for Snug Harbor. As usual, we planned to fish out of Snug for one or two periods before the fish moved up the Inlet. It was a little overcast but calm, and we were enjoying the trip until we spotted a ship that was bow-down and apparently dead in the water. We changed course slightly and moved toward the ship, which was about seven and a half miles off the east side, between Kenai and Kasilof. As we approached it we began to smell and then saw oil on the water. We could see that the disabled vessel was named *Glacier Bay* and that it had launched an inflatable boat that was surveying the spill. When we pulled up to the inflatable and hailed the guy, asking if everything was OK, he yelled back, "Everything's cool. We just lost a little product." The vessel wasn't aground, but was bow down because they were transferring oil from one tank to another. When we arrived at Snug Harbor later that day we heard the first reports of the *Glacier Bay* oil spill.

That spill put a scare into the fishery but did not greatly impact our season. Fish and Game wanted to prevent any contaminated fish from making it to market and thus threatening or possibly ruining the good name of Alaskan salmon, but they curtailed our fishing for only a short time. Although some oil had drifted toward shore and fouled a number of nets, it appeared that the fish themselves would avoid the oil and arrive safely in the spawning grounds up the Kenai and Kasilof rivers. We were all lucky that time, but two years later the tanker *Exxon Valdez* ran aground on Bligh Reef in Prince William Sound. The tanker disgorged as much as two hundred thousand gallons of North Slope crude oil per minute, and early reports warned that this would be one of the worst environmental disasters in world history. Hearing about it in Arizona, when I was midway into the spring semester's academic work, I hoped that the oil would not drift out of the Sound, into the Gulf of Alaska, and around the Kenai Peninsula before finding its way up into the Cook Inlet. That's quite a distance, but that was a lot of oil.

By the time I arrived in Kenai on June 15th, there were reports of oil being found in the lower Inlet. When the season opened to set-net fishermen on the west side, the price of fish began to fall. And Fish and Game, again trying to prevent any oiled fish from reaching the market, closed the Inlet to drift fishing for the rest of the year. Confusion and depression reigned in the fishing communities, but Exxon assured fishermen that we would receive quick, preliminary compensation for our lost season. They devised a complicated formula that tracked individual fishermen's catches in recent years and soon distributed checks intended to compensate each fisherman for the number of fish that he might have caught for the season. These preliminary payments helped cover expenses and boat payments, but there was no way to compensate us for what we had lost. It was something like this. Let's say you were making your living playing music. Exxon apologizes for upsetting your work, saying, "We're sorry, and here's a nice check. Let's forget about it now, but just don't plan on making any music this year." We all needed the money and took it, but it didn't make us whole, any more than it began to remedy the ecological aftershocks that continue to this day.

Few if any salmon were killed in Cook Inlet by Exxon's spilled oil. But because the fleet didn't catch any fish at all that year, far more fish made it to the spawning grounds than normally. This was a disaster in the making. When the fry emerged the following May, there were too many for the lakes' food to sustain, and the state biologists were alarmed by their low count of outmigrrating smolts. It looked bad for the return years, three and four years ahead, and for future years that should have followed in that cycle. Prices for Cook Inlet permits and gill-netters fell precipitously. Biologists working for both the state of Alaska and Exxon predicted that Cook Inlet would have its last good run in 1992, the return year for the last fish to spawn before the spill. There would then be a series of very lean years until the runs recovered. They were right about 1992, which was a very good year, and over that fall and winter I agonized over how to protect my thirty years' investment. I finally sold *Ishmael* and my permit in the spring of 1993. As it turned out, though, the biologists had simply missed finding many of the outmigrating smolts from the return of 1989, and the returns in 1993 and 1994 were better than expected. But after the Exxon spill hammered the price of fish, the farm-raised salmon industry drove the price of wild salmon even lower, leaving the fishery in decline.

For the first time I began spending my summers in Tempe, where the Sonoran Desert heat is not so dry when the monsoon begins in July. I taught summer classes for a couple of years, needing to supplement my income in order to see Todd through college. Once in a while a fishing friend from Alaska would FedEx a fresh sockeye to help me handle being away from the Inlet, or one would tell how he'd see *Ishmael* on the grounds and still think of it as my boat. Members of my old fishing group still used *Ishmael* as a point of reference. Radioing to others in the group, an old friend would report, "I'm over here by Bert's boat and we're catching a few."

With those summers on my hands, thanks to Exxon, I was at least free to burrow into my scholarly work on Darwin. That was dry work, though, even when it led to a number of publications, and even as it focused on Darwin's vital theory of sexual selection. Exxon, the public-minded corporation that brings you Masterpiece Theater and, unwittingly, this extra dab of crude. But one summer, wanting to escape both the Arizona and the academic heat, I spent a couple of weeks on the Inlet, deck-handing for fun for a day each with three of my old friends. A few years later, in August of 2001, Judith and I leased *Ishmael* from the present owner, Tim, and vacationed like yachtspeople in Seldovia and Kachemak Bay, and in 2002 I worked as Tim's deck hand for no share, just my airfare. In those poor years, there wasn't enough money in it to hire a deck hand. I just wanted to work on the boat again. Tim has taken good care of it, and even though *Ishmael* is now nearly thirty years old, it still looks good.

The year Judith and I leased *Ishmael* for a week, I got to Homer a few days early. I wanted to visit friends and give Tim a hand cleaning away the season's fish scales. For the two nights before I was due to meet Tim at the boat, my friend John let me stay on his boat, *Buckwheat*, which was docked alongside *Ishmael* in the small boat harbor. Tim was out of town and I just hung around, waiting for him and enjoying life in the harbor. *Buckwheat*'s cabin is a little higher than *Ishmael*'s, and as I sat drinking my morning coffee or having dinner in John's galley, I could see down into *Ishmael*'s cabin. It was just like it used to be, and I was looking forward to getting aboard. Once in a while I'd glimpse someone moving around in the other cabin and think, "Ah, there he is. Tim's back." But it was just my own reflection in the two cabins' windows.

Part II: The Ebb

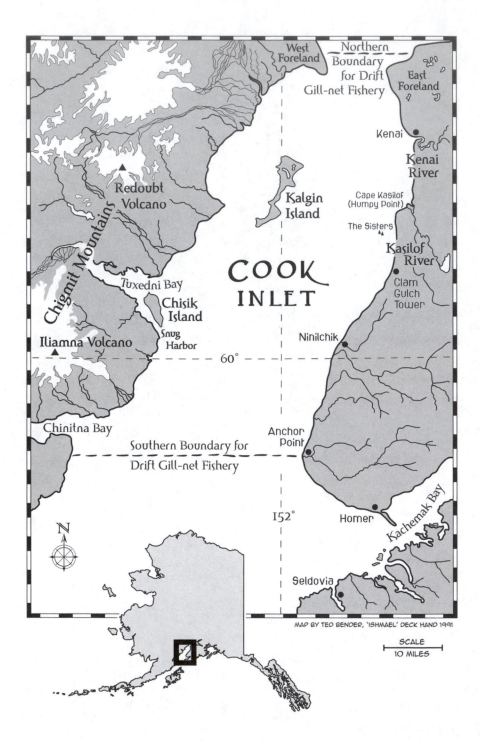

West
Foreland

Northern
Boundary
for Drift
Gill-net Fishery

East
Foreland

Kenai

Kenai
River

Redoubt
Volcano

Kalgin
Island

Cape Kasilof
(Humpy Point)

The Sisters

Chignit Mountains

Tuxedni Bay

Chisik
Island

COOK

INLET

Kasilof
River

Clam
Gulch
Tower

Iliamna Volcano

Snug
Harbor

60°

Ninilchik

Chinitna Bay

Southern Boundary for
Drift Gill-net Fishery

Anchor
Point

152°

Kachemak Bay

Homer

N

Seldovia

MAP BY TED BENDER, 'ISHMAEL' DECK HAND 1991

SCALE
10 MILES

Catching the Ebb

COOK INLET WAS CLOGGED with ice that seemed to stretch all the way across and buckle up into the Chigmit Mountains. You couldn't imagine a boat out there. Dick and I were driving along Cannery Road toward the Kenai River and the cannery called Columbia Wards Fisheries. We'd driven from Anchorage through the dark January morning that led to this crystalline day, and we had another two hours of daylight to find the boat we had come to see. Our first trip to Kenai hadn't worked out. Our friend Herb was still trying to talk us into spending the summer vacation gill-netting on the Inlet, and now he had another lead on a boat that we might want. Herb had been fishing on the Inlet for several summers and was a history teacher at Central Jr. High School in Anchorage. Dick was the band director that year (1962-63), and I was a first-year teacher of social studies and what they called language arts. Maybe twenty years older than we were, Herb was a tall, heavy, good-natured man. Judging from his gentle manner, the glasses he wore, and his slow-shuffling walk, you wouldn't think he was the adventurous type, but he must have thought that Dick and I might be. There were other younger teachers he might have approached that year to pass on his love of fishing. I think he singled us out because he knew that, as friends and potential partners in this new adventure, we might be more willing to give it a try. I certainly wouldn't have considered getting into it on my own.

Herb also knew that Dick had his own plane and wanted to be a bush pilot. Like other men on the faculty, Dick and I had hunted moose that fall. And on one of our hunting trips I had been impressed with my new friend's physical strength. As a former shot-putter, I could heft a good load and did my share of the work when we packed the butchered meat back to the frozen lake where Dick had landed on skis. But Dick rigged up a tumpline, picked up a hind quarter, fitted the strap to his forehead and walked off with a load that would have defeated a much larger man. He was about five eleven and weighed only around a hundred and seventy-five pounds, but he had burly shoulders and walked with a forward-leaning gait that reminded me of a bear. He was a formidable player under the backboards in the faculty's after-school pickup games. But if you saw him direct the school band, or the Anchorage symphony orchestra, which he did for a short time, you might not believe that this man, who had an MA in music and a passion for Brahms, could survive in the bush. He told me how he'd once made a believer of a client whom he'd flown to a remote beach on a clam-digging expedition. Dick was using those fat, low-pressure tires for that trip and his client was alarmed when they hauled their clams back to the plane and found that it had a flat tire. Dick lay down next to the tire and asked the client to lift up on the strut to take a little weight off the tire. Then, using the embouchure he'd developed as a specialist in wind instruments, he proceeded to inflate it with his own breath.

On our earlier trip to Kenai the day was even shorter and we arrived in the cold gray twilight of early afternoon. All we knew was that we were looking for a guy named Ike Johanson who had a boat for sale. Herb knew Ike as a fisherman at Columbia Wards and thought that his boat would be perfect for us. It was the same kind as Herb's, a thirty foot "conversion." Herb was in love with these seaworthy little double-enders and explained that they had been around for a long time. They had been built as sailboats for gill-netting in Bristol Bay, when only sailboats were permitted, but after the regulations changed in 1952 the graceful old double-enders were converted from sail and fitted with gasoline engines. Herb told us we couldn't go wrong with a conversion and that we might be able to find Ike at the Rainbow Bar. There were two bars in town. The Rig attracted people who worked in the oil business, at the fields northeast of town or on the offshore platforms further up the Inlet. Fishermen hung out at the Rainbow. We knew from Herb that the previous summer's run had been one of the best in years, but, drinking our beer, we saw a couple of fishermen already drinking off a tab against next season. Ike wasn't there but we heard that he'd been in earlier. We finished our beers and listened to a few raucous numbers on the jukebox, then left the dim smoky bar with directions to Ike's house.

Ike lived with his family in a cold-looking little frame house near the center of town. He was a thick man of about five foot eight with a complexion and eyes that suggested he wasn't long back from the Rainbow. I wondered if he was also drinking against next season's catch. When his wife and young son let us have the bare little living room to ourselves, Dick broke the ice. "We came by because we heard you might want to sell your boat." Ike was quiet and almost sullen, and he told us right away that he'd thought of selling his boat and getting a bigger one. It had been a good season. But they were having a hard winter and anyhow it was too late for him to find another boat. He didn't know of any other boats that we might want to look at. We thanked him and didn't stay long. He was friendly enough but we wanted to get out of the house, which didn't seem too cheerful. Only over the next few years would I see Ikey Johanson in his element, as I came to know him at the cannery. He was a dogged and damned good fisherman, one of the best of the Kenai fishermen. Ikey held his own against any of the "outside" fishermen who came up in July each year and then returned to either the Columbia River or Puget Sound, where they fished their own waters. They might have bigger, faster boats, and more experience fishing other salmon runs, but Ikey knew the Inlet and fished it both earlier and later each season than the guys from outside. After I had fished there for a good many years and he'd accepted me as another fisherman, not just a schoolteacher playing around in the summers, he shared some of his thoughts about where the fish might be next time, or where he'd found them last time. And I came to appreciate his integrity and the quiet wit that he sometimes expressed in talking while hardly moving his mouth.

Before we left Kenai that day we drove over to the old Russian Orthodox church and then a little further, to the edge of the bluff. The church seemed ghostly in the half light, and on the bluff a cold breeze from off the Inlet gave the gray expanse a sense of desolation that drove me back inside the cab of the truck. We had just enough time to drive by the big cannery on the river bank just inside the mouth. We knew it was called Daubenspeck's, and we thought we might be able to see some other boats with For Sale signs. It was easy to find, but the cannery was all shut down for the winter and we couldn't see much beyond the fence, only the big metal buildings that seemed to be on the bank of the ice-clogged river and some long rows of snow-covered boats that looked like they were all the same and made of aluminum. Leaving Kenai that afternoon on our three-hour drive through the dark back to Anchorage, I remember thinking it was a poor, gray, dismal little town, something like the windswept places I'd seen when I lived in Casper, Wyoming in the late forties, and I couldn't imagine ever coming to love it as I do.

⌁

Unlike the discouraging gray day we'd had on that first trip, this one was full of light. After Cannery Road left the Inlet and wound back into the snow-covered black spruce, we caught sight of Columbia Wards' gate and the buildings ahead. There was a line of boats in winter storage off to the left of the main buildings. The first building we came to was a little white frame house on a hill, where we were supposed to talk with the winter watchman and ask if we could take a look at a boat called *Margaret*. The owner was a preacher from Fairbanks who used his two- or three-week summer vacations to fish the peak of the run. We didn't know why he wanted to sell out, only that his boat was another conversion and that it would come with the nets. The watchman lived there with his wife and they seemed happy enough to have visitors. Hardly anyone showed up around there over the winter because it was about fifteen miles over the unpaved road to the nearest town, Soldotna. From Soldotna you could cross the only bridge over the river and drive on for another ten miles on a paved road to Kenai. Although it was a long drive to Kenai, the town and another cannery were clearly visible across the river from Columbia Wards, just a couple of miles down-stream, around a bend and beyond a big tidal flat.

We had a cup of instant coffee in their kitchen before the watchman took us down to see the boat. When we left the house he turned away from the line of boats we had seen and headed back toward the cannery. We walked by the old wooden buildings and out onto the main dock, where there were fifteen or twenty little boats blocked up and resting on their keels. "Here's where they keep the conversions," he said. "They can pick 'em out of the river with a crane and set 'em here. They'll be the first ones to go in next spring." They all looked exactly the same and were painted dark yellow, and the watchman told us that the cannery owned this little fleet of boats and leased them to fishermen for a percentage. The double-enders were about thirty feet long and nine feet wide, each with a little half-open cubbyhole cabin up forward. They were open boats with only low bulkheads that you'd have to crawl over to get from one end to the other. Each of them had a little hydraulic roller for bringing in the net over the stern. They didn't have names, only black numbers painted on the side of the cabin. In among them was one with flaking white paint and a much bigger house. There was no name painted on it, but the watchman was sure this was the one that belonged to the preacher from Fairbanks.

We didn't really know what to look for, other than to take note of the flaky paint, to tell ourselves that the little propeller looked in pretty good shape and that the bottom looked sound enough. There weren't any holes or broken planks, but some of the seams needed caulking. Since the hull was exactly like those of the company conversions, we guessed that it was just as good as they were, though it seemed that the preacher hadn't maintained it very well. The best thing about all these conversions was that you could see where the masts had been stepped, and most of them still had the old wooden rudders. The watchman found a short ladder and we climbed aboard to take a closer look and check out the boxy little cabin.

Stepping down into the boat we saw that it wasn't decked over and there wasn't even any flooring nailed across the ribs. A crude wooden box built against the back of the cabin covered the engine. A rickety door on the starboard side of the house opened to a dim little space where, just inside, the front half of the little engine sat uncovered and overgrown with rust. Between the engine and the windshield there was enough space and headroom to stand up at the wheel. The wheel caught my eye. It was a neat old wooden one with spokes, though a few of the handholds were missing. It was fitted to a corroded sprocket and chain that were coated with grease. A narrow bunk on each side footed into the crowded space just beneath the foredeck. At the head of each bunk there was enough head-and-shoulder room for a person to sit up, and in the space between there was a flimsy drop-down table. Behind the wheel, a plywood shelf was fixed to the back wall, on the port side of the engine. This seemed to be the galley, because the wall was grease-stained and the shelf looked big enough to hold a Coleman stove. Well, the cabin wasn't much, but there was definitely enough room for two people to stand up and move around between the engine and the bunks. And, crude as it was, it was much more inviting than the little open cubbyhole cabins on the company conversions. If we bought it we'd be living in here for three months or so. We knelt down to take a closer look at the engine. The preacher claimed that it was good and dependable—a little four-cylinder Willys—but I couldn't imagine how anything that rusty would turn over at all.

Behind the cabin *Margaret* was an open boat, arranged like the other conversions, except that there was no hydraulic roller to help you pull in the net, only a well-worn wooden roller. Clearly, we'd be pulling in the net by hand, but we didn't know enough about gill-netting to give it much thought. If the preacher had done it, we sure as hell could. There was a work area between the roller and a low bulkhead that separated the work space from the hold. The open hold was about eight feet long and ended in a forward bulkhead about two feet aft of the cabin. A narrow rusty gas tank was fixed to the forward side of this bulkhead, leaving less than a foot between it and the engine box.

When we climbed back down to the dock we walked to the edge and checked out the huge chunks of broken ice that jammed the river, and on our way back to the winter watchman's house we looked over toward the other boats, which sat next to each other high off the ground on double rows of big timbers. We didn't walk over to take a closer look, but now we could see how much bigger these were compared with the conversions, and most of them had good-sized cabins and big drums in the stern– power-driven reels for pulling in the net.

It was dark by the time we got into the mountains on the drive back to Anchorage. We stopped at a roadhouse near Kenai Lake that was well known for its homemade pies, and over coffee and huckleberry pie we talked it out. You couldn't really fall in love with *Margaret*. There wasn't anything about her that was beautiful. But she did look pretty much like the other conversions and to our eyes she seemed workable and well seasoned. The hull looked to be in good shape and the cabin seemed big enough for us to squeeze into for the summer. We needed to find out more about the little Willys engine, and we wanted to talk more about it all with Herb, but for now we decided that we should go for it. The price was twenty-five hundred dollars. We didn't have that kind of money, but we could put something down on it and then pay it off in May, when we could take the rest of our year's teaching salaries in lump sums. I don't know what Dick was earning that year (he already had a couple of years' teaching experience in Seward), but my salary as a first-year teacher was sixty-four hundred dollars. We shook hands on the deal, and it worked out. The preacher sold us the boat and our three-years' partnership in *Margaret* was as solid and balanced as anything I can imagine. We were already good friends, but our time together with *Margaret* cemented the friendship and changed our lives.

Over the rest of the school year Herb told us all kinds of things about fishing. We were all attention but couldn't really appreciate much of it. "Never throw out your anchor when you have your net in the water; remember, you're *drift* fishing." Or, "It can get rough out in the middle rip." And, "Slow down if you're running into big seas, otherwise you might dip into one and pitchpole." This last one stuck in my mind because he illustrated it with a pencil doing a headfirst somersault. Of course we had to wait until we got to the boat itself to figure things out, especially all his advice and information about the nets and how to handle them. Mainly we learned that the fish usually swim north or south, with or against the tide, so you want to set your net across the tide, to the east or west. To set it, all you had to do was throw out the end buoy, a watertight keg that was tied on a short line to the end of the cork line, put the boat in gear, move ahead, and let the net peel all the way out behind you. When the net was all out, you'd just turn off the engine and drift with the tide.

The school year finally dragged to a close, and by the end of May we were living in the cannery's river world, where we measured time by tides and the ever-higher sun. We needed the longer days and also the lift we got as the new owners of *Margaret*. Having taken over the preacher's rig, we were immediately accepted as new members of the cannery's little community. The cannery wanted the fish we'd sell them, and in exchange would put up the boat for the winter, sell us fuel and supplies on credit from the company store, charge us the going rate for any help we needed from their mechanics or shipwright, and provide a range of other services.

Our plan was to take a week or two to work on the boat before we launched it, and then—before the fishing season opened in the last week of June—to take a shakedown cruise that would also help pay some bills. We would run down the Inlet to Homer and then across Kachemak Bay, where we heard there were plenty of harbor seals. I know it sounds awful today, but at that time there was a three-dollar bounty on seals, and the pelts were worth two or three times as much. We were already in debt to the company store at Columbia Wards. Also, we had heard that seal liver was about the best meat you could get. As it turned out, we did find plenty of seals, enough to learn how smart they are, and we did enjoy one very tasty dinner of seal liver. But we gave up that plan and resolved to make our way as drifters. We knew we had a lot to learn about all that. Still, there was an appealing simplicity to the term "drifter"—you just put out the net and catch fish while you're drifting with the tide.

Before we launched *Margaret* early that June, we scraped and painted her, even giving her the first coat of copper bottom paint that she ever had. We wanted to treat her right, but other fishermen must have been amused to see that we didn't know how to paint the water line. We followed a plank line and didn't realize until we launched her and viewed her from a distance that we'd given her a kind of smile, with the upturning lines of red paint fore and aft. Still, this touch fit oddly with the cabin's crude lines. Comical as it might have looked, *Margaret* was now our home. We were glad to be able to get out of the weather, and took a degree of pride in our new boat. Besides, a few people around the cannery who seemed to know what they were talking about assured us that, with her pointed bow and stern, the aging *Margaret* was "a damned good sea boat."

After the crane lifted *Margaret* into the river, we spent a few days checking it out in trial runs near the cannery and then took on provisions for our two-week sealing adventure. Finally, on a clear day in early June, we were ready to pull away from the floating docks at the cannery, anxious to begin our first trip into Cook Inlet. On the advice of a wiry, white-headed old Norwegian man named Tut, we waited till just after high water at the cannery. Tut was the web boss (overseeing the work in and around the web house, where the company's nets were stored and repaired), and—already aware of how much he was revered by everyone at the cannery—we were pleased when he took enough interest in us to offer his advice: "If you're plannin' to make that eighty- or ninety-mile run down to Homer, you'll be wantin' to catch the ebb."

It was a relief to be under way and to see how fast we were moving even at low throttle. Our rusty old Willys engine put out only about forty-five horsepower, but we were making time! And the little ten-foot skiff we were towing was doing just fine. We rounded the two big bends in the river, and when we approached the mouth we could see the Chigmit Mountains stretching from north to south on the other side of the Inlet, dominated by the snow-capped volcanoes Mt. Redoubt and Mt. Iliamna. Below the mountains a low haze hung over the Inlet. A few whitecaps showed on the bar ahead, and a pod of beluga, the little white whales that are about twelve feet long, seemed to be on their way out of the river, too, humping over and spouting nearby. The whitecaps ahead seemed normal because we had seen them several times from the bluff near the old Russian Orthodox church, when we'd driven there to get the fine, breezy view of the Inlet stretching far away to the south. Neither of us had ever been on that large a body of water. In fact, our combined experience consisted mainly of Dick's several canoe trips in Canada when he was growing up in Minnesota. He knew quite a bit about navigating in places where there were no prominent landmarks and about getting around in shallow water. My only experience was one short trip on a charter sport-fishing boat for salmon in Monterey Bay.

There was a little breeze from the southwest and we began to catch some spray on the windows. Dick was at the wheel and began to use our single, hand-operated windshield wiper. It could have used a new blade. An electric wiper would have been great, but our only piece of electronic gear was an old five-watt marine-band radio. We had a compass and could measure the depth with a weighted line. The incoming swells were bigger when we got out toward the first buoy. We began to pitch and plunge into them. Dick throttled back and gave up on the windshield wiper, finding it much better to keep his hands on the wheel. Some tin cups and other things we'd stored on the narrow shelves immediately jumped the low rails and crashed to the floor. I held on to something and grabbed the stuff before anything slid toward the engine and into the open bilge, then jammed everything in place wherever I could. We stood almost shoulder to shoulder in the little cabin, Dick holding the wheel and I bracing to keep our balance. We already had a few leaks around the windshield, so I stuffed our sleeping bags into the driest place I could find, way forward in the foot of the bunks. I couldn't do anything about the mattresses; they were already damp and would be soaked before long. The engine was chugging away just inches behind us and now generated enough heat to steam up the windows. I hooked open the door to ventilate the place, and that helped disperse some of the engine noise and the smell of gasoline.

Everything seemed to be going OK, though, and before long the seas calmed a bit. Dick sped up a little, and I stood at the door, where I had fresher air and a clear view behind us. I could barely see the channel markers, and the old Russian church looked smaller on the bluff. We began to settle into it and looked forward to a smoother trip ahead. Our main worry was all the brown water that surrounded us. At the cannery the river was always muddy on the ebb, and we had seen lots of logs with big limbs rolling and drifting by the cannery dock, but we expected to find clearer water this far out in the Inlet. Dick thought we might have drifted outside the channel and over a bar, and wanted me to check the depth. He slowed way down and I grabbed our weighted line and made my way out onto the bow. We had no handrails or safety lines, but I managed to throw over the lead and was relieved when I couldn't find the bottom.

When we thought we might be four or five miles out of the river, I spelled Dick at the wheel. The buildings in Kenai still seemed close, but the next point of land south of us, Cape Kasilof or Humpy Point, was just barely coming into view. We headed outside the point, determined to clear the rocks that our chart showed just a few miles below—the Sisters. Steering out that way we found a little smoother water, so we decided to have the last of our morning coffee. It still passed for warm when Dick poured it from the Thermos bottle, but there was no place to set a cup. We just swayed with the boat's movements and managed to get most of it down.

Humpy Point began to take clearer shape to the southeast, but it didn't look like what we'd seen of the place when we drove down there to look at the mouth of the Kasilof River. About then we began to see a change in the water up ahead. Dick checked the chart and satisfied himself that we were well outside Karluk Reef, but he stood up on the engine box behind the cabin to get a higher view of whatever it was. We had heard that there were rip tides in the Inlet but didn't know that this was the East Rip. It was a long line running north and south, brown on this side and greenish on the west side. When we got closer it didn't look bad. There was a fair bit of scattered driftwood and kelp on this side, but there didn't seem to be anything on the green side. I throttled down when we came to the center of the rip, avoiding the wood, and as we passed through the churning turbulence between the muddy water and the green, we felt the boat fishtail on its own. This wouldn't be a good place to fall in. It felt good to speed up again.

Dick lengthened the line on the skiff so it rode our wake more smoothly and wouldn't take on so much water. *Margaret* itself had taken a fair amount of spray, and the bilge was sloshing around under the engine. We had been using the hand-operated bilge pump that was fixed to the wall outside the cabin, but it was slow and ineffective. So, whenever we dipped into a swell the alternator belt picked up a little water and threw some onto the engine. We didn't want any electrical problems. But it wasn't only the collecting spray. Dick noticed a lot of water seeping through the seams in the bow. That didn't look good. We didn't find out till later that *Margaret*'s planks of Port Orford cedar were still dry above the water line and would take a few days to swell tight.

By the time I took another turn at the pump it was slower than ever. We'd have to take it apart in Homer. But when I went inside to tell Dick about it, he pointed down to the bilge and said we had to find a better way to keep ahead of it; the belt was throwing more water all the time. I got the deck bucket but there wasn't a good place to get at the water. It would have been better if we were running level, but the dipping and plunging kept sloshing the water forward, around the engine and over the floorboards. The best I could do was to stick an old coffee can down into the little space just ahead of the engine. I could fill up a bucket pretty quickly, dump it overboard, and then do it again. That worked pretty well and I got ahead of it in just a few minutes. Then I stayed outside for a while because I was queasy from the smell of oil and from having my face so close to the rattling engine and the sloshing bilge.

Before long the swells began to build even more, but they weren't breaking too badly and we found that we could still make pretty good time by quartering them. We could still see Kenai but we seemed to be gaining on Humpy Point. We had no way to estimate our speed except to line up prominent objects alongshore with a peak or glacier in the distant Kenai Mountains. This way we could see ourselves move southward at a promising rate. After a while though, when Dick had the wheel again and the seas had built noticeably, it seemed that the push we were getting from the ebb was being offset by the building southwest breeze. There were more whitecaps now, and we guessed they were stacking up against the ebb.

By God, though, we told ourselves, we were making pretty good time. We were steadily inching down on the Kenai Mountains and were soon off of, and then just below, Humpy Point. When we began to see great flashes of white spray just off shore and to the south, we knew we had spotted the Sisters. I had never seen anything like that, even from shore, and as we plunged ahead, taking our own high spray, we couldn't resist swinging in for a closer look. We got no closer than a half mile from the scene, but it made a lasting impression—the peaked gray-black rocks pounded again and again with breaking seas and then disappearing in high bursts of spray. Years later, I pictured the Sisters again, in reading *Moby-Dick* and trying to imagine what Melville suggested in his short chapter "The Lee Shore." Melville's picture of the breaking shore is far less vivid than his image of the open ocean—what he calls "landlessness" or "the howling infinite," where he glimpsed "the highest truth . . . indefinite as God." But my imagination was fixed on the Sisters. If *Margaret* had still carried her sail, we would have been in the kind of trouble Melville imagined. As it was, we were relieved when the little Willys pushed us a bit further toward open water, if not toward Melville's highest truth.

It was good to take our eyes off the Sisters, but it made me realize how chilled I was, and hungry. We had a couple of the cheese sandwiches we had packed that morning, happy to eat them standing up as we swayed with the seas and braced ourselves against the bigger plunges. And when we had gone on a mile or so to the southwest we caught sight of the only other boat we would see all day—a tender that seemed headed for the Kenai River. It was running with the wind and wasn't throwing as much spray as we were, and partly for this reason we saw it as a huge vessel— maybe seventy or eighty feet, invulnerable to the seas that ran several feet above us. As the tender moved past us and out of sight, I thought about how far we had to go and how cozy it was back at the cannery.

We continued to plug on at a pretty good rate, leaving the Sisters well behind and then even another well-known landmark on that beach, the high radio tower that's visible from far out in the Inlet, the Clam Gulch tower. Going by the chart, we thought we should be able to spot the village of Ninilchik before long. When we'd driven to Ninilchik it seemed like the Russian church in the village would be visible from a long way out. But even standing up outside, with my feet on the bulkhead behind the fuel tank and hands braced against the top of the cabin, I couldn't see a thing. Maybe we'd been making better time than we thought and were already past it.

It did seem that we were pretty far off shore, though, and when we looked out to the west we began to make out another rip. We saw what looked like smoother water just this side of it, so we decided to move further that way to take a look. Before long the smooth water disappeared and we began to catch sight of something black all along the rip. We slowly edged over that way, wondering if it might be a sandbar and not a rip. We couldn't see anything like a sandbar on our chart, and then we began to get glimpses of something like dark fingers sticking up in the air. There was a vast line of debris over there, and even though the water was getting a little rougher and we didn't want to waste any time, we couldn't help heading that way to check it out. Before long we began to get our first good look at a churning Cook Inlet rip, with its jumble of huge trees jostling in a chaos of spinning limbs. Even above the noise from our engine and the sloshing waves, we could hear the rip's low hissing groan. We'd seen enough and quickly headed back to the southeast, hoping again to catch sight of Ninilchik. Gradually, over the next few years, we would learn to appreciate the allure and treachery of these rips. Sometimes the only fish you can find are along the edge of, or actually *in*, the rips, right along with the debris. If you're quick and lucky, you can pick up a few fish and get your net back aboard before it gets drawn into the current and suddenly bunches up into a great tangled glob.

I took my place again, braced between the gas tank and the back of the cabin, making the most of the higher and wider view this offered before my glasses would take too much spray. These quick look-arounds beat the hell out of what I could see through the foggy windshield down in the cabin. There were only breaking swells for as far as I could see, but we had to keep a sharp watch for stray logs. Even this far from the rip we'd caught sight of a few big ones that were plunging half-submerged. And I wanted to keep an eye on the shoreline and distant mountains to gauge our speed. I couldn't tell if we were making any headway at all, and shortly after Dick changed places with me, he came back into the cabin to say, "Yeah, looks like the tide's beginning to change on us. We're barely inching south. But, you know, I think I caught sight of Ninilchik. We're still quite a way above it it."

Seeing Ninilchik, even at that distance, kept us feeling good for another hour or so, despite the bigger seas and despite the constant need to bail and then bail some more. But we were both still unnerved every time we'd come down off a big one and hear the engine rev out of control when the prop came out of the water. We didn't need instructions to back off on the throttle just before we began to plunge, and that's the way we ran for the rest of the day. Sometimes the waves were so big that all we could do was slow way down and head straight into them. The pounding sounded like hell and of course it forced more and more water through the seams in the bow.

The wind picked up and the seas were bigger, the breaking white tops blasting downwind and leaving long streaks in the water. We were taking constant spray even when we weren't plunging directly into the seas. At least they were regularly spaced now and the water had turned a clear blue-green, which was much more encouraging than the murky water we had left behind. By now we'd edged below Ninilchik, but we had mixed feelings about that. We wondered if the wind would pick up even more and briefly thought about trying to make it into Ninilchik. When we'd driven there, we had gone down to the little harbor and seen fifteen or twenty fishing boats crowded into it. Only a narrow tidal creek led out to the Inlet, and we had heard that the channel was hard to find and impassable if the surf was up or if it was less than half tide. It wasn't worth the risk, and since there's no island or point along that whole shore where you could get any protection from a southwest wind, we knew it was Homer or nothing. We figured that left us with about forty miles to go, but we weren't really worried. We were encouraged by our own lack of experience. Maybe this was just the way it was on Cook Inlet. Probably so, and we told ourselves, "By God we can handle it." Besides, having popped back up after taking some pretty good seas that covered the whole cabin, we were beginning to believe that *Margaret* really was a good sea boat. She was sure as hell a better sea boat than I was a sailor, because by now I had thrown up everything. The worst part was bailing while leaning over the engine. Every time I took a full bucket out to the downwind side of the boat, I heaved and heaved some more. And there was no place to lie down in the open air to ease the nausea.

Dick never got seasick, and after that day over forty years ago, I rarely did either. The two times I did get seasick, it was the same problem: not just rough weather but wafting fumes from the engine or a diesel stove. A little later that day, though, I forgot about being seasick and focused my attention on something else that scared us both. We began to notice several pinhole leaks in our rusty old gas tank. Gasoline steadily oozed from the pinholes, and each time we came down hard off a wave little streams appeared. The leaks weren't bad enough to threaten our fuel supply, but it didn't help to look too closely at the tank's flaky rusted surface. We were afraid of a fire because the tank wasn't far from the well-heated exhaust pipe. Only later, after we got to Homer, did we learn of a simple solution to this common problem among aging fishing boats: you could keep things together for quite a while by rubbing a bar of Ivory soap across the tiny holes. We just kept a close eye on the tank and held our breath for the next several hours.

After we got well below Ninilchik we finally caught sight of Anchor Point and began to think we had it knocked. But we had no way to know that it would take hours to reach and round the point. We were now bucking both the wind and a pretty big flood, and, judging from what we could tell from looking ashore, we seemed to be making no headway at all. The swells now came straight in from Shelikof Strait and rose to fifteen or twenty feet, but they were farther apart and didn't seem to break with such violence. It was still tricky trying to quarter them as we ran on toward Homer, but it was a kick maneuvering them without having to worry too much about taking a bad hit from the side. Our little Willys never missed a beat. But when we finally began to get around Anchor Point—well off shore—we saw yet another point ahead, Bluff Point, which doesn't even look like a point on the chart. At last, though, we began to make out the Homer Spit and, ever so slowly, inched our way toward it. Even with the powerful engines of today, you try your best to avoid making that run against the tide. We were exhausted, cold, and hungry, but we inched along the spit and finally had our harbor in sight. At the same time we were buoyed by the spectacle of the glaciers on the other side of Kachemak Bay. With all that, we didn't much mind the further couple of hours it took us to make our way to Land's End and the entrance to Kachemak Bay. When we finally made the turn into the Bay, we caught what must have been the last of the flood as well as a great last push from the big incoming swells. With all that speed, accentuated now by the way we seemed to fly past the nearby buildings on the end of the Spit, and our great relief at being there, we entered the harbor with a sense of exhilaration and confidence that I have seldom known since. I was twenty-five and Dick was twenty-seven.

I won't forget our surprise and pride at learning not only that we had made it in during a gale, but that we had been the only boat to do so that day. After we docked *Margaret*, straightened up the cabin, and draped our sleeping bags over the cabin to dry, we wobbled up to the bar at Land's End, on the very tip of the Spit, where there's a fine view of the glaciers and the entrance to the harbor. We were red-eyed and grubby, and the bartender asked if we were the guys he'd watched on that little boat pulling in to the harbor a while ago. We nodded that we were, and before he took our orders he pointed to a wind gauge behind the bar and said, "That's a gale, man."

We had caught the ebb, riding it not only part of the way to Homer that day but also into careers that changed our lives. We made a go of it that summer, earning enough to cover the twenty-five hundred dollars we'd paid for *Margaret*, pay off our bill at the company store, and still pocket about three hundred dollars each. We learned a lot about boats, salmon, gill nets, and Cook Inlet. We were hooked on this new way of life. But we didn't know that over our next thirty years we'd be riding another ebb, the gradual decline and transformation of this simple and exciting kind of work. There were good and bad years, varying with our luck, the market, and the size of the runs. The industry changed dramatically as the boats got bigger and faster and the gear more efficient, and as the Japanese market for frozen salmon displaced the market for canned salmon. There were some rich years toward the end, but things began to fall apart with the *Glacier Bay* oil spill in 1987 and then the disaster of the *Exxon Valdez*. At the same time, the fishery for wild salmon began to take a deadly blow from the farm-raised salmon industry.

The sockeye still return to Cook Inlet in good numbers and fishermen gear up to pursue them. But it's not the same. Because of the greatly enlarged human population in Anchorage and on the Kenai Peninsula, Fish and Game had to devise more complicated regulations to apportion the runs among the competing interests of sport, subsistence, and commercial fishermen. With all this—the depressed market for wild salmon, and the much more high-powered and technologically sophisticated equipment that is now required in order to compete on the grounds—the Cook Inlet gill-net fishery grinds on, like an overloaded boat dragging across the bar at low water. The way of life that I commemorate here began in the 1870s, was revived in the late 1940s, and thrived for nearly another half century, but I can't imagine a tide that will lift it again.

First Drifts with *Margaret*

 AFTER SEVERAL DAYS EXPLORING the fjords across Kachemak Bay, we knew we couldn't make a living hunting seals. We had to get back to the cannery and get ready for the fishing season. There was a lot to do and a lot to learn, and we needed to buy more provisions on our tab at the company store. We left the harbor at low water and rode the flood to just above Ninilchik before the tide turned and reduced our speed to almost nothing. But it was sunny and flat calm for the whole trip back to Kenai, as though we were on a different body of water. We took hours to gain ground on the Clam Gulch Tower and the Sisters, and even more to round Humpy Point and finally make it into the Kenai. Over the next few days we tried to seal the leaks in the cabin and built a new gas tank from an old fifty-five-gallon oil drum.

Then we focused our energy on figuring out the net and imagining how it would work from the boat. The gear that came with *Margaret* was stored in the web loft above one of the cannery buildings. The loft was a long, dimly lit rectangular space beneath the rafters, lined along each low side with cubicles or lockers that were framed in with two by fours and enclosed by chicken wire. All the boats had gear lockers here and ours contained seven bundles of gear, each tied up in burlap and holding one shackle, a piece of net fifty fathoms long. By tying three shackles together we'd have a legal-sized net measuring a hundred fifty fathoms, or nine hundred feet. We picked what seemed to be the three newest shackles, hoisted them down onto a wooden cart, and hauled them along a boardwalk to a series of net racks at the edge of a grassy tide flat. Even that early in the afternoon, mosquitoes rose from the grass to swarm around the few fishermen who stood working with their nets. At least the mosquitoes were big and slow enough to make easy targets. And they weren't bad enough to keep us from glancing across the flats to take in the view of Mt. Redoubt on the other side of the Inlet.

Only when we draped the cork line over one rack and the lead line over the other, with the web hanging in between, could we begin to see how it all worked. The cork line was strung with evenly spaced floats, and the lead line had little pieces of lead clamped to it. The web would hang from the cork line and be pulled down into a long wall of net eighteen feet deep. It was a network of countless diamond-shaped meshes each measuring five and an eighth inches when stretched tight, just the right size to slip behind a sockeye's gills when it tried to swim through. A couple of our old nets were made of linen and the floats were football-shaped pieces of cedar, about six inches long, with a one-half-inch hole drilled through them for the cork line, and they had been dipped in paraffin. The newer gear was made of nylon and the orange-colored floats were made of spongy plastic. It helped to see the gear stretched over the net racks, but how in hell were you supposed to work with it from the boat? We checked out some of the other conversions that had already loaded their gear, and the nets sat piled in the stern compartments like little stacks of hay. How could they keep a net from being just a tangled mess?

For now, though, the main problem was to repair all the tears and holes we could see. Other fishermen worked at lightning speed, using wooden needles to mend their gear, and we knew at once that we'd never learn to do that in just a few weeks. We talked with Tut, the cannery's web boss, and arranged for a cannery worker to mend our net and bill it to our account at the company store. Tut, whose real name was Trygve Ellingsen, was in his early seventies, and we were fortunate that he liked us well enough to take us under his wing. He loved kidding us about being school teachers, and showing us how to mend a hole or tie a knot, always demonstrating it in a blaze of speed that he knew would mystify us. The mischievous twinkle in his eye and his dry sense of humor accompanied the music of his Norwegian accent. Over the next few years I got to know him well enough to talk about many things, from family to politics, and I was especially drawn to him as an early, vehement critic of the war in Viet Nam.

We finally got our gear in decent shape, tied the shackles together, stacked it all in one huge bundle, and wheeled it to the dock. When the crane operator lowered it into our stern, *Margaret* rode level in the water.

This diminished the comic effect of our newly painted water line, but even we could see how ungainly our boat was compared with the other conversions. We were especially impressed by three that were privately owned, including the one we'd wanted to buy from Ike Johanson. He had added a plank all around to beef it up and raise the freeboard, decked it over, built a solid and well-designed cabin, and, most important, installed a reel for pulling in the net. We also admired our friend Herb's conversion, *Suzy Jo*. He had fished it for several years with his wife, but she had recently graduated from law school, and her new practice left him to fish it alone. We couldn't imagine how she had lived and worked aboard it for all that time because, a victim of childhood polio, she wore a brace and walked with a painful-looking limp. Although *Suzy Jo* was decked over and therefore much easier to get around on, and although it had a hydraulic roller for bringing in the net, its tiny cabin would have been a tight squeeze for the two of them. But my favorite of the private conversions was one owned by a local man, Alfred Wik, who fished it with his two sons. Well maintained and painted aqua-marine, it struck me as the most beautiful conversion, an impression I got partly from the way Alfred and his sons worked on it together and mostly from what still strikes me as its dreamy name, *Nereus*.

Still, we took pride in *Margaret* and were by now well adjusted to our life aboard her. We were also anxious to get to know *Margaret* as a fishing boat and itched to make our first drifts with her. Needing to get as much practice as possible before the run really got underway, around the Fourth of July, we were determined to be the first boat out on opening day. We knew that most fishermen would sit out the first period or two, and even this gave us a little lift: no one would see us fumbling around as we tried to learn the ropes. Following Herb's advice, we decided to fish somewhere fairly close to Kenai. That way we'd avoid making the long run to the lower Inlet and also have a shot at stragglers from an early run of reds that were already headed up river toward the spawning grounds. If we left a day or two before the first opening, we could cross the Inlet and anchor at the north end of Kalgin Island, where we'd be in a good position to head out. After the first fishing period, we'd run farther down the Inlet to a remote place on the west side called Snug Harbor, at Chisik Island. We could buy fuel and groceries at the cannery there and then be ready to fish the lower part of the Inlet over the next few open periods. The main run would begin to enter the Inlet in late June and gradually work its way to the north, adjusting to the smell of fresh water before entering the Kenai and Kasilof rivers. As soon as the fish hit the river in late July, fishermen from the Columbia River or Puget Sound would put up their boats and head south to fish later runs down there. Dick and I had already decided to fish as far into August as seemed worthwhile. Fishing would be slow, but we'd still have a month before school started to catch whatever we could and pay down our bill at the cannery store.

We loaded the boat with two weeks' supply of groceries, purchased on credit at the company store, and bought a few fifths of the cheapest whiskey we could find on our last trip to town. It was hard to sleep during those last nights at the cannery, not only because we were keyed up, but because there was so much daylight now. Also, I still wasn't used to the sound of water running by just inches from my head. When the tide ran hard it sounded like water was gushing into the boat. Sometimes in the middle of the night, at slack water, you could hear a fish jump, and once in a while you could hear nearby beluga surface and spray as they followed the salmon upstream or made their way back out of the river. Lying there at the waterline, I heard their *whhhsssh, whhhsssh* and imagined their white shapes surging by just a few feet away.

We left the river at about midnight, just after high water. It's only a twenty-mile run to the north end of Kalgin. You can see it from the bluff—a low line in the water out to the west and a little south, with a bump on the north end. But you can't see it from a boat, even in good light. It was cloudy that night and we were the only ones headed out. We knew we'd have to cross the middle rip, which had a bad reputation. But we also knew that beach fishermen from Kalgin Island sometimes crossed the Inlet in skiffs; with their outboard motors they could wait for good weather and dash across with a load of supplies from Kenai. As we chugged along through the slop that night, it took us about two hours to find the middle rip, but even with the cloud cover, we couldn't miss seeing the white water out to the west. We had to slow down even more to pick our way through a wide stretch of driftwood. We went through some

Beluga in the Kenai River

swirly water that looked like the beginning of whirlpools, and, crossing through it all, we again appreciated the power and turmoil of a Cook Inlet rip: the seas had no pattern and were so jagged and disorganized that you couldn't tell how to steer through them. The pointed caps leapt straight up as though agitated by some colossal vibration below. Before long, though, we passed into calmer seas and throttled up. But we hadn't yet heard that there's another rip out there, the west rip. When we saw some awful-looking flashes of white water up ahead, we took them for rocks that we hadn't seen on our chart, so we made a big, wide circle to the north. At about five that morning we finally dropped the hook off the north end of Kalgin Island.

We spent the next day drying out our wet sleeping bags (we never managed to make *Margaret*'s cabin watertight) and taking our skiff ashore to walk the beach. I learned how stupid it is to stand up in a skiff while getting onto a beach, and after that mishap some people appeared and invited us into their cabin. They had seen me fall in and knew I'd want to dry out and warm up. They were one of two families of set-netters who spent their summers at the north end of Kalgin. They welcomed our company and impressed us with their isolated, simple way of life. We'd lived on *Margaret* for almost a month, and it seemed a luxury to enter their dark little cabin, where a fire glowed in their woodstove and the teakettle steamed. Over tea and cookies, we were drawn to the way the family concentrated its energies on the coming season, and we envied their set up. They had a good water supply from a nearby creek, unlimited firewood, a solar shower, and even an outhouse. But we also sensed that, from their point of view, it might be better to fish from a boat. You don't have to take your chances and wait for the fish to make their way along your beach. You can go find them.

Of course we wanted to find the fish the next day, but we also wanted to play it safe and use our first day of fishing to get a feel for how it all worked. Looking at the chart we liked the idea of fishing close in on the west side of Kalgin Island because this area seemed more protected from the wind, and it was a long way from the middle rip. We didn't know that drifters seldom find it worthwhile to fish that area. Our only idea was to stay well offshore and to set the net across the tide. But where? It looked the same everywhere, and we didn't see any fish jumping. Herb had told us to look for jumpers, emphasizing that if you saw just one you could be sure that it wasn't alone. Our main problem was what to make of the water that churned in great muddy swirls and, again, we worried that we were over a sandbar. I got out on the bow and took soundings with the lead, but we couldn't find the bottom and didn't know what to think. Would the fish even swim in this muddy stuff? We finally came to a place where there were no muddy swirls and thought that we'd try it there.

We put the boat in neutral and both got in the stern with the high wobbly pile of net and got things sorted out, ready to throw the buoy keg over. The keg was tied to a twenty-foot line that was fixed to the end of the cork line. When we were ready to set the net, Dick went to the wheel in the cabin—our only steering station—and shifted into forward. I threw over the keg and we moved slowly ahead until the line tightened and the net began to peel off the pile and into the water. Dick aimed the boat straight ahead and then ran back to the stern, crawling over the bulkheads along the way, to help me get the net out. If we kept the lines separated as the net peeled out, the web would spread out on its own. We had pictured our net stretched out in a straight line, a floating wall of web spread to its full nine hundred feet and gilling everything that swam its way. But as it peeled out of the boat, the wispy web caught on anything and everything—a button, a sliver of wood along the rail, or the head of a screw that wasn't quite flush. We'd hear the web tear, scramble to free the snag, and when it jerked free the pile of net would topple over on itself in a tangled mess. Still idling ahead, the boat would turn with the breeze or tide, and one of us would run forward to turn the wheel. When we finally got the whole net in the water, we looked back and saw it meandering about and stretching to only a third of its full length. Still, the net was out. Now all we had to do was turn off the engine, drift with the tide, and wait for the fish to swim our way.

Our little Willys was not a noisy engine, but when we turned it off the sudden silence made the Inlet world seem much larger and a bit mysterious. No longer driving through the water, in seeming control of everything, we felt it take us in. We drifted along on the imperceptible current, hearing only the water lapping against the boat. Inside the cabin, something on one of the shelves shifted its weight and tipped back and forth, tapping gently against a tin plate or cup. We stood outside, listening and watching. I went inside to get the last of our morning's coffee. Sipping at it, we watched the net and tried to gauge the speed of our drift. We couldn't tell if we were moving at all, but the tide book showed three hours till slack water. We tried to appreciate our fine view of Mt. Redoubt and the west side of Kalgin Island. Then we turned on our marine-band radio—the scratchy little five-watt set that had belonged to the preacher. There were only a few faint, intermittent words from out of nowhere. We watched the net and waited. There had to be something in all that water.

After about an hour and a half we decided to pull it in, so we put on our rain gear and cotton fish-picking gloves and began to haul. The net came in so easily that we wondered why the other boats bothered with hydraulic rollers or reels. One of us pulled it in while the other stacked it in a neat pile that we hoped would make it easier to peel it out when we set it again. If you grabbed the cork line and lead line together, the net bunched together without tangling. It took us about forty-five minutes to pull it in, and we pulled in all nine hundred feet of it without finding a single fish. Later we learned that even the best fishermen have to put up with a waterhaul once in a while—all that net with nothing but water.

Moving a little closer to shore, we tried again. Then we moved a little further out and tried again. Then we moved a little south and tried again. We had drifted south on the ebb and then drifted up on the flood, never seeing a jumper or another boat all day. But late in the afternoon when we had drifted back up toward the north end of the island we were pulling in what looked like another waterhaul when a fish came in over the roller, and we gave a whoop. It was all tangled in the loose web, a salmon, and presumably a red. It wasn't very big, maybe five or six pounds, and it had been dead for so long that it was stiff. It took us a minute or two to sort through the web to find where it was gilled and then pick it. You had to pull a mesh back over one of the gills and then pull the fish out tail first. We could barely appreciate how much work it would be to pick a net full of fish. But we admired the beautiful fish, its blue-green back, the line running its length and separating the dark back from the silvery sides and white belly. It was our first one after all these weeks of getting ready! and we shook hands. But that was the only one, and after one more drift we decided to call it a day. We had learned a lot and we didn't want to keep fishing all night.

We were ready for dinner when we dropped the hook again at the north end of the island. After Dick cleaned and filleted our fish, we got out the whiskey and drank a toast to our first dinner of fresh-caught salmon. I can't remember what we had with it—though there certainly weren't any fresh vegetables or lemons. We rolled it in cornmeal, fried it in our black iron skillet, and ate it all. Red, firm-fleshed, tender, and moist, it had to be the best fish anyone had ever enjoyed. In recent years, I'd have lemons aboard and fry it only in olive oil, with no cornmeal; and if there was anything to drink it would be a glass of wine or beer. But the cheap whiskey accompanied it well that night, and to top off our feast we had the finest dessert our meager provisions would yield—a batch of bilge pudding. This was a package of instant pudding whose directions called for mixing the powder with cold milk, canned milk in our case, and putting it in the refrigerator to chill and set. Having neither refrigerator nor ice, we mixed it in a plastic pitcher and suspended it over the side in the cold water of Cook Inlet. We called it bilge pudding because we realized that if necessary we could just lift a floorboard and chill it in the bilge. We never actually tried that, but some years later on a camping trip I discovered that it wasn't necessary to chill it at all. With whatever thickeners it contained we could have used it to caulk our seams. Would we have survived all that summer's bilge pudding, I wonder, without our daily ration of the solvent whiskey?

The next day we caught the ebb and ran south to Snug Harbor, on the southwest corner of Chisik Island. Lying at the entrance to Tuxedni Bay, Chisik is a wedge-shaped island, twenty-eight hundred feet high at the north end. You can see it from Kenai on clear days. People had pointed it out to us, sixty miles across the Inlet to the southwest, near the base of Mt. Iliamna. But you can't appreciate the dramatic setting or the appeal of the name, Snug Harbor, until you round the southern tip of the island and pull into the entrance after a day on the Inlet. The channel between the island and the mainland is less than a mile wide and carries the strong tides running in and out of Tuxedni Bay, but as soon as you get inside the water's almost always calm. Even though we'd enjoyed a fine day on our run down the Inlet that first time, we were stunned to enter the calm channel and take in the scene ahead. From the distance, the south end of the island seems quite low, compared to the north end, but, approaching it on the inside, you see its high rocky cliffs dropping straight down to the beach. Hundreds of screaming gulls soared over the channel, and thousands tended or defended their nests in the high cliffs. A bald eagle patrolling the cliffs set off riotous flights of the screeching birds. The high slopes on the island and mainland were carpeted in willow, alder, devil's club, or salmon berries, in the varying shades of vibrant green that only the Alaskan summer solstice can produce. Moving further into the channel we caught sight of the cannery nestled in a cove and what seemed like a throng of people along the dock and boardwalks. We couldn't wait to explore that little world, and as we passed through the cannery's fleet of anchored boats we knew we were in the right place.

We ran on past the cannery and anchored under the north end of the island, near other boats from Kenai, and close to a high thin waterfall that fell to the beach. We had our lunch, glassed the island and the mainland, then rowed ashore to walk the beach and visit the cannery. Because our cannery had a working relationship with the Snug Harbor Cannery, we were welcome to use these facilities. We walked along the boardwalks that connected the buildings, went to mug-up (coffee break), took showers, and charged a few items at the cannery store. At mug-up we talked with a few fishermen we recognized from Columbia Wards, and they seemed to appreciate our common goal—to get this early start in the season, while most of the fleet remained at the dock in Kenai. We were happy to be among these other boats, both for the sense of security we felt and for the opportunity to learn from their example. It seemed a rather tight-knit little community here at Snug Harbor, and we couldn't imagine how it would swell over the next week. Within that time well over a hundred gill-netters would hole up here, and there would be a big Fourth of July celebration.

That Thursday morning we followed a group of boats out of the harbor at about 3 a.m., watching as they threw spray when they left the protected water and caught the southwest breeze. We gulped down the last of our coffee and scrambled to secure things in the cabin. This wasn't going to be like our first leisurely day of fishing, but at least we could see other boats and hear people talking on the radio. We didn't know which direction to head, and before long it looked like the boats were beginning to thin out in different directions. We wanted to keep in the middle of them, but with all the spray and whitecaps it was hard to keep them in sight. *Margaret* was slow and the Inlet seemed bigger than ever.

By opening time we were somewhere near the middle of the Inlet and the ebb had pushed us south of Snug Harbor. When we got close enough to the only boat still in sight, we could see it was drifting with the net out. We ran on for about a quarter of a mile and began to set our own net. As soon as we slowed down enough to put out the net the wind began to push the boat and it was clear that it would have its way when we began to drift. The net went out fast and kept taut with only a few spots where the lead line crossed over the cork line. We had wanted to keep it running from west to east, across the tide, but the southwest wind soon pushed the boat to the north and the ebb pulled the net to the south. All we could do was hope that the fish didn't always swim north or south, with or against the tide. At least the net was stretched in a straight line for its whole length.

Before long we noticed that the boat near us had moved away, giving us the impression that we were alone. Maybe it was too rough for the others, we thought, or maybe they were all catching fish somewhere else. We decided to pick up the net to see what we had, and then got our first feel for what it's like to pull in the net by hand on a windy day. The net drags heavily in the water, so when you pull it in, you're actually pulling the boat against the wind. The greater the wind, the harder it is to pull, and for the first time we understood why the other name for "deck hand" in this fishery is "boat puller." You can get quite a workout pulling in nine hundred feet of net. We alternated, one pulling in a shackle while the other stacked, but we didn't have a single fish. When we got the net into the boat we listened to our scratchy little radio and heard a few boats talking, some that seemed to be catching fish. The trouble was, we had no idea where they were.

"*Blue Sky. Lucky Lady.* You on there, Toots?"

"*Blue Sky* back. Yeah, howzit goin', Jack?"

"Ahhhh, drew a blank on that first one, but we moved over here and got a hit or two settin' it out. How on that?"

"Yeaahh, sounds good. 'Bout the same here. Maybe they'll show on the flood. How on that?"

"Wellll, don't think we'll be gettin' much till the tides begin to build next week. How?"

"Yeaahh. Thinkin' the same thing. We're gonna pick it up and try to get on that streak over east. Let ya know what we find, OK?"

"Roger. We'll keep an eye on ya. *Lucky Lady* out."

"*Blue Sky* out."

Their voices sounded so big and sure and, having seen these famous boats at the cannery in Kenai, we imagined how warm and comfortable it was inside their cabins and how wonderful it would be to have a power reel like theirs.

We fell back on our main plan, to stay close to the other boats and imitate what they were doing, so we started the engine and agreed that we'd run east till we spotted some other boats. The guy on *Blue Sky* had said he was heading east, but of course we didn't know where he was in the first place. The wind kept up, and it was slow going, but we finally spotted some boats and got close enough to try it again. As I put out the net while Dick steered, the wind caught some of the loose web and it caught on the head of a bolt, making a long tear when the lines drew taut. It was hard for Dick to steer in a straight line at slow speed, which caused our net to meander, but as soon as we got it overboard, the wind pushed us away from the net and it began to straighten out. We gave it an hour before we picked it up, and had nothing again. We moved a little further to the east and tried it again. We picked it up again, and still had nothing. All day, the same thing. We laughed it off and told each other that at least we'd have big arms and shoulders by the time the season was over.

By around eleven that night the sun had dipped toward the mountains in the northwest, and because of the clouds we were expecting about three hours of semi-darkness. The sun would finally "go down" behind a peak in the Chigmit Mountains and then emerge on the other side about an hour later. We had no idea at all how or where to make a night set, only that we had to make one. The period didn't end until 6 a.m. Besides, we'd heard that, down here in the clear water, where the fish could see your net, the best fishing was at night. As the sky darkened we made out a light from another boat in the distance and headed that way. When we finally got the net out it looked like we had lots of room, so we took off our rain gear and went inside to have a bite to eat. We'd leave the net out for about an hour, one of us taking the watch while the other slept; Dick took the first watch and woke me up after what seemed like only five minutes. We could barely see the net, and we didn't like putting on the cold wet gloves. We knew we'd get another good workout, because the breeze hadn't let up, but we had high hopes for this first night set. I pulled in the first shackle. Nothing. Dick pulled in the next one. Nothing. I pulled in the last one. Still nothing. Not a damned thing. Now what do we do? we wondered. "Well," Dick said, "let's try moving a little closer to that boat out there," pointing to a dim light in the distance. I was up for it, so we started the engine and moved that way. We got as close as we thought safe and then set it out again.

This time I took the watch and Dick crawled into his bunk for an hour's nap. I'd worked up a sweat pulling the last one, so put on some warmer clothes and sat outside on the engine cover to keep an eye on things. It was as dark as it was going to be now, and I could see only a few feet of our net, but the main thing was to watch for driftwood and other boats. The other boat's light came in and out of view in the distance, and the dark water stretched around us forever. With the cold breeze and the sounds of low waves and sloshing bilge, I took comfort in the little warmth that the engine cover retained. Then I heard something bump the side of the boat and jumped to my feet. Shit! I'd fallen asleep. Dick came scrambling out the door, yelling, "What's goin' on?" We had drifted into the other boat. A light came on in the other cabin and a guy came running on deck to see what was going on. He was alone and apparently hadn't wanted to leave his net out while he took a nap. He started his engine, yelled, "That was close!" and pulled away from us, taking care to stay clear of our net.

The shot of adrenalin had me wide awake and stumbling all over myself to apologize for fucking up. "Damn it! Dick. I'm sorry!! When I sat down there he was a long way off, and the next thing I know he's banging against the side. Shit!"

"Hey, it's OK. We lucked out. Besides, my hour's about up. Let's just check the net and get out of here."

Dick was cool, but I felt like crap. He'd never let himself fall asleep like that. We didn't talk about it any more but just put on our rain gear and the cold wet gloves and pulled in the net again, taking turns, one shackle at a time. *Another* waterhaul. Something like eighteen hours and not a single fish. But the sun was coming up, or rather was edging out from behind the mountain, and we were damned well going to keep fishing until the period closed at 6 a.m. So we started the engine and moved off slowly toward the northwest. That would at least take us a little closer to Snug Harbor. We didn't want to run too far, because we'd heard that "you can't catch 'em if you don't have your net in the water," and in about twenty minutes we decided to try it again. We knew nothing about how to read the water, only that you wanted to spot jumpers. Everything looked the same in every direction. Whitecaps. We were someplace in the middle and could see only a few other boats in the distance to the north. But we decided to put it out and make a pot of coffee. Dick watched the net while I held the pot on the camp stove and boiled the water, and we poured out big cupfuls before the grounds had a chance to settle.

The tin cups warmed our hands as we slurped down the strong coffee and it, with the emerging sun, helped us face the prospect of pulling in the net again. We still had about three hours to go and noticed a small group of boats gathered a few miles to the north. We figured it was a good time to play our main card: stay close enough to the other boats to see how they did it. So we put on the cold gloves and began pulling it in. Nothing but water, water, and a few stray bits of kelp—and then, toward the very end, a single squirming fish. Well, we had dinner at least, but the poor thing looked awfully lonely when we threw it into our hold. As the two of us worked together we at least had the comfort of joking about twenty hours of fishing for one fish. But we got under way again and headed as fast as we could toward the group of boats to the north.

As we got closer we could see a half a dozen fishing fairly close together, and two more approaching them from the east. That seemed like a good sign, and as we got even closer we saw another good sign—a streak in the water that ran north and south, on up to where the boats were drifting. We got onto the streak, which we took to be a rip that was beginning to form, and began to follow it north. It had drawn in scattered bits of kelp and other debris, but no big stuff, and we hadn't been on it long before Dick yelled from outside, "Hold on! I thought I saw a jumper." I backed off the throttle, took it out of gear, and went outside to help look around. There were still quite a few small whitecaps, so Dick couldn't be sure, but we stood as high as we could get, held on, and looked. We both saw it at the same time and yelled out, "Yeah! Over there!" It jumped again. I ran back to the wheel and we headed that way. When we got in that vicinity I looked back to Dick and shouted, "This OK?"

"Yeah! Let's try it here." And, pointing toward Mt. Illiamna, he yelled, "Head her west." He threw over the keg, I shifted to forward, and we began to move slowly to the west. The net was peeling out much better this time, but it still took us about fifteen minutes to set it. I turned off the engine, and we began to drift. We watched the cork line intently, squinting into the sun. And waited. We began to drift upwind and the lines grew taut, promising that we'd have another hard pull, and we waited. A whitecap would break along the cork line, and we'd lean forward and point. "Was that one?"

"No, I don't think so." But we really didn't know. We were getting to the end of our second day of fishing and still hadn't seen a hit. Our only two fish had been tangled deep in the net, so we never saw them splash. We watched. We waited. It was getting close to five. I finally asked, "How about another cup of coffee? I need something to warm me up."

"Yeah," Dick said. "Might as well." And then we both saw a bow form in our cork line about fifty feet from the boat. Some of the leading floats jerked down into the water and then we couldn't believe our eyes. The floats shot up and out of the water and a half dozen fish broke the surface on the other side of the net in a series of violent and irregular splashes that were nothing like whitecaps. Again and again—for nearly half a minute—they leapt up, beating ahead and fighting to break through the net. Then they continued to struggle under water, tugging at the floats for a minute or so until their energy was spent. Dick and I were pounding each other on the back and jumping up and down, yelling like fools. And before we were settled down we did it again as another bunch hit further out in the net. A blast of white water and beating spray. Glimpses of fish twisting in the air. We were tingling, hoarse, tense—wild and more pulsingly alive than any teacher had a right to be.

We forgot the coffee and just stood, swaying with the boat and watching the net. We wanted more. Another hit. Just one more. We watched more intently than ever and babbled on in disbelief and renewed exclamations. "Did you see the bow they made in the net on that first one?!"

"I almost pissed my pants when they came out of the water like that!"

"Yeah! I thought we were on another waterhaul, and then, BAM! There they were!"

"How many do you think we have?"

We watched for as long as we could, without seeing anything more, but we had to leave time to get the net in the boat by six. Picking it, we found only those two bunches and two other single fish caught deep in the net, and learned a little more about how to hold a fish by the head and pull a mesh back over the gill plates. There were nine in the first bunch and seven in the last one, making eighteen fish in that one drift, and nineteen for the day. Keeping one to eat, we had eighteen to sell, and at $1.47 each, that added up to $26.46 for the day. We talked about that on the long run back in to Snug Harbor, knowing damned well that we wouldn't break even for the day. We'd forgotten about how sleepy we were, and each time I went outside to pump the bilge, I looked into the hold and counted them again. Nineteen. They didn't even begin to cover the bottom of the hold, but there they were, beautiful in themselves, just fresh in from the ocean all silvery and blue-green. And no matter what everybody else had caught that day, we were going to be proud to deliver them.

When we finally pulled into the channel at Snug Harbor, into the calm water and under thousands of screaming gulls soaring near the cliffs, we probably didn't quite know what had happened to us. We tied up to the tender, *Pintail*, and delivered our few fish, pitching them one at a time with a one-pronged pitchfork called a peugh (or pew), a practice that ended in the late seventies, when the Japanese demanded higher quality and taught us how to handle the fish. We got our first fish ticket, a pink slip showing that we had delivered eighteen reds, and learned that other boats had been delivering two or three times that many. We pumped the little fuel we needed, signed a receipt for that, and then pulled away toward the anchorage at the north end of the island. Then our exhaustion set in. We'd kept out the biggest fish and Dick filleted it. Again, we dipped it in cornmeal and fried it to perfection. Sitting at the little table that dropped down between the bunks, we drank another shot of whiskey to celebrate our good luck and rehashed the events of what seemed like a month-long day. The salmon was as good as it gets. It was only about 2 p.m., but we soon slumped down in our bunks, and I fell into a dark numbness that wasn't quite sleep. Again and again, some visceral spark kept flashing a brilliant scene—repeated blasts of white spray, fish bursting out of the water and twisting in the air.

The Cannery

WHEN THE OLD COLUMBIA WARDS cannery on the Kenai went out of business in 1998 two of my friends wrote to tell me about it. We all had close ties to the cannery and noted its closing almost as we would a death in the family. Bill was especially moved because he'd been a close member of that family for thirty years. I've seen similar sentiments expressed by people being interviewed when a steel mill or garment factory shuts down in the Midwest or South: people mourning the loss of their livelihood, their way of life, and the community's economic base. Not that Columbia Wards' closing had such tragic social consequences. No one was thrown into poverty or cut off from health care; no town's Main Street was sentenced to a slow death; no wealthy owners sold out a community for tax breaks or lower labor costs outside the country. It was as though a streambed had been diverted years ago and an old cottonwood finally died.

In 2002 Wards Cove Packing Company (as it was then called) announced that it was closing its remaining canneries in Alaska because of "competition from farm salmon and weak overseas and domestic markets." The company had begun in 1928 when the Brindle brothers of Seattle bought a small cannery in Wards Cove, near Ketchikan, and eventually developed it into the largest family-owned fishing operation in Alaska. The site of their cannery in Kenai was first developed as a saltery in 1910. Libby, McNeil, and Libby purchased the saltery in 1914, but, realizing that salteries were already outdated, soon converted it to a cannery. It was not the first salmon cannery on the Kenai, the first having been established near the mouth of the river in 1888. Those were also the very last years of sailing ships, and up through 1926, at least, Libby brought in supplies and personnel on its schooner, *Henry Wilson*. The schooner no doubt played a key role in helping to salvage the operation when the cannery burned down in 1921 and was rebuilt the following year. The Brindles bought the old Libby cannery in 1959 and named it Columbia Wards Fisheries, or CWF. For several years after I first saw the cannery in the winter of 1963, the plant looked very much as it does in existing photographs from 1926. The words Libby, McNeil, and Libby were still faintly visible on the front of the main warehouse, and Columbia Wards' scows and its fleet of conversions were painted "Libby yellow."

The first road to the cannery was put through in 1959. But even with the new long dusty road connecting it to Soldotna, the cannery remained an isolated place up through the late 1960s. The company brought in most of its summer crew from Seattle, housing and feeding them in a self-contained community with its own water supply and generator, as well as machine, carpentry, and mechanics shops. There were bunkhouses and mess halls for cannery employees and fishermen as well as a laundry and a company store that also served as the mail room. If you worked or fished at the cannery, you might make the trip into Soldotna or the more distant Kenai only once or twice all summer. As the roads gradually improved and a new bridge over the river made it a much shorter trip to Kenai, more workers began to drive to the cannery from their homes in town, and fishermen began to acquire beat-up old cars to use in the summer and leave filled with antifreeze for the winter. A few fishermen pulled camp trailers up the highway from Washington or Oregon, parked them on the cannery grounds, and lived there during the season, finding that more agreeable than living in the fishermen's bunkhouse or on their own small boats. For many reasons, the once isolated and intimately interconnected community began to dissolve.

While it was intact the cannery was, again, somewhat like an old cottonwood tree that lay dormant over the winter but leafed out early each spring. A skeleton crew arrived in late April or early May to begin de-winterizing the place, and a key part of this was the job of driving pilings to reconstruct the docks. Because the winter ice flows would tear away the pilings, cannery crews pulled the pilings each fall and drove them again each spring. A period of intense life peaked in July and lapsed into dormancy by late August.

I arrived at the cannery in late spring every year after a long push to get out of the academic life and back into the northern light, always riding a wave of high hopes for the season ahead. You had to count on losing a lot of time the first few days to brief but rewarding encounters with people you hadn't seen since last season, meeting them on one of the boardwalks or near the boats still in winter storage on the ways, and stopping to catch up on each other's news. Inevitably, in these greetings, you would hear of veteran cannery workers or fishermen who had died over the winter. Wes had a heart attack, you know; or, did you hear about Spike? Such jolting news somehow strengthened the bonds of the community, and also provided a dark accompaniment to the season's new life. The burst of energy from over twenty hours of sunlight each day lifted you, as well.

Away from the groves of black spruce, blue swaths of lupine overtook the open ground. In each leaflets' palm lay a perfect jewel of collected rain. Along the tide flats across the river throngs of gulls noisily protected their eggs or first grey hatchlings. You might spot flashes of white in the river, as beluga whale humped over to spout, or see a cow moose with her calves emerge from the black spruce woods to graze on the tide flats. If you saw a jumper in the river you knew the early run of sockeye had returned, and by the same pulse more and more fishermen arrived from the Columbia River or Puget Sound. The cannery's beach gang began launching boats on the highest tides, first firing up the steam-powered winch, greasing the skids, and pulling one boat at a time along the timbers to the cradle. They'd wedge the boat in its cradle and then ease it down into the river.

As soon as I got to the cannery I'd set down my bags and go directly to the ways, find the boat, and go aboard to see how it had survived the winter. Even after the earthquake in 1964 the boat was always intact and exactly as I had left it ten months before, except for the years when it was thinly covered with a powdering of volcanic ash. But I had to see it, find the nearest ladder, climb up, and go aboard. In its awkward wintry state on the ways, the boat was not the living, floating one I had dreamt about over the winter, the boat that yielded to your weight as you stepped aboard. Only when it floated from the cradle several days later would it come to life again.

But the cannery itself was already abuzz with life, and I have often wondered how much its ability to function as a congenial community derived not just from its isolation from the outside world or its single purpose—to process the largest and best possible pack—but from its

Columbia Wards Fisheries on the Kenai

well-defined social structure. Everyone knew his or her place in a semi-segregated society that was overseen by the superintendent. His summer home was located on the bluff above the river, just behind the main office. Just below the office and immediately downstream lay the fish-processing plant and warehouse. The company store and the mail room occupied one half of the office building, and from it a boardwalk led away from the river past a high wooden water tank to a cluster of buildings that included the laundry, the "henhouse" (the women's bunkhouse), the kitchen, mess halls, and another bunkhouse called "knob hill," which housed the carpenters, storekeeper, machinist, and other key figures. A woman named Frances presided over the henhouse and the cannery's considerable house-keeping industry. She spoke with a soft German accent and wielded her authority in a friendly but firm manner, especially in her dealings with residents of the henhouse. It was often necessary to ask Frances about this or that, and she could be found wheeling her linen cart to or from the bunkhouses and the laundry. The three mess halls were segregated by occupation, one being reserved for the superintendent, accountant, and other officials, such as the beach boss (director of all work along the docks), web boss, and shipwright. Fishermen and some cannery workers ate in another mess hall, and a third was reserved for the Filipino crew who butchered the fish. These distinctions seemed natural at the time and I was never aware that anyone felt the pinch of class.

Another bunkhouse along on the boardwalk next to the river housed the beach boss, the web boss, and boat mechanics. It had a kind of front lobby, with an old barber's chair and other chairs where people could socialize at the end of the day and still keep an eye on the boardwalks and the boats tied to the floating docks below. The barber's chair was often occupied by the friendly old Norwegian beach boss named Ingolf or his close friend and fellow Norwegian, Tut, the web boss. Occasionally someone else would sit in the chair to get a haircut from Tut. Behind this boardwalk bunkhouse, and at the edge of the woods, was another that was reserved for fishermen, usually a rather closely knit group of fishermen from the Columbia River. The bunkhouse on the boardwalk seemed free and open. You could sit in the lobby or go back into the individual rooms if you needed to talk with one of the mechanics. Outside but connected to this bunkhouse was a separate toilet and shower room for use by fishermen or other cannery workers; once in a while, when this outside facility had been occupied, I used the inside bathroom. But one day during my first year there Ingolf took me aside and told me gently but firmly that some of the fellows didn't like it that I had used their bunkhouse bathroom.

When everyone at the cannery gathered three times a day for mug-up, the structure of segregated dining was greatly relaxed but still subtly at work. Here, at tables set up in one of the mess halls, or, when the canning began, on the dock, people all helped themselves to the cookies, fresh-baked cinnamon rolls, and coffee or tea. People tended to gather in groups, cannery workers, fishermen, foremen, and such, because they were naturally associated by their work. As a fisherman I gravitated to one of the small groups of fishermen gathered here and there. But among fishermen, as among cannery workers, I suppose, there was an acknowledged order. Fishermen who knew each other from the Columbia River might cluster together, but there was also an informal hierarchy of fishermen, from the highliners down to those who never seemed to catch many fish. If there were several clusters of fishermen, you could tell by posture and gesture which fisherman within a group was catching the most fish. Everyone throughout the cannery knew who the best fishermen were. As something like a rookie on a professional baseball team, an inexperienced fisherman like myself wouldn't feel comfortable shouldering very close to a conversation among highliners. After the superintendent, and perhaps the bookkeeper, who was second in charge, only two or three acknowledged highliners enjoyed unquestioned status throughout the cannery. The superintendent himself stroked the highliners as a major league manager might his best pitcher or hitter. And if a highliner had his own boat and was single, his social attraction was as great as a boatsteerer's in the heyday of Nantucket whaling.

Two other obvious measures of status among fishermen were what boat you fished and whether or not you were an actual, that is, an experienced fisherman. Lowest in this hierarchy were those who fished the cannery's fleet of conversions, the aging, ill-equipped little boats that were typically assigned to beginning or less-productive fishermen. If a cannery worker wanted to break into fishing, in order to make more money, or to have a more adventurous kind of work, he might be able to convince the superintendent to let him have a conversion. For one-third of your catch, the cannery would provide and maintain the boat and nets, which was a very good deal. In my first few years in partnership with Dick on *Margaret*, our place in the society of fishermen was only slightly higher than that of a fisherman with a company conversion. *Margaret* was a conversion, but it was our own boat and thus conferred upon us something like the status of a farmer who worked his own acre and a half. However, we fell into yet another class, that of "school teachers." Because the Cook Inlet salmon season coordinated almost exactly with the school-year calendar, a number of adventurous teachers fished either as drifters or as beach fishermen. It was difficult for teachers to break out of that identity, and some never did. There was a definite sting in being called a "school teacher," but it was possible to live that down after a number of years if you demonstrated that you could take care of yourself and, most important, catch lots of fish. Whether it was one of the company's mechanics, Tut the web boss, or another fisherman, people took good-natured fun in referring to your being a school teacher if, say, you didn't know how to bypass the solenoid in order to start your engine, or if you didn't know how to mend your net, or how to maneuver your boat at the dock.

The fishermen who came up each year from the Columbia River had no problem in maintaining their own boats and gear. Like farmers who have to be mechanics as well as crop- or stock-growers, these long-term, year-round fishermen were self-sufficient and worked expertly on their own engines or nets. But others of us, not just the few school teachers, often needed help from the cannery's mechanics and web boss, who were mainly responsible for maintaining the boats and gear that the company leased to fishermen. But, needing to insure a supply of fish, the cannery also did all it could to help private fishermen maintain their boats and gear. The official procedure was for the mechanics or the web boss to tell the office the cost of materials and the number of hours they had worked for you, and the cannery would deduct the bill from your earnings. But the traditional practice was for the web boss or mechanic to do the work, billing you according to the official rates, or possibly quite a bit less, and then let you know that the favor would cost you a quart. If Tut had mended a big hole in your net in time for you to fish the next period, you'd thank him for saving your butt and he'd remind you, "Well, that'll be a quart." A "quart" was definitely a quart—not a fifth—of Canadian whiskey, preferably McNaughton's, though Canadian Club would do. Dwayne, one of the mechanics, set me straight on the quart/fifth distinction, one time, in a good-natured way. But if you kept that straight, and if you didn't wait too long to get into town to fetch the quart, this was a flawless mechanism for getting the help you needed. I never saw Tut or any of the mechanics wiped out on the whiskey, but, isolated as they were in doing their work and living at the cannery, they were as pleased to have a few quarts on hand as you were to get the help. In their own social interactions in the bunkhouse, the mechanics and other workers would invite fellow workers into their rooms for a drink or two at the end of the day.

Again and again in my early years as "a school teacher" at Columbia Wards, I was impressed with the employees' high-quality work—Tut's in the magic he worked at the net racks out at the edge of the tide flats, or a mechanic's ability to keep a rusty old marine engine ticking away. One man impressed me especially, the quiet, stooped, slow-moving old shipwright named Ole, who was still working in his early eighties. Ole presided over a wonderful shop full of sawdust, an ancient belt-driven band saw, and all sorts of other tools. You would see him walking with a tool or a piece of wood along the boardwalk that led from his shop to the floating docks, where he might be repairing something on one of the company's fleet of wooden boats. Only years later when I was involved in building *Ishmael* did I come to fully appreciate the craftsmanship required of a shipwright. Everything has to be fitted in place, without help of levels or squares, but I got a good sense of Ole's artistry when I watched him replace some planks and ribs in one of the cannery's skiffs. When he had a job to do on a boat down at the floats, he'd go to the boat once to measure things and then walk slowly along the boardwalks back up to his shop. In a short time he'd pack the crafted part back along the boardwalk and down to the boat. Ole was master of the philosophy, "measure twice, cut once," and I doubt that anyone ever saw him make more than two trips to a boat.

Among the fishermen, certain old-timers impressed me by never seeming to work at all. I often saw one such man on my repeated trips from the boat to the parts shop or the mechanics' shop, where we were allowed to use some of the tools. Passing back and forth in front of the dockside bunkhouse I'd nod to one of the Columbia River fishermen, Harold Forsberg, who sat there with some friends. That was a perfect place from which to note and comment on people's performance in maneuvering their boats at the docks. Harold was a formidable, almost frightening-looking man, with a walleye and forearms the size of Popeye's. But when you got to know him, he was as gentle as could be, and could make a humorous observation with an economy of words that seemed related to his ability to take his dock-side seat so frequently. Harold had a sturdy wooden boat that you could spot from a long distance because of its spiffy green and white paint job, and its name, *Black Label*, always struck me as a further reflection of his wit. I assumed that he'd named it after his favorite beer. Howard often nodded back and smiled in a friendly sly way as I hurried past him with a greasy part or a broken fitting.

Other fishermen from the Columbia River impressed me not only by catching lots of fish, but by their acknowledged brilliance in everything involved in a fisherman's work. The brothers Toots and Jack Fisher were masters at everything, and when you heard them talking on the radio during a fishing period it seemed that they were always catching fish. In his calm, deep drawl, Toots would call from *Blue Sky* to Jack on *Lucky Lady,* always ending his short report with, "How on that?" They designed and built their own boats, masterpieces of marine architecture that continued in the fishery for many years after the Fishers' deaths. And they were self-confident enough as mechanics to use unconventional engines, like an old eight-cylinder Packard that simply purred. You never saw these guys in a sweat, even if they were picking a load of fish on the grounds and being sucked into a dirty rip.

Not that the Columbia River fishermen were the only ones who impressed me. A number of local fishermen from Kenai and Kasilof not only caught lots of fish but further distinguished themselves one day when Columbia Wards was attacked by the Alaska National Guard. The Guard was conducting a training exercise one summer in the mid 1960s and had picked the cannery as its objective. No one seemed to have noticed the C 123s that flew over that day, because low-flying aircraft sometimes passed nearby on their way to or from the Kenai airport. And no one saw the parachutes deploy somewhere upriver. But many of us did see the invasion from the docks, when several overloaded skiffs came down on the cannery from upriver. There was a big ebb at the time, with a strong current of several knots. The little aluminum boats—maybe twelve or fourteen feet long—were scooting straight on downstream at a rate that seemed suicidal to anyone who knew anything at all about the Kenai River. And it was clear that the little boats were not only overloaded with men and equipment—M-1 rifles, mortars, and machine guns—but way under-powered, with outboard motors that were probably ordered up by someone who enjoyed trout fishing on calm lakes.

When they drew abreast of the cannery and began turning across the current to execute the surprise attack, they began to capsize, quickly, one after another, leaving a string of boats bobbing upside down in the tidal current that sped them toward the open Inlet. Flailing infantrymen were scattered in their wake. I doubt that any of these men would have survived had we not witnessed it all from the docks, first wondering, "What? Are we being attacked?" and then quickly realizing that a bunch of people were about to drown. A number of fishermen who happened to be on their boats at the time quickly started their engines, untied from the floats, and raced out to the bobbing Guardsmen. They picked them all out of the water, gasping for air and frantic from the shocking cold. But a lot of equipment sank into the silt and was never retrieved. Just a few years earlier, shortly before the outbreak of war in Viet Nam, I had commanded an infantry basic-training company at Fort Ord. And now, already astonished at what was beginning to develop in Viet Nam, I lost a little more confidence in our leaders' ability to plan for war. It's hardly better today—witness their gloating certainty that American soldiers would be greeted as liberators on the streets of Baghdad. We could still use some leaders who know something about human nature, or even a bunch of gill-netters who know something about the reality of tidal currents in places like the Kenai River.

The cannery's social hierarchy, its division of labor, and such social mechanisms as the quart helped it run smoothly, almost as parts of the well-oiled, belt-driven machinery that clattered along the processing lines or in the room above the warehouse where new cans were stamped into shape. Everyone worked together in ways that seemed natural and just to achieve the single purpose of catching and processing as many fish as possible. But even within this relatively happy order there was occasional strife and also a quiet but steady undercurrent of cultural-racial difference, though this was less troubling here than in American life in general.

The strife arose only a few times in the years I was associated with Columbia Wards and was always sparked by the price of fish. Most of the fishermen, including myself, belonged to the United Fishermen of Alaska and sometimes came together under that banner to challenge the fish prices posted by the cannery. Once in a while there were short-lived strikes, but they never seriously interrupted a year's production or, as far as I could tell, resulted in significant increases in the prices we were paid. Sharing my dad's history of union membership and his distrust of management, I joined the others in sitting out several fishing periods over the years. I often felt that we were getting ripped off, and could never understand why fishermen get so little and the middlemen so much, based on what I could tell from the price of salmon in the supermarket. Even now, I feel that disparity; and at the same time I doubt that Columbia Wards' owners, the Brindles, enjoyed extreme wealth. They had enormous overhead and took very high risks each year, while always being subject to fluctuating world markets. But when we threatened to strike or actually did strike, we still remained within the cannery's sphere, taking our meals at the mess hall and attending mug-ups. Fishermen would meet in one of the mess halls and talk about the price of canned salmon or what we had heard they were getting in Copper River. One or two fishermen would stand forth as our angry spokesmen and meet with the superintendent. The management would play its own game in settling the dispute, telling our representatives that they were powerless to negotiate and that only the people at the head office in Seattle could make such decisions. In particularly tense situations word spread that old man Brindle would be flying up from Seattle to represent the company, and we waited for someone to catch sight of him.

Such disagreements would begin to take shape over the winter as markets fluctuated and the company tried to dispose of its previous year's pack, and they would come to a head at the beginning of the season. By then fishermen would be feeling the economic pinch as well. We would have spent our last season's earnings and probably have taken on considerable debt to finance the coming season's costs, for nets or boat repairs. When we decided to strike we would hang together loosely, our identities as independent fishermen tested to the breaking point. But that point never came in my years at Columbia Wards. There was never any violence and fishermen rarely broke ranks to fish for what the cannery offered. The two sides always found a way to agree just before the run was due to appear in strength. Thereafter the tension dissolved into the rush of fishing and management's eager determination to put up the largest possible pack for the year. The natural resource itself—the season, the tides, the pulse of the run—helped us all avert the kind of labor disputes that arise in mills or mines. It was good to catch your fish and be able to deliver them, and it was good to receive them.

The undercurrents of race or cultural difference never caused a serious rift in the cannery's ability to function as a community, but you always knew that they ran deep and constantly wore away at the Alaska Natives' economic security and self-respect. A few of the local peoples, the Kenaitzes and Chickaloons, had established themselves as productive fishermen, one of the best being Archie Sunrise, but very few were included within the higher ranks of cannery employees. The only one I knew from the early years was the night watchman, Ephim Baktuit, who made his rounds each night, carrying a clock that he punched according to schedule at various stations—the warehouse, the web loft, the parts shop. It was probably because of my own low rank as a new fisherman in the early sixties that I came into brief contact with two Natives and glimpsed something of their lives that still tugs at my conscience as an American. The first was Alan, a man who was probably in his early thirties and lived alone in a ramshackle dwelling at the edge of low dunes along the beach a few miles from the cannery. The shack seemed held together by pieces of driftwood and other materials that Alan had salvaged from the cannery dump, but it made a cozy refuge from the buffeting Inlet winds. Just yards from the high-tide line, it had only a very small window facing on the Inlet. But standing outside in sunny, calm weather, you would be stunned by the view across the Inlet to the Chigmit Mountains from Mt. Spurr to Redoubt and Mt. Iliamna. At high water on grey windy days the Inlet's muddy surf seemed to eat away at everything.

It must have been a lonely place to live. Dick and I first saw Alan standing outside his shack as though hoping for a visitor. It was on one of our first trips to the cannery and we were strangers to the place, but he welcomed us in. Later, during the Viet Nam years, Alan flew an American flag that seemed to claim his place in the America that others said we should leave if we couldn't love it, but his flag was always frayed from being so exposed. On our first visit he invited us back to join him and a few friends in the small bathhouse he had built outside. When we returned, bearing a six-pack as our gift, we stripped to our underwear and entered the bath hut, where Alan had already built a bed of coals that he'd covered with a pile of rocks. When he threw pans of water onto the rocks we gasped in the sudden clouds of steam, and then, following their lead, beat ourselves with branches. I wonder if we sweated out some of the old sorrow that lay behind and between us as we gathered there in that strange intimacy. When we'd all had enough we went outside, where Alan told us that to finish it off we should really run to the water's edge for a chill plunge, but we all laughed in rejecting that idea and got back into our separate identities. Alan later found work for a few years as a deck hand and cook on Columbia Wards' tender, *Whale*, but even in that role he was something of an outcast because many concluded from his effeminate manner that he was gay. The last time I drove in to Columbia Wards, I looked for Alan's shack but there was hardly a trace of it and at the cannery I heard vague surmises that he had died.

I met the second Native person a few years later, when I was returning for the fishing season and landed at the Kenai airport. I shouldered my duffle bag, walked to the main intersection in town and headed out the paved highway toward Soldotna and then the long dirt road from there to the cannery. As soon as I stuck out my thumb on the highway in Kenai, someone picked me up—it was easy to hitchhike in those days—and drove me all the way to Soldotna. There I walked across the bridge over the Kenai River to the dirt road leading to the cannery. I knew there wouldn't be many cars on the road, but I couldn't afford a long cab ride. I hadn't walked a mile when a beat-up old car stopped to give me a lift. I don't think they recognized me, but I saw at once that it was a couple I had seen around the cannery over the years. He was a red-haired man with a sickly complexion, who went by Red and who owned, but never seemed to be able to operate, an old derelict named *Big River*. I would see him working on it once in a while, but he never got it ready to fish. She was a Native woman with a couple of missing teeth. I had talked briefly with one of their two children who worked at the cannery, a high-school boy who was hoping to make the wrestling team and then find a way to go to college in Oregon. I let him know that I was pulling for him. His sister was a few years older and seemed intent on finding a boyfriend among the cannery workers.

I loaded my duffle bag and climbed into the back seat and they drove on toward the cannery, another fifteen miles away. I could tell they had been drinking but that didn't bother me. He was driving slowly enough. Red didn't say much but the woman began to strike up a friendly conversation, and my heart went out to her immediately when she told me what had just happened back in town at the bar. She had got into a fight with another woman—a regular knock-down, hair-pulling, on-the-floor fight that had left her with a black eye. But she was proud to let me know that she had won, proud she had started the fight when the other woman insulted one of her heroes, Harry Truman. I can't remember what it was about Truman that made her admire him so. Maybe it was his reputation for being a little pugnacious, as when he let it be known that the buck stops here (on his own desk), or when he said, if you can't stand the heat, get out of the kitchen. Truman was one of my heroes, too, and I was proud to tell her that my Grandpa Stroud knew Truman and that I had once seen him in person; Grandpa frequently met Truman in the early years of his political career when he would ride the Frisco Railroad and Grandpa would chat with him while he performed his duties as conductor. And I had seen Truman when he made a campaign stop in Casper, Wyoming, where we lived in 1948; he took his famous brisk morning walk, waving and smiling to the crowd. And my brother, who played in the high-school marching band that led a small parade, told us how the secret service had appeared the previous day to inspect the instruments for possible concealed weapons. I never learned her name, but I'd become a kind of comrade in arms with this little woman who had fought to defend Truman's reputation.

I seldom saw her after that. *Big River* had been towed someplace to fall apart, I think, but I did see the kids once in a while. It seemed that the boy's dream of going to college had slipped from his reach, and his sister had gotten pregnant. But one day as I was working around my summer camp, a tent that I had pitched among the birch and black spruce on the outskirts of the cannery grounds, my friend appeared from the trees and greeted me. She didn't look any better than she had when she and Red had given me the ride. I'm sure she sought me out because she knew I kind of owed her a favor, and so when she asked me if I could help her—"My cupboard is bare," she said—I reached for my wallet and gave her ten or fifteen dollars. I was happy to do it, and for vague reasons that went back way before I first met her and before we had established our odd bond as defenders of Harry Truman. She was grateful but embarrassed and soon went on her way.

I went about my work and then, several hours later, I was surprised to see Harold Brindle make his way toward me through the trees. Harold was the new superintendent that year, and, finding that we were roughly the same age, with a few other things in common (we had both attended the University of Washington, where we had both been athletes), we talked occasionally. We weren't friends, exactly, but we had found a way to address each other almost as though we were on equal footing. The purpose of this unexpected visit, however, was to chide me in a good-natured way for having given in to my friend's appeal for help. She had shown up later someplace else around the cannery with a half-empty fifth of whiskey, and Harold had found out where she got the money. I was only a little embarrassed for having been so naive, but Harold said, with a tight smile, "You know, Bert, you just can't help them." I remember saying something like what the hell, and I still think what the hell.

Another undercurrent of racial conflict at the cannery involved the "iron chink," famous not only at Columbia Wards but at canneries all over Alaska. If you were visiting the cannery for the first time someone would be sure to tell you about it, or even take you to see it in operation when the cannery was processing fish. Entering the main building, you would see great holding bins of bloody, whole fish ready to be cleaned and canned. There was a deafening noise of clanking machinery and lots of spraying water that washed away the blood and gore along channels in the concrete floors before emptying into the river. Workers in rain gear stood at conveyor belts that led from the fish bins to the other end of the great noisy room, where sealed cans packed with raw fish would be collected in large trays and then rolled on tracks into massive retorts to be cooked. "That's the iron chink," your guide would yell over the din, pointing to the line of machinery just below the holding bins. "It took the place of the Chinese butchers who did this in the old days." As fish fed into the machine at a number of points, it grasped them in place for the split second it took a blade to whack off the heads and then sent the gutted carcasses along their way to other conveyor belts.

The term "iron chink" reminded me of the national hysteria over "the yellow peril" when white America happily exploited the Chinese railway workers and then wished them away, and I had heard a story about the Chinese cannery workers from long ago. If one died here, so far from his home, his body would be salted down and shipped home in a keg. That sounded plausible because I'd heard how the young Joshua Slocum and his wife had lost a child in the Philippines back in the 1880s, and how, not being able to bear the thought of burying the child there or at sea, they had preserved the body in a keg of brandy until they could bury it back in North America. But there was also a tiny old cemetery on the outskirts of the cannery, in a peaceful setting among the lupine, birch, and black spruce. It contained only three graves, each marked with a wooden post about eight inches by eight inches and four or five feet high. These were pointed at the top, and each bore hand-carved Asian characters that ran the full height of the post. The sites were surrounded by picket fences that were worn and half rotted, but still showed slight traces of white paint. A depression was visible in one of the graves, as though it had caved in; but the story around the cannery was that a desperate cannery worker once dug into the grave in hopes of finding opium. One of the markers had rotted at the ground and fallen over. I wondered about the lives of these people who died in this remote place and were buried with such devotion. The beautiful carved script. People at the cannery called this the Chinese cemetery, and I guessed that the dead were among the people who were later replaced by the iron chink.

In my early years at Columbia Wards there were plenty of Asian workers, and they, too, were fish butchers, but they were all Filipinos. Their expertise at this work was so valued that they were flown up from Seattle every year. They lived and ate separately and were overseen by the Filipino boss, Pete. Every Fourth of July they would have a party for the whole cannery, setting up tables of wonderful food that they had prepared, such as barbecued pork and noodles, and they held a modest fireworks display. It was the cannery's only big social event, and fishermen would count themselves lucky when the Fourth fell on a non-fishing day and they could attend. But after the Fourth the Filipinos would return to their more or less separate existence, and you would see little of them when they weren't at work butchering fish. I never had any reason to believe that they were looked down upon as Asians, but I had no way to tell what they had experienced in their lives or how they felt about their place in this community. Over the years, their numbers dwindled and then they were no longer there. But not too many years after that a new group of Asians began to appear at Columbia Wards and every other cannery in Alaska. The market for salmon shifted from canned to fresh-frozen fish that were highly prized in Japan. Salmon suddenly became much more valuable, and the Japanese taught us how to take care of it, demanding that we treat this valuable food with much more respect than we ever had. We had once unloaded our fish by jabbing each one with the single tine of a peugh and throwing it aboard a tender; now we learned how to pick up each fish, not by the tail, but by the body, using both hands and carefully throwing it into a bin. And now that the eggs had become so valuable as Sujiko, the iron chink was modified in order to extract the eggs without damaging them. The booming Alaskan salmon industry no longer exploited an Asian workforce but was now overseen by Asians.

That, too, began to pass as the Japanese market shifted to the much more economical farm-raised salmon. When I last visited the cannery, in 1998, I didn't know that it would be shutting down just two months later. Making my way through the trees, I kicked up the usual swarm of mosquitoes but was happy to see that the little cemetery was still undisturbed, though now more overgrown than ever. The pickets and grave markers were a little more decayed, and seemed to be heading in that direction at about the same rate as were some old cannery boats that rested not far away, off the edge of the road that leads into the cannery. The old boats were hauled there twenty or thirty years ago and the undergrowth had begun to overtake them, as well. I took some pictures of the cemetery and, using some butcher paper I had brought with me for this purpose, carefully made rubbings from two of the grave markers. The carved script had always seemed so beautiful and mysterious to me, and I wanted to find out what was written there. I planned to take the pictures and rubbings to a university colleague, Tim Wong, a professor of Asia Studies and Chinese literature at Arizona State.

When I went to Tim's office that fall I told him about the iron chink and my interest in the old Chinese graves. Could he read the script on these two markers? He was intrigued by these remnants of Chinese history in North America, and was pleased when I told him that I wanted to write a little piece someday that I might title, "The Iron Chink." I unrolled the rubbings and placed the pictures beside them on Tim's desk. He looked at them closely for a few minutes and then turned to me with a smile. "I think you'll have to change your title, Bert. 'The Iron Jap.' These are Japanese graves." Then, pointing from top to bottom as he read the script on one, he translated for me: "The late, or the former . . . Fujuda Aijirō . . . grave, or the grave of." Another read similarly and could be translated as "The grave of the late Katayama Asajirō." Tim explained that Katayama is the surname and the "rō" suffix indicates "male" or "son." At the time, I was disappointed that the script included no dates, nor any indication of how these people died, as old gravestones often do in the Western world. Now it seems better to see these details as simply being overtaken by nature, something like the little temple I've seen in pictures from Angkor Wat. The temple is hardly visible within the base of a magnificent tree that grew around it it long ago and now towers above it.

After I made the rubbings that day, I walked back toward the river. It was late in July and, though I didn't know it, the cannery was processing some of the last fish that would pass over the dock at that old site. I saw a few people who remembered me and greeted me as though I were a visiting member of the family. I talked briefly with Emery, a Kenai Native who had been beach boss for several years, as indispensable now and as much loved as Ingolf ever was. This was on a fishing day and most of the boats were still out in the Inlet. Some had already quit for the season, though, and Emery was keeping his eye on the new hydraulic boat lift as it maneuvered to pick one boat out of the water. I recognized some other boats anchored in the river, waiting to be lifted out. It was just after high water and they were starting to swing the other way on the beginning of the ebb. I remembered how good it had been to make my way back into the river after a wild day on the Inlet, with a decent catch, and to head upriver toward the cannery, my first harbor.

Bowline Bill

EARLY IN AUGUST OF 1963, our first year as fishermen, Dick and I were on a drift a few miles out from Clam Gulch tower, not catching a thing and wondering if we should "bunch it." The fishermen from the Columbia River and Puget Sound had already bunched it a week before—bunched their nets together to be lifted off the boat. That was the first step in the process of ending their season, winterizing their boats, and flying out in order to get ready for other short seasons at Astoria or in the Sound. We'd hear guys talking on the radio and one would say, "Well, that's it for us. Had ten on that two-hour drift, mostly dogs and a few silvers. We're bunchin' it. See ya in the river." We had no other fishery to think about and didn't want to quit too early in our first year. It seemed best to follow the lead of the local fishermen who knew that the run was over—most of the fish had gone up the river—but were content to keep at it for a while longer. Scratch fishing—there wouldn't be any more big catches, but "you might be able to scratch out a few." We'd caught enough to pay for *Margaret* and this first year's expenses. Now we were edging a little into the black, and that felt pretty good. Still, when it looks like the fish are gone, and when you're the only ones out there, you can't help wondering if it's worth it.

We hadn't seen any other boats and assumed that we were the only ones out there that day. We had ten or fifteen fish for the day, dogs (chum salmon) mainly, which added up to about seven dollars and fifty cents, but it was a beautiful day. Sunny and flat calm. So, largely because we didn't know what else to do, we just left the net in the water and waited for the flood to push us up a little closer to Kenai. It wasn't costing us anything, though it sure would have been nice to see a hit.

We heard an engine someplace in the distance and began to look around. There was some smoke on the horizon out toward the middle and we finally saw a speck of a boat. It gradually drew a little closer and we guessed that it must be heading in above us, toward Kenai or Kasilof.

We returned to watching our net, hoping to see a hit or at least a bobbing float. Anything to avoid picking it up. Nothing.

It was surprising how far away you could hear that engine. *Margaret*'s little four-cylinder Willys hardly made a whisper by comparison, and we guessed from the sound and the smoke that it was a diesel. It was still a few miles away but now it changed course slightly and was pointed towards us. "Looks like we're about to have company," Dick said. That was normal. If you're looking for fish and see another boat on a drift, it's worthwhile to check it out. Especially if the boat's been there for a while, all by itself, you think they might be on some fish. You might see fresh hits in their net, and if not you can keep on, run along their net, and look down to see whether they've already caught some that are still hanging in the gear. Sometimes it pays off. On the other hand, if you're the only boat around, and another one appears on the horizon and then turns to come toward you, it could be a friend or maybe someone who's either in trouble himself or about to bring some to you. This one began to make us wonder, not just because of the noise it was making, and the black smoke it was putting out, but because it had a definite list. Dick reached for the binoculars, and in a second he said, "You know, I think that's *Martha K.* We're gonna have a visit from Bowline Bill."

We had seen Bill and his boat at the cannery, when someone pointed him out, but we'd heard of him even before that. We finally we met him at mug-up, where we learned his name was Bill Thies and that he was an interesting guy. He had a master's degree in some kind of engineering, and some years ago he'd come to Alaska to get out of the engineering rat-race in California. Something about his looks, the glasses, maybe, and the way he dressed, in those hard twill pants, made you think, yeah, this guy could have been an engineer. But once you heard how he came to be called Bowline Bill, that's the only way you could think of him.

Sometime in the late fifties he was fishing alone toward the end of the season. Most of the other boats had quit, but he was still scratching. He was somewhere north of the river, on the east side, around the Forelands, and for some reason he ran in toward the beach and decided to tie up at one of the scows anchored a mile or so off the beach. They were little wooden, unmanned scows about ten by twenty feet, painted Libby yellow, anchored here and there along the beach to take fish from the set-netters. Fishermen along an isolated stretch of beach like that could haul fish out there in their skiffs, pitch them off into a bin with their name on it, cover the fish with burlap, and leave them to be picked up by one of the cannery tenders. The tender made scheduled stops after each period. Set-netters could also send in orders by radio and the tender would drop stuff off on the scow—fuel, maybe, a new set of spark plugs, a few loaves of bread. There's no telling what Bill had in mind that day, but he was probably tired of running the boat and wanted to tie up to the scow for a while, maybe work on the engine or take a nap. Maybe he wanted to make a drift at the change of tide, close to the beach, and decided to tie to the scow instead of dropping his own anchor to wait for the tide.

I can imagine how it happened:

It was late afternoon. He was tired and wanted to let go of the wheel for a while. "I'll go in and tie up to that scow again for the rest of the flood. Don't wanta get pushed way to hell up past the deadline. Be good to turn off the engine and lie down. Then I'll run in to the beach and make a last set at high water slack. If there's anything around they ought to show up then. Take the ebb back down to the river and hang it up. Sure as hell not gonna make any night sets up here." So he headed over toward the scow, slowed down, eased in a little closer to it and then, timing it just right, took his boat out of gear. Drift in against the tide and get out on the bow before it bumps. Not that he had to think it through like this. If you fish alone for very long it's automatic. Perfect. Flat calm, no need to put out a bumper, just ease right up to it. Boat's j-u-u-ust coming to a stop against the tide. Not even a bump. Grab the bowline, step off onto the scow. Take the cleat. Yeah. He stood up to stretch his back and glance ashore, quickly noting that there was nobody around.

"Great. Get a good nap. Now the stern line," and then, "What the FUCK!?" running the few steps to the end of the scow in time to see the bow of his boat ease just out of reach, drifting up the Inlet on the flood. "No! Don't try to jump for it, you dumb asshole." The bowline had slipped off his bow cleat, and the boat end now floated on the surface, pointing straight from the scow to the boat, whose engine purred steadily on. "Son of a BITCH!!" Not a boat in sight and nobody along the beach. "Shit!   Go ahead and yell your fuckin' head off, you dumb bastard. Nobody's gonna hear you."

He was on the scow for only about twelve hours before a beach fisherman came out in his skiff to pitch off his fish. Bill must have spent a cold night there, with nothing to eat or drink and nothing but a piece of burlap to wrap around him. When he heard the outboard approaching he stood up and no doubt surprised the hell out of the fisherman. Here's a guy you've never seen before standing alone on the scow, just nodding to you as you approach, and nothing else in sight. Bill hated telling his story to the set-netter, and then had to do it again, when the tender made its rounds and picked him up. The captain listened to his story, trying not to laugh, and then got on the radio to pass on word about Bill's boat. That part ended luckily, because somebody found it and towed it in later that day. It had drifted up on the flood, back down on the ebb, and up toward the Forelands again. There it was, drifting along in the east rip, surrounded by tidal debris, and the engine still idling away. Bill didn't realize it at the time, but when he got off the scow and went aboard the tender for the trip back in to the cannery, he was a new man.

As Dick and I saw him approach that day, we thought he might need a hand. *Martha K* was a square old slab of a boat, some kind of World War Two landing craft that he had bought as salvage and then fitted out as a gill-netter. It was the kind of boat that made you wonder about Martha. Whoever she was, could she have been proud that this slab bore her name? Bill was a capable engineer and probably put his rig together for next to nothing, but the bad list, the loud, smoking engine, and the general disarray on deck made us proud to have *Margaret*, as small, aged, and ill-equipped as she was. You might smile at our boxy little cabin and the ridiculous job we had done in painting the waterline, but next to *Martha K*, *Margaret*'s classic, double-ender lines made her a thing of beauty. Bill slowed down to come alongside, being careful to keep clear of our net, and we got ready to take the lines. We noticed that *Martha K* didn't smell too fresh, and Bill was looking pretty scruffy. His pants were greasy from working on the engine, and he looked like he hadn't washed or shaved for several days. A good-looking German Shepherd came up out of the cabin to greet us from the bow. Bill shut down his engine and asked, "How's it going? You guys doing any good here?"

We gave him our disappointing report, our few dogs for the whole day. We had been on this one for a couple of hours and hadn't seen a thing. How about you? Any luck out there? "Yeah, I did OK. That's what I wanted to talk to you about. I got about five hundred dogs on a night set, on the middle rip off Ninilchik." Boy, did that sound good to us. That was about two hundred fifty dollars worth of fish. Damned good for that late in the season. He took off his hatch cover to show us, and the smell of old fish surged up. They didn't look really old, not flat-out rotten, but they were a long way from fresh—late-season dogs, soft and with those brownish-yellow stripes. Nobody packed ice in those days, and nobody was even thinking about insulating his hold. You just tried to protect them from the sun, using burlap if you didn't have hatch covers, and remember to throw a few buckets of water on them once in a while. You rarely saw a tender captain go aboard a boat that was delivering to see what shape the fish were in, the test being to pick one up and sniff the gills. It was all going to be cooked in the cans, anyhow, and the stuff that ended up too mushy would just be graded a little lower. *Margaret*'s hold was only a big open bin with no cover, and we'd delivered lots of fish that year that you wouldn't want to cook for dinner. Especially some that had been on the bottom, soaked in gurry and often mashed out of shape against a rib. We'd even pitched off a few that had been scrunched in too close to the exhaust pipe and were half cooked.

But Bill's load looked enough on the edge for one of us to ask how long ago he'd caught them. "Well, it was night before last, and that's the thing. You know, I had an argument with Archie the last time I was in at the cannery, and I don't think he's gonna take these." Archie was the superintendent at that time, and he was a little crusty. "Didn't like me having the dog aboard. Shit, I've always had a dog on the boat, and I told him he could go to hell." This dog certainly looked sleek and well fed. He came aboard to check out our boat, sniffed around in the stern as though looking for a place to go, and then obeyed Bill's soft command to go back aboard *Martha K*. Bill had set a big pot of boiled salmon on deck. I was impressed with the dog because everyone knows they don't like to crap on their own boats. You have to watch that one doesn't come aboard your boat and do it on a piece of net that might be lying around in the picking area.

"I was thinking maybe you guys could take 'em. I'd split it with you. I'm guessing you might be planning to go in on the next tide. We could pitch 'em off in a hurry, if you're willing. *Are* you about to pick up and head in?"

We were quiet for a second and then I said, "Yeah. We're about to pick it up. But, you know, I don't think Archie would take them from us, either. We had a little run in with him, too." I told Bill how, one day early in the season, we were having lunch in the fishermen's mess hall and were planning to sneak out a couple of spoons. We needed another one or two on the boat, and we didn't know when we could get to the Salvation Army store in Kenai, where we'd found most of our other stuff. I'd scooted the spoons under a napkin when the waitress began to clear away the plates and she saw me. "What are you gonna do with those?" she asked. "Nothing," I lied, turning a little red, I'm sure, but trying to bluff my way through it. She kept her eye on us until we got up to leave, and of course I didn't try getting away with them. Two or three hours later Archie came down to the floating dock where we were tied up. He went aboard the boat we were tied to, stepped to the rail and waited for us to acknowledge him. You'd often see Archie pacing the boardwalks along the main dock, but we had never seen him down on the floating docks with the boats, and certainly not bothering to talk with new fishermen like ourselves.

"I heard you guys were up at the mess hall at dinner, and you tried to steal some silverware. That right?"

"No!" we lied, again, feeling about as cheap and stupid as you can be.

"Well," he said, "The waitress told me she saw you trying to sneak something out of there. I don't know. Pretty lousy if you ask me. You're gettin' free food, and damn good food, and you pull something like that. Aren't you two supposed to be school teachers?! For Christ's sake!" He turned around and left us there.

Regrettable as that incident was, we were relieved to be able to tell about it. Bill understood immediately and didn't push us any farther to try to sell his punky fish for him. We talked a little bit more, drank some coffee with him, and then he got ready to go. He fired off his diesel and we let go the lines. We could hear the engine noise for a long time and then still see the black smoke as he made his way north. We never heard how he got rid of those fish. Probably ended up pitching them overboard.

That's the way it seemed to go for Bowline Bill. Nothing seemed to work out for him. I was talking about him once with our mutual friend, Poopdeck, who told me how he'd twice rescued Bill from remote areas on the west side of the Inlet. The first time, Poopdeck had pulled into Chinitna Bay on his way to a seal-hunting trip and seen Bill's disabled boat. He'd never met Bill, and found that Bill was over there as a guide, with a moose hunter from Seward. They had been broken down for several days, and Poopdeck towed them across the Inlet and all the way around the Kenai Peninsula to Seward, a trip of nearly two hundred miles. Then, just a couple of years later, Poopdeck heard somehow that Bill was again stranded on the West side of the Inlet, below Kalgin Island. Looking for shelter, he'd run his boat up into a creek at high water and then couldn't get back out. Poopdeck geared up, crossed the Inlet, found him, pulled Bill's boat out of the creek, and then towed him back to Homer. Those were both pretty big messes to get yourself into, but I'm sure there must have been others.

I was never involved in any of Bill's serious predicaments, but I was almost drawn into his web of misfortune one time in the early seventies. We were both still fishing out of Columbia Wards and he told me about his winter work. Somehow he'd acquired a license to run a winter commercial fishery for trout on Kenai Lake, fishing with a gill net that he strung under the ice. I doubted that there was such a licensed fishery, and didn't give it much thought, except to imagine what it must have been like to pull nets and fish up onto the ice and have them freeze solid within minutes. He processed the fish into smoked trout pâté, put it up in quarter-pound cans, and then tried to market wherever he could. He knew that I was a university teacher in Arizona in the winters, and talked with me about representing him down there and perhaps elsewhere in the lower forty-eight. He gave me a can to sample, and it wasn't bad. But having some on crackers, I couldn't help thinking about what I'd seen aboard *Martha K.*

Even if this was a legal operation, I could imagine what it might have been like. He was probably doing it mostly alone, and I didn't want to think about what-all was in it, how he processed the stuff, how often he cleaned the grinder, and so forth. Fortunately, he never called me during the year to follow up on it.

I didn't see him or hear anything about him for a few years after that. Wondering what became of him, I asked Poopdeck if he knew what Bill was up to these days. "Oh, shit," he said. "Thought you heard about that. Poor bastard blew his brains out last fall. Somebody said it was over a woman. I never knew a guy with such a string of bad luck, and sometimes I thought it was just him. Didn't have enough sense to pour piss out of a boot. But I always liked the guy."

Anna A

AFTER THE GILL-NETTING SEASON that summer in 1963, I had nearly two months to scrape up some more money. My half of the earnings on *Margaret* amounted to four hundred dollars, and that wouldn't go very far. My predicament had arisen earlier that year when, teaching junior high "language arts," I realized that I wanted to learn more about English literature. As a first step, I took a night class offered in Anchorage by the University of Alaska. It was a survey of British literature from the Romantics to the twentieth century and the teacher, Richard Gaines, sparked a love of literature that I hadn't felt before—certainly not in the two classes I'd taken a few years earlier at the University of Washington. Even if Gaines had been my professor in those years, I doubt that he could have rescued me from my absorption in collegiate athletics. A recent master's graduate from UCLA, Gaines had begun a new career in teaching, after a long and impressive career in acting on Broadway and in Hollywood. You can see him in old movies like "Double Indemnity," with James Cagney. Gaines could make poetry come alive by reading it aloud. When he read a poem aloud, it made sense, as sentences, and this helped me get over the feeling that poetry is a mysterious other kind of language. Deciding to become an English major, at that late date, I gave up my teaching position and planned to return to the University of Washington in the fall. Now I needed money.

There wasn't any work in the Kenai area, but I heard that there might be some in Kodiak, where there was a king crab fishery as well as a salmon fishery. You can't get there by road, so I wouldn't have to compete with a lot of other people looking for seasonal work. I needed only another six to eight weeks' work and decided to spring for an air ticket to Kodiak.

The day I got there I was lucky to find a cheap bunkhouse near the harbor, but it was too late to check in at the cannery offices. There was still lots of daylight, though, so I walked through town, checking out the harbor and admiring the spectacular setting. I walked up the hill to the Russian Orthodox church, which was a little older than the ones in Kenai and Ninilchik, and stopped for a beer and a bite to eat at one of the several bars "down town." The prices were way higher than in Kenai or Anchorage, and I knew I'd have to get out of there soon if I couldn't find work. There was a lot of talk about the booming king crab fishery, and lots of bars and tourist shops displayed mounted crab that were often over ten pounds each. The first place I tried the next day was a cannery called King Krab, Inc. But the guy at the office told me they weren't hiring. The salmon season was about over and the crab season hadn't quite got going. He didn't know of anyone who was looking for help.

Just as I was turning to leave, a heavy-set guy walked up to the counter and told the man, "Well, he's not back, and we're pullin' out in a couple hours. Prob'ly drunk up at the B and B."

The guy at the counter looked back at me and said, "Hey, can you cook?"

"Yeah," I said, stretching things quite a bit by telling him I'd cooked on a fishing boat and at a fraternity house. He hired me on the spot, had me sign some papers, and told me that the pay was six hundred dollars a month.

"Get your gear and be back within forty-five minutes, OK?"

When I showed up with my duffle he took me down to the dock and we went aboard *Anna A*. She was an aging halibut boat of about seventy feet width with an eighteen foot beam, and was working as a tender for salmon until the crab season got going. From the back deck we entered the cabin and passed through the galley. It looked well equipped, with a table that would seat six to eight people. Just then a tall guy who looked like he was in his early sixties came through the galley's forward door, and the man who had hired me said, "Here's your cook, Andy." Then to me, "This is your skipper, Andy Hegerberg." I introduced myself but soon found that my name here would be only "Cook."

Andy seemed a little suspicious and aloof, but he showed me to the forecastle, just forward of the galley, where there were six or seven bunks. Two looked occupied, a third held the few things that the previous cook had left behind, and two others were full of stored supplies. Andy pointed to the two empty bunks and told me to take my pick, so I put my duffle on the bottom one. A ladder led up from the forecastle to the captain's quarters and pilot house. The skipper took me back into the galley and briefly showed me around. He had a thick Swedish accent that was full of that Scandinavian music with lots of "Ja"s and "Vell"s. There was a big diesel-oil stove with a pot of foul-smelling coffee sitting in a corner at the sea rail and, pointing to it, he told me to keep a fresh pot going all the time. Other than that it was three meals a day, and I'd always need to have something on the table for mug-ups and other snacks, especially if we were putting in long hours taking fish—a bowl of cookies or leftover cake or maybe some canned fruit.

To the left of the stove there was a good-sized sink and then a door that led out to the starboard side of the boat. To the right of the stove was a large refrigerator/freezer. There didn't seem to be time for any conversation, but I found a chance to let the skipper know that I owned my own boat and had just finished the season in Cook Inlet. Unimpressed, he cut things short and said that I'd better head up town and buy groceries for the trip. We were going to pick up fish on the other side of the island and would need supplies for about a week. There would be only four of us—himself, the engineer, a deck hand, and myself. The guy at the office would tell me who to see at the store and how to get the stuff back to the dock in time for us to leave, in about two hours. This was looking very good, six hundred dollars a month plus room and board, and the man at the office made it clear that I could get whatever I wanted at the store, no questions asked.

The store was well supplied, and since the galley had a huge refrigerator and freezer, I really stocked up. This was an amazing luxury after what Dick and I had made do with on *Margaret*, where we ate only what we could find at CWF's company store and had no refrigerator or ice chest. I got quite a load, including lots of bacon and eggs, coffee, canned orange juice, a few sacks of potatoes, a couple of dozen big ribeye steaks, a leg of lamb, a pork roast, some chickens, lots of bread, canned goods, cookies, ice cream, and cake mix. All the most expensive stuff.

Back at the boat the guy who'd reported the cook missing was working on deck, getting things ready for the trip. I introduced myself—his name was something like Steve—and then started taking the supplies into the galley. I was putting things away when a grey-haired little old guy in an oil-stained white tee shirt came out of the forecastle, headed for the starboard door and down into the engine room. He stopped, took a wet cigarette out of his mouth, and told me he was John, the engineer. I told him my name was Bert, but he cocked his head and cupped his ear and nodded when I repeated my name. He was a bit stooped and looked like he was in his early seventies. Heading out the door, he flashed a quick smile and had a kind of twinkle in his eye.

I continued storing the groceries until Andy came in from upstairs and told me that we'd be pulling out in a few minutes. I'd need to be on deck and take some lines. We were heading outside on a run down to Old Harbor, and it looked like it'd be a little sloppy. I should start dinner once we got underway. He yelled something to Steve on the back deck and then went up the port side stairs to the pilot house. I had most of the things put away and went out to take the sternline while Steve took the bowline. Even this little bit of work on deck was better than being in the galley, and it was a thrill to be working on a boat in such a picturesque harbor. It was alive with other fishing boats of all kinds, from thirty to a hundred feet, heading in or out, or tied to the dock with crewmen working on their gear.

There was a little breeze, though, and as soon as we got outside the harbor we began to roll and sometimes plunge. It was late afternoon and as soon as we got outside I headed back into the galley to start dinner. I knew I'd have to work fast and keep it simple, but the stove was already good and hot. I put some potatoes into the oven and began to run water over four of the frozen steaks to thaw them out as quickly as possible. But I had to set that aside and get things secure. Everything on the table, the counters, and the stove was beginning to move around, and a half-empty coffee mug slid across the table, leapt a sea-rail and crashed to the floor. Cleaning that up, I quickly learned how to make my way around the galley, going up or down the sloping deck with one hand on a rail. The wind had picked up and a little bit of diesel smoke was wafting from the stove. I remembered Andy's directions about the coffee, so threw out the old stuff and put on a new pot of water. I'd never cooked on an oil stove and soon learned how long it takes to boil water, even when the stove's hot. I decided that once the potatoes got going I'd cook the steaks on the top of the stove, a large black iron griddle with a surrounding channel to drain off the grease.

The diesel fumes from the stove were getting to me so I stepped out on the back deck and ducked behind something to stay out of the spray. Going out the galley you stepped down to the deck, which was awash with water rushing in and out at the scuppers all along the rails. The only dry place was on the hatch cover for the hold, in the center of the deck. It was good to get some fresh air, but I was surprised to see how much a big boat like this rolled and plunged in heavy seas. I realized that when Andy had said we'd be running "outside" he meant not just outside of town but out into the Gulf of Alaska, and since we were headed down the island, there wasn't anything to do but run more or less broadside to the seas. I didn't know how long a run we had to Old Harbor but it looked like we'd be rolling all the way. I heard something crash in the galley and ran back inside. I hadn't secured the coffee pot with a corner sea rail. The stove-top was a cloud of steam, the steaks were drenched with hot water, and the pot was rolling around on the floor.

I got that cleaned up and went into the forecastle to talk with Steve, who was trying to read in his bunk. He seemed cheered to know that we'd be having steaks, and when I asked him what the routine was, he told me that when it was ready, he and John would eat first. Then he'd take the wheel while Andy ate. Back in the galley I unrolled and spread out the rubber mesh mat that kept things from sliding around on the table, but even then I couldn't set out plates or anything else. The only things that stayed put were jammed together in a little box/tray in the center of the table—salt and pepper shakers, a bottle of ketchup, jars of mustard and pickles.

The potatoes were getting close to done, though, so I got ready to cook the steaks. The stove was hot as hell by now, making the galley even stuffier. The doors and windows were closed because of the wind and spray, and the diesel fumes coughed back down the stovepipe into the room. Following Steve's remarks about the routine, I decided to cook one steak at a time. I'd get his ready first and then get things ready for John, who was still working down in the engine room. I soon yelled to Steve that his dinner was ready. I was impressed with how he kept the food on his plate and managed to hold himself in place on the bench. The smoke from the steak didn't mix well with the fumes, but it didn't seem to bother him a bit. He ate with gusto and topped it with a large bowl of ice-cream and some frozen strawberries that I'd thawed.

I wasn't at all hungry. In fact I was wondering if I could keep from throwing up while I finished making dinner for the other two. It helped to duck out to the lee side once in a while for a breath of fresh air. It was dark now and I couldn't see anything of the island. Back inside I put on John's steak and began to get things ready for him, while holding on with one hand and trying to keep things from sliding and banging around. Steve put his dirty dishes into the sink, where they rattled around like mad, and on his way back to his bunk told me to let him know when Andy's dinner was ready. I threw on the other steak and, seeing that John's was about done, headed down to the engine room to call him up for dinner. I barely made it outside the galley before I had to grab for the rail and puke. It went all over the deck walkway, but it didn't matter because the deck was awash. This was the second time I'd been seasick and it seemed worse than before, the diesel fumes being even more nauseating than the gasoline fumes that got to me on *Margaret*. I dry-heaved for another minute or so, then got myself together and made my way forward to the door that led down to the engine room. The door banged open in the wind and I stepped down onto the metal grill stairway. The engine was roaring in the dim light and I caught sight of John squatting next to it with a wrench. I yelled but of course he couldn't hear me, and I didn't want to go down any further.

I backed out the door and as it slammed shut dry-heaved again. Then, afraid that the steaks were burning up, I ducked back into the galley and moved them to a cooler spot on the griddle. I had to get John before his steak was crisped. When I got back to the engine room John still had the wrench in his hand and was trying to reach a fitting on the engine without getting too wet. I had never seen so much bilge slopping around. John nodded when he saw me signal that his dinner was ready, but I couldn't take my eyes off the sloshing bilge, and worse—the ribs and some of the planks. They were all moving! As *Anna A* rolled and plunged, the flexing ribs looked like they were made of rubber. How in hell could it all hold together?

It was good to be back inside the galley, and somehow I managed to get John's plate ready. He came in, washed some of the grease off his hands, propped himself into his place at the table and dug in. I told Steve that Andy's was ready and he went up to relieve him at the wheel, but he came back in a second and said he'd take Andy's plate up to him. Andy didn't want to give up the wheel in that kind of weather and would nibble away at his dinner when he could.

I washed the dishes, made a fresh pot of coffee, and then sacked out. John and Steve were asleep in their bunks, and Andy stayed at the wheel for about five hours. At some point in the middle of the night we stopped rolling so much, and once or twice I caught sight of Andy coming down and heading back up from the galley with a mug of coffee. Just about daylight he yelled down to us and we got things ready to drop the hook at Old Harbor. After we anchored it was time for breakfast, and the pancakes, bacon, and eggs I served up seemed to fill the bill. The other three ate at the table while I kept the stuff coming, and they exchanged only a few words. The gist of it was that a few seiners would be coming alongside later in the day to deliver their fish and take fuel. And they laughed in talking about this somewhat remote village. There were only a few scattered ramshackle houses. "All they do here is fish and fuck," Andy said, and John added the punch line: "And they don't fish in the winter."

I noticed Andy's bloodshot eyes and wondered if he ever slept. When I poured some more coffee, Andy said, "Cook! The coffee's old, and how'd you make it, anyhow?" I told him I'd washed the pot, put in the fresh water and coffee, and then boiled it for a few minutes—just regular sheepherder's coffee. "You *never* boil it!" he said. "And don't wash the pot. Just boil the *water*, stir in plenty of grounds, and set the pot there on the corner so it won't get too hot. Never let it boil. And you got to keep it fresh, OK?" I have to admit it was a good method, and I wanted to do everything I could to keep Andy alert and coming back for more on those long nights at the wheel.

We hung out there for a few days, taking fish and pumping fuel, and when we had two boats alongside at once, I worked as a deck hand and tallied fish on one side. The fishermen pitched off the fish one at a time, stabbing each with a peugh and throwing it onto the deck, where the deck hand kept a tally by punching one of four little counters that were fixed to a board and marked red, pink, silver, or dog. These fish were mostly reds, but most of them were covered with gurry, especially the shapeless ones from the bottom of the hold, and sometimes it was hard to tell a red, worth a dollar and a half, from a dog that was worth a third of that. Of course the fishermen kept an eye on the tally, and so did Andy. Once, looking over my shoulder he said just loud enough so the fishermen couldn't hear him, "Goddamnit! That wasn't a red. Said you were a fisherman!"

I was more confident with my cooking, where I could take time to get things right, and over those few days I tried to please the crew with a pretty damned good roast leg of lamb or some baked pork chops. But these guys weren't keen on that kind of fare. They were polite enough, but there was lots of lamb left over. Occasionally a boat would deliver a steelhead, and since the cannery couldn't take them, I once put a fat one aside for dinner. Getting ready to clean it, I began to sharpen a butcher knife with a stone from the galley, and when Andy saw what I was doing he showed me how to do it better and more quickly with a file. I appreciated the tip, and thought that the interest Andy had shown in what I was doing meant that he was looking forward to dinner. But when I put the baked steelhead on the table and seasoned it with a few hard-to-get lemons, it too fell flat with the crew. The pie I'd baked went down OK, but neither this fine steelhead nor any of the other special cuts of meat I'd prepared seemed to interest these guys.

After about a week, we were on the hook waiting to take fish in another bay, and sitting around the galley table over our morning mug-up. By now, Andy seemed a little more open and friendly toward me, maybe because I kept a clean galley, put decent meals on the table, on schedule, and hadn't snuck any whiskey aboard. Telling a story or a joke, he would glance my direction once in a while. I had never worked for a captain on a boat, but I didn't have to know about Captain Ahab or Wolf Larsen to feel the weight of ship-board authority. Still, I'd grown less wary of this new captain and was more receptive to his wit and good-heartedness. It seemed a good time to try to find what he and the others really liked for dinner, the roast lamb and pork roast having fallen flat. So I asked what they'd like that night. They glanced at me and then Steve and John looked to Andy. He kind of cleared his throat, smiled, and then very delicately said, "Vell, Cook, what we really like is salt cod and potatoes."

"Let me show you," he said, getting up from the table and motioning me to follow. He went out the door to the starboard deck and then up the stairs to the smaller deck outside the pilot house. "Here you go," he said, pointing to a large, covered plastic bucket. He bent down, took off the lid and picked a chunk of grayish-white fish from the brine. The bucket was half full of these rigid chunks and I remember wondering why anyone would want to eat this stuff when there was an endless supply of fresh salmon or steelhead, not to mention the choicest cuts of meat that the grocers could stock in Kodiak. Andy must have sensed what I was thinking because he gently coaxed me into considering this unlikely-looking delicacy. "All you need to do is take it out in the morning and soak it in fresh water. Change the water once or twice before dinner. Then make a nice big pot of potatoes. Just peel 'em, don't mash 'em. Then, when everything's ready, boil the cod for just a few minutes, until it flakes good. If you boil it too long it'll get tough." He told me all this with a kind of motherly care and a sense of reverence for an old family tradition.

As we headed back down to the galley he told me that he got the cod off a boat in town, but sometimes they put out their own lines when they were anchored up somewhere. "Well," I said, "let's have some tonight."

Andy beamed and said, "You betcha!" So I got a pan from the galley, fetched several of the rigid chunks from the brine, and followed Andy's instructions. I have to admit that it was an excellent meal, even all-white as it was—just the boiled cod with lots of boiled potatoes and butter. No parsley or anything fancy. After that we had it maybe three times a week—interspersed with steaks, meatloaf, or chicken—and they ate it up.

In a few days we had a decent load of fish to take back to the cannery in Kodiak. It was an easier run going back, and after we got unloaded and cleaned up, Andy told us we'd be there for a couple of days and then make a run to Karluk, on the Shelikof Strait side of the island. Fish and Game would open Karluk Lagoon for a few days the next week, and it looked like there'd be lots of fish. That afternoon Andy retrieved a nice steelhead he'd been keeping on ice and wrapped it in newspaper. In a few minutes he reappeared, all spiffed up and wearing a clean white fisherman's cap. He told me not to bother with dinner that night because Steve lived in town. Andy would also eat in town and John would probably hang out at the B and B, one of the bars. Then he stepped off the boat and headed up town, carrying the steelhead under an arm and whistling a tune. I heard Andy come aboard late that night and John came in sometime in the wee hours. Andy looked like he might have had a date, but I didn't want to ask. He'd already told us that his wife was coming up from Ballard toward the end of our charter in a few weeks. They'd stay on the boat while it was on the grid for repairs, and then both head home.

On the two-day layover in Kodiak I got to know a little more of John. He was an interesting old guy who said that he'd lost a small fortune when he had to leave some kind of a business he had in China when things fell apart for Americans there in the late forties. He'd worked with Andy for several years and made eight hundred dollars a month. He didn't have family or any other home and deposited his monthly check at the B and B. With his room and board on the boat, he didn't need much else. He bought his cigarettes and drank off the rest. I'd gone to the B and B for a beer one night and seen him at the bar, really wiped out and letting some other guys rip him off by drinking on his tab. I'd hear him come back early in the morning, soused but never stumbling drunk. Andy could count on him to keep the engine in perfect order. One night when we were both lying in our bunks reading, he proudly showed me his new glasses—a pair he had found at the Salvation Army for three bucks. I agreed they were a bargain but thought eight hundred a month and you get your prescription glasses at the Salvation Army. We talked a while, he cupping his ear to catch, or actually miss, most of what I said. His eardrums were about done in from all that pounding in the engine room. I don't know how it came up, probably from something he was reading in his magazine, but we'd begun talking about women, and after a while he said, "Well, the old sailors all say a porpoise is the *best* fuck."

"Huh?" I said.

"Sure. You've seen 'em. They're friendly as hell, and curious." True, we had seen plenty of them swimming alongside or playing in the bow wake. But John didn't elaborate and my imagination couldn't take it any further.

It was a pretty long run to Karluk, north of town and around the island through Kupreanof Strait, then something like a fifty-mile run down Shelikof to Karluk. Again, we left at night and Andy didn't sleep until nearly noon the next day. On long, clear stretches he put it on iron mike (the autopilot) from time to time. From the forecastle you could hear the electric motor and the chain-drive turn back and forth, searching for the heading and constantly adjusting to the wind or swells. Once when he had it on iron mike I was standing at the rail on the back deck and Andy came out through the galley door. He'd come down to grab a cup of coffee and stepped outside to keep his bearings while he took a piss. Keeping his watch to the port side, with a cup of coffee in one hand and the constant wet cigarette in his mouth, he pissed right on the deck. He didn't see me, and I understood at once how much better this was than for him to have ducked into the head or to have risked pissing over the rail. The low deck was awash, as it often was. Later that night, when we got a little further into the Strait along Raspberry Island there were patches of fog and it was pretty narrow in some places. Even in that murk I could see some awful looking rocks as we passed close by.

We anchored at Karluk for two days and took on all the fish we could, filling the hold and finally the whole back deck up to the hatch covers. Fish and Game had more escapement than they wanted, so they kept the lagoon open, and a few of the local seiners really loaded up. One afternoon a seiner was coming alongside to deliver when its engine died, just far enough away so they couldn't throw us a line. They were dead in the water there for a few minutes, trying to get their engine started, but they gave up, tied two lines together and finally managed to throw us an end. They'd had a hell of a good day and were all drunk, celebrating the unexpected bonanza at the very end of the season. When they were tied alongside and getting ready to pitch off their fish, one of the guys opened the hatch covers and another man crawled out, totally covered with fish gurry but apparently happy as hell. They delivered over six thousand reds, which, amounting to about ten thousand dollars worth, was quite a payday. But they didn't make it out of the village the next day, even though everyone knew there were still lots of fish around. The boats that did fish that day came in loaded, but the fish were old and dark red, with the hooked noses they get at spawning time.

As soon as we took on the last fish we could carry, Andy got underway for the long, all-night run back to the cannery in Kodiak. When we tied up to the cannery dock, in the dark at about four in the morning, Andy was a red-eyed ghost with a wet cigarette drooping from his mouth and a mug of coffee in hand. He went up to the cannery to arrange for the delivery but came back in a few minutes, red in the face, and pissed. "The bastards won't take 'em till the morning crew shows up," he told us. "Probably be three hours or so. Let's get some sleep."

I was awakened a few hours later by the awful din of screeching seagulls and got up to look on deck. The cannery crew hadn't showed up yet and the sun was blazing down on our foot-deep deckload of fish. They were all soft and old in the first place. Now the sun was beating down on them and the whole mess was aswarm with gulls feasting on pecked-out eyes and guts. We could hardly keep them off and barely managed to hose off the leavings and the gull shit by the time the cannery crew showed up. The fish would be stuffed into cans and cooked to near mush, anyhow, but it made me wonder about the product. We heard a rumor that this batch was going to some institution, an orphanage or something.

Later that day Andy filed the butcher knife, took care of the bright king he had set aside, and again wrapped it in newspapers. Before long he emerged from his quarters, all spiffed up in his good clothes and white fisherman's cap, and carried his prize into town.

Our last run that summer was around to Larsen Bay, not far from Karluk on the Shelikof Strait side of the Island. We'd take fish from a few boats in the Strait and then deliver them to the cannery in Larsen Bay. There we'd take on a load of canned fish and haul it back to Kodiak. It was a leisurely trip into beautiful country, Larsen Bay itself ending in a sweet little cove where the cannery was situated. Coming into the bay we saw three brown bear along the beach, a sow with two cubs. Because of its remote location, the cannery had to bring its crew in by float plane or boat, and this seemed to make it a very tight-knit little community. I went ashore to catch mug-up and imagined that all along coastal Alaska the same scene was being played out. The whistles for mug-up blew at 10 a.m. and people gathered as they did here, talking about how the season had been and how many days it would be till they could leave for home. Fish butchers and slime-line workers in their aprons and rain gear, carpenters, mechanics, plumbers, electricians, laundry workers and housekeepers, cooks and bakers, fishermen. Both the cannery's setting and its community charmed me, but when we pulled away from the dock the next morning, the propeller churned up a suffocating stench of rotting fish heads and guts that spilled out a great pipe from the cannery whenever they were processing. The screaming gulls could snatch only so much of it before it sank to the bottom, where it remained until an especially big tide might sweep it out into the strait. I knew that the bodies of the dead fish formed an essential part of the cycle in the spawning grounds, but what about this foul mess? The best I could imagine was that it fattened the crabs.

The salmon season closed toward the end of September, and Andy arranged for *Anna A* to go on the grid for some bottom work. Then they'd have to get ready for the crab season. Steve took off, so for the last few days I had to cook for only the three of us. The day we went on the grid was my last day, and I had my air ticket for a flight to Seattle. We got the boat on the grid at high water. John told me goodbye and then headed for the B and B. Andy's wife had arrived, but she'd gone into town; so just he and I sat down at the galley table for a cup of coffee. He seemed relieved to have the boat safely on the grid and pleased at the prospect of two weeks' break. He and his wife would play around a bit and then fly back to Ballard for a visit with the family. Andy and I had become much easier with each other over the weeks, and this was more of an enjoyable conversation than we'd ever had. Our work was done, and he was something less than the captain. I was sort of free and detached from my identity as "Cook." I don't remember if he actually called me by my name, but he did tell me I had been a good cook. I was proud of that. But the next time I saw him he told me that I had been the best cook he ever had. That was a strange situation, though. It was a little over two years later, Andy was in a bad way and, oddly enough, I was captain.

I was back in Seattle, finishing my second year as an English major at the University of Washington. I was passing through Ballard on my way home from an Army Reserve meeting at Fort Lawton, and stopped into a little store to pick up a snack. I had on my Army greens, and by now I was a captain in the infantry, still a little uncomfortable with that identity, but thankful for my share of the GI Bill and for having escaped the horrific mess in Viet Nam. I'd picked out a package of cookies and, turning toward the cash register, bumped right into Andy and his wife. He greeted me warmly; I was glad to see him, but he looked more than two years older. That's when, introducing me to his wife, he said that I'd been the best cook he ever had. Then he asked, "Did you hear about the accident?" I shook my head and he told me the story. No, there wasn't an actual glitter in his eye, but the old fellow did tell me a kind of rime.

He had been running another tender in Kodiak that summer—not *Anna A*, which was on another charter—and he put it on the rocks. He was coming through Kupreanof Strait, headed back to Kodiak with a deckload of fish from Karluk. It was foggy and the windshield was a blur; so he put it on iron mike and stepped outside the wheel house for just long enough to get a clearer view ahead. But the iron mike was searching back and forth and locked to one side. It was just for a few seconds, he said, but it put them right on the rocks. He and the crew all got off, but they lost the fish and the boat. We didn't go into the details and implications of all this, but I remembered Andy's red eyes after his long night runs through those straits on *Anna A*, always pushing to make the tides and deliver the fish before they got too old. I realized how easily it could have happened—the tide, the wind and fog, all those rocks and narrow channels, not to mention the damned iron mike. I also guessed that a skipper in his sixties probably couldn't salvage his career after an accident like that. Andy seemed moved by the genuine shock and sympathy of my response, but I sensed that no matter how many people he found to listen to his story, nothing could take the pain away.

Poopdeck's Hand

You would wish long
and long to be with him, you would wish
to sit by him in the boat that you and
he might touch each other.
Walt Whitman

POOPDECK'S REAL NAME was Clarence Platt, but about fifty years ago someone nicknamed him Poopdeck (after the cartoon character Popeye's father), and it stuck. Before he died at age ninety-six he was so well known and beloved in Homer that they named a street after him. If you were introduced to him after his accident in 1965, you might offer your hand in greeting and be surprised when he extended his left hand. You might cringe in noticing his mangled right hand. He had only the thumb and forefinger on that hand, and over the years it began to look like a beak or hook. He would sometimes rub it, and if he knew you well he might explain that the missing fingers still itched.

I met him in 1963, when he was only sixty, but by then he was already well known and respected around the cannery as an eccentric old guy who caught lots of fish and knew his way around the Inlet. He fished an old steel boat that you could spot from miles away because of its odd, stubby lines and a high safety rail on the bow. He had named it *Bernice M*, after his wife. If you were at first a little intimidated by his cast-iron features, the prominent chin and brow, you would be all the more charmed to see them break quickly into his wide smile and to hear his ready laugh. Even then he walked with a characteristic shuffle, leaning forward slightly at the waist, and wearing a scrunched-up old Stetson and jeans that were rolled up in an uncool, old-fogey kind of way. The day I met him I was talking with Herb aboard his boat, *Suzy Jo*, when *Bernice M* came up the river to the cannery's floating dock and seemed to be aiming to tie alongside the boat next to us. Wanting to be helpful and also looking forward to meeting

118

this semi-legendary figure, I stepped over and waited to take a line. As Poopdeck pulled closer I reached too far and fell in, causing a commotion and making a fool of myself. Poopdeck didn't take much notice, just pulled away to avoid crushing me between the boats and circled to make another approach. By then I was ready to take his line, and all he said was, "Howdy, and thanks. Bet that was cold, huh?

That was the first of Poopdeck's two years as the cannery's winter watchman. Bernice died of cancer the following year, and it was early that July that Poopdeck had his accident. Dick and I were fishing that day and, like most of the fleet, had made our way out toward the middle, between Ninilchik and Snug Harbor. It was blowing about twenty-five that day, making it hard pulling when Dick and I brought in the net. This was early in a twenty-four hour period, and it looked like it was going to be a long, slow day. We'd just set out net after getting a waterhaul on our first drift when we were jolted by Poopdeck's "Mayday!" His voice was faint and all he could add was that he'd hurt himself and was losing lots of blood—then nothing else. We learned later that he'd caught his hand in the machinery that drove his reel. Dick and I were about three miles away and could see *Bernice M*'s unmistakable silhouette in the distance to our west. The Inlet was all whitecaps with that smoky haze that makes you wish you weren't quite so far out in the middle. But right away people nearby him began talking on the radio and we knew that boats were hurrying that way. The first boat to reach him called the nearby tender, *Chatham*, and asked the captain to use his more powerful radio to call in a helicopter. After that people stayed off the air, wanting to keep it open for the Coast Guard and the helicopter.

We just stayed on our set and kept looking toward *Bernice M*, knowing that we couldn't do anything and hoping that the helicopter would get there in time. It must have been a half hour before we saw it flying in from the northeast, but shortly after we saw it stop and hover in the area, the pilot came on the radio to say it was too rough. He asked fishermen on nearby boats to crowd in close and upwind of *Bernice M*, hoping that they could break the seas just enough for him to pull it off. It worked, and before long the helicopter lifted Poopdeck aboard and flew back toward Kenai. Poopdeck's nephews, Brian and Ken, had been close by on their

Poopdeck's Hand-carved Hanging Needle

own boat, *ValRay,* and Ken had gone aboard to help Poopdeck and then run *Bernice M* back to Kenai.

Poopdeck was back fishing the next year and continued for the next eighteen years, when he retired at age eighty. All he needed was a deck hand (he would have laughed at the pun) and a larger boat. He sold *Bernice M* and bought a thirty-six-foot aluminum boat named *Hummingbird,* and in a few years replaced that with an even more comfortable and well-equipped fiberglass boat that he also named *Hummingbird.* Not long after his accident he began to amuse himself and his friends by letting it be known that he was going to live to be a hundred, and from then on he could tell you exactly how many days it was until he turned a hundred. Looking back through my collection of letters from him, I see one that he wrote in 1982, telling of his plan to sell his boat and permit the following year. "You se," he wrote in this letter, which as always, he'd pecked out on his old typewriter, using only his hooked forefinger, "I'm pretty near a hundred years old (only 7872 more days till my 100th birthday) and I find that fishing just ain't as much fun as it used to be. Incidentally, if that sounds like a lot of days, they are clicking off awful fast." He died of leukemia at age ninety-six, but until then he continued to live an active and adventurous life, traveling throughout the world on investments he closely tracked in the stock market, working on gill nets for old friends, keeping up on his reading by subscribing to all kinds of magazines, and tending an amazing garden from which he supplied himself, visiting friends, and what he called "the ancient people" who lived in the retirement home in Homer.

Poopdeck was famous among his friends for keeping a wine cellar of homemade wines that he produced from his own garden or from fruit that friends might ship him from California or Oregon—dandelion, elderberry, blueberry, peach, raspberry, whatever was available. He called it "bug juice" and liked to explain, as he did in a letter to me in 1991, that "instead of calling it wine like sensible folks I call it bug juice because you have to remember all those billions of little bugs that had to comit suicide in order to make it, you start them working and keep them working till they comit suicide and then its ready to drink." When you visited him in Homer he would take you down into his musty cellar lit by a dangling electric bulb and show you his rows and rows of gallon jugs all labeled by fruit and year. You would happily sample five or six and return to his living room upstairs with a glass of your favorite, primed for a good conversation. After he retired and if I was fishing out of Homer early in the season, I would visit him and he'd send me on my way with fresh produce from his garden and a bottle of bug juice. One year he wanted to fill a bottle for me to take with me on the boat, and I grabbed an old brown whiskey bottle from the pile of bottles that he saved for this purpose. When I saw him a few weeks later we had a good laugh about the bug juice. I'd been nipping on it every day, but once or twice got something in my mouth that seemed like a bit of steel wool. I took a closer look and saw that we'd neglected to rinse out the bottle and that two or three spiders had crawled into it and died.

Sometimes, when I tell people about my long friendship with Poopdeck, they wonder how I could have been friends with someone whose life was so different from my own. He was thirty-six years older than I, but I didn't consider him a kind of father or even an uncle. And our friendship was not affected by the difference in our educational backgrounds, he having graduated from high school and I with many years of graduate school. The closest we ever came to discussing literature was once when I mentioned Jack London, and he told me how much he'd admired London when he read him as a boy. But, although he read widely, especially in magazines, he wasn't drawn to fiction or poetry. Yet he was literate—and witty—in a different way. He kept several short typewritten definitions pinned above his desk, one of which was, "A pessimist is a man who thinks everybody is as nasty as he is and hates them for it. Quote from George Bernard Shaw." Below this was another: "A pessimist wears a belt and suspenders and carries a safety pin. Quote from Poopdeck." Or this one for "Stress": "The confusion created when your mind overrides your body's basic desire to choke the living shit out of some asshole who desperately needs it!!!"

I always enjoyed his playful way of disarming the thought that my academic identity made any real difference between us. The year he retired from fishing he began his letter to me, "Well I done went and did it (that sounds awful to an english Prof I know) but I've been practiceing talking like a hillbilly for 70 years and I aint about to change now or nohow," and then he told me he had sold his boat and permit to his grandson. Several years later, he resorted to sending his long list of friends a duplicated annual letter, but he always added a handwritten personal note and a cartoon drawing of himself—a bald, round-faced man with a mustache and smile. In one of these letters he reported on his trip that year to Angel Falls, in Venezuela, including a boat trip down the Orinoco River, and he told of stopping to see me in Arizona on his way back from Miami to Alaska: "I flew to Phoenix where my good friend Bert Bender met me, Bert is a fisherman on Cook Inlet in the summer but in his spare time is a collage

Proffeser at Tempe Arizona." He added that the trip gave the two of us "time to catch up on our B.S. which had got away behind in the 8 years since I quit fishing."

Poopdeck and I held political views so opposed that they might have disrupted our friendship if we hadn't had the sense to avoid the subject altogether. I was, and still am, a long-time liberal Democrat, and he was both a long-time Republican and member of the National Rifle Association. In my visits with him I ignored the mass-produced "autographed" photo that he displayed of Ronald Reagan thanking Poopdeck for his support. We both knew that this essential difference in our makeups was somehow irrelevant to the bonds that connected us. I share similar political views with most of my fishing friends, like John, for example, with whom I enjoy a comradeship in our opposition to the present war in Iraq; or my friend Thor, who once told me how much he was enjoying Howard Zinn's *A People's History of the United States*. Yet other fishing friends such as Poopdeck, Ted, and my former partner, Dick belonged to the NRA, occupying the opposite end of the political spectrum from my own. I've wondered about this and can't imagine sustaining such relationships with academic colleagues whose political views differed so dramatically from my own. It takes more than just working together to help people overcome the political barriers that can divide us. Poopdeck knew about these differences that can divide us, and I think he would have counted them, as he did a number of other things, as "just one of the hazards of being people." But I also think there's promise in the way friends in the fishing life overcome their political differences by recognizing the larger, natural reality and our small place in it.

Poopdeck came to my rescue once in the early years of our friendship. I was fishing alone on *Sounion* and suddenly began taking on water through a loose fitting. When the water came up to the engine and threatened to short out my electronics, I gave the only "Mayday!" I ever sent out, and Poopdeck was the first oneto reach me. He had been only a few miles away and rushed over to pump me out and keep me afloat until another boat with a larger pump arrived. By the time he got to me I had stopped the leak, but the water had reached the higher, drier planks and was coming through the seams. Fortunately, it was calm weather and my life wasn't really in danger, but the boat would have certainly gone down if Poopdeck hadn't been there. He said it wasn't any big deal, and when the larger boat arrived, he pulled away and went on with his own fishing.

Beyond this help, he also gave me some friendly advice, some that he would dispense freely to many others and some that was more personal. The first was how to survive in the stock market: "You can make a lot more money with your butt than you can with your head," he used to say. Just get an investment and then sit on it. He offered the personal advice when my first marriage ended in divorce in 1980. "For cripe sake," he wrote,

> *next summer lets get together on the radio befor hand and come to Homer with me some cloeser [meaning a closure or closed fishing period] (how the hell you spell that) anyhow lets do it, I like to brag a little occasionally and that would give me a good chance.*
>
> *Next morning; Got side tract here last night, and now I've forgot what it was I was going to say if any thing Mabey a little good advice would be in order, not that anybody ever pays any attention to it, but don't make the same mistake I did when my first wife kicked me out, I hated wemon or was afarid of them I don't know which for sure, but I waited for nine years befor I got another and if I had it to do over I'd start looking right away.*

I respected and admired Poopdeck for his ability to survive such terrible losses as Bernice's death and go on with cheerful determination. After she died he lived alone in the isolation of being winter watchman at the cannery. But he could smile at that, as he did in telling me one of the things he'd done that first winter to take his mind off things. He had begun to think about the wonderful rye bread that the cannery's baker, Old John, featured every summer. So, wanting some rye bread that winter, Poopdeck decided to go up to the kitchen and find where John kept his rye flour; he looked and looked but finally gave up. When he asked John about it the following summer, John laughed out loud and told him his secret: he just used regular old white flour and added shots of bottled rye flavoring and food color.

I was also impressed with Poopdeck's relationship with his mother. She lived to be almost a hundred, and when she came up from Oregon to visit him after Bernice died, I was amused to see this man, then in his middle sixties, scurry around the place to hide his home brew. He explained that he wasn't ashamed of his drinking but was only protecting his mother from the fear she would certainly feel, because two members of their family had destroyed themselves with alcohol. I enjoyed many drinks with him over the years but never saw him drunk or anywhere near it. He had lost other relatives to cancer, and both his children had died young. On his visits with me in Arizona we had opportunities to talk more intimately. He told me about his bout with prostate cancer some thirty years before and how that had ended his sex life. And, most memorably, sitting in our living room one night, he mentioned his dead son. The only time I ever saw him falter in his cheerful determination to accept losses and go on ("them's just part of the hazards of being human") was when I asked how his son had died. "It was an accident," he said, adding that it had happened somewhere up toward Fairbanks. "He drowned." And when I asked how it happened, his voice broke. There were tears in his eyes and he said, "Hurts too much to talk about it." I heard later that his slightly retarded son had drowned in a bathtub at home. Again I'd glimpsed something of Poopdeck's capacity for love and tenderness, feelings that I recognize in the face from an old picture I somehow came to own. The photo is dated 1950-51 with the inscription, "Poopdeck with baby seal." Poopdeck is in his late forties, on a beach somewhere, dressed in his oilskins and wearing one of his shapeless felt-brimmed hats. This was the time when he fished briefly as a beach set-netter, and his right hand is intact, protected by a cotton fish-picking glove. He has a baby harbor seal cradled gently in his right arm and looks down on it as a doting father might look upon his own child.

The day after his accident back in 1965 a few of us were sitting around his kitchen table in the winter watchman's house, rehashing it all. He was in the hospital in Anchorage, and we hadn't heard how he was doing. We were missing him and drinking some of his home brew. His nephews Brian and Ken were telling us how they'd been the first to get to *Bernice M* after the accident. They'd found lots of blood in the boat, and Poopdeck had looked bad when the helicopter lifted him off. We were sitting there together the way people do after any loss, disoriented but finding relief in this eddy in the current of it all. Going over the details again and again, and forgetting about the season that was just beginning to sweep us along in our different directions. Then Ken said, "I got a problem." He had gone aboard Poopdeck's boat and brought it back to the cannery. After he tied up the boat at the cannery dock, he began to clean up the mess. "I found that chunk of his hand."

Nobody said anything for a second. Ken was troubled, and we could picture his situation. You couldn't save it. There wasn't any way to rush it to the hospital and hope for them to sew it back on. It was a bloody piece of meat and bone.

"Well, whadja do with it?" one of us asked.

"Man," he said, wincing, "I didn't know what to do. . . . I just picked it up and threw it in the river."

All we could do was nod in support. I didn't want to think about it and reached for another home brew. But at some point about fifteen or twenty years later—long before Poopdeck died and they scattered his ashes in the Inlet—I came to love the thought.

Like any of his old friends, I remember Poopdeck sitting in his easy chair with a glass of bug juice. Always keeping up his hillbilly pose, he'd propose this toast: "Here's to'd you, here's toward you, if I hadn't a seed you, I wouldn't a knowd you." But mainly I see him on a boat, as I first did. I've been absorbed in thoughts about him these last few days, and yesterday felt his presence again. I heard Stanley Kunitz on National Public Radio, celebrating his one-hundredth birthday by reading his poem, "The Long Boat." A year younger than Poopdeck would have been and speaking in his shaky, gnarled voice, Kunitz told of an old man drifting off into death, as though in an unmoored boat. Shrouded in fog and beneath the crying gulls, the exhausted old man would lie down to take his rest. What relief to be cradled against the storm and float off into the infinite sea! But he thinks of home and the garden-earth he loved to tend.

Ngul-a Fatica!

IN EARLY JULY OF 1967 I pulled into Snug Harbor for a two-day layover. It had been a pretty good period for so early in the season, and my spirits were up. I was fishing alone on *Sounion* and, after pitching my fish off onto the power scow *Beaver*, I dropped the hook just off the beach and about a mile above the cannery on Chisik Island. There were thirty or forty boats anchored along the beach, several from Columbia Wards, and while I was cleaning up and fixing something to eat, Jon pulled in and tied alongside. We both wanted the company. Jon was fishing the cannery's little bowpicker *Carol Lee* that year, his first on the Inlet, and he seemed a little wired. From his point of view I was probably something of an old hand. I was in my fifth year on the Inlet and owned my own boat. But I think we were both a little high on the sense of freedom and independence you get from running a boat on your own. You're self-contained in the little boat-world and feel the charge from being your own man. You can take off in any direction you want, when you want, and there's nothing like the edge you get from knowing all the time that what you make, and whether you make it at all, depends on nobody but you. Jon and I had struck up a budding friendship, though it embarrassed me a bit when he called me on the radio and butchered the name of my boat. I pronounced it "soon-yun," but he'd always say, with a little excitement in his voice, "*Sow-own-ion. Sow-own-ion*. Do you read, Bert? *Carol Lee*."

The next morning we did a little work on our boats. Jon had a problem with his hydraulic roller, but mainly he was worried about a gasoline leak that he wanted to track down. There was a sheen of gas in his bilge, and enough fumes to make you nervous. I was interested in that, too, since we were tied up together, and I helped him track it down. Like so many of the old boats, *Carol Lee* had an aged gas tank that was beginning to dissolve into rust. Gas oozed from innumerable pinhole leaks, making the boat a floating bomb. Jon didn't smoke, but he cooked on a camp stove that burned white gas, and a spark from the stove or from the engine's rusty old electrical system could easily set off the fumes that collected in the bilge. I showed him how to stop the leaks with a bar of Ivory soap, and that was enough to keep him going until he could get back to Kenai.

We went ashore to the cannery in time to catch the ten o'clock mug-up, where we could have a couple of fresh cinnamon rolls and, more important, hear the talk among fishermen about how they'd done the day before and what they thought about the next opening. We wanted to know what time people were planning to pull out the next morning, whether they'd head straight out or work their way south against the flood. You wouldn't want to be swept too far north for the opening set. And we were hungry for rumors about the price of reds and about what was going on in Bristol Bay. If they were slugging them over there, it'd play hell with our price here in the Inlet.

After mug-up we hung out for a while on the boardwalk outside the store, where each of us picked up a few things we couldn't do without, maybe a can or two of condensed milk and an extra jar of peanut butter. A loaf of bread from their freezer to replace the one you had, now a mass of powdery green mold. In the office adjoining the store, the owner-superintendent Joe Fribrock was busy talking on the radio and checking over some charts, while his wife Dorothy helped fill orders at the counter. Outside the store we bumped into an Italian fisherman Jon knew, a short, animated guy named Frank, who had a cigar in his mouth and talked a lot with his hands. He lived in Los Angeles, near San Pedro, where he used to fish, but now he just fished the Inlet in the summer and sold Christmas trees in the winter. Frank drove up the highway each summer in a van stocked with his summer provisions—a variety of pastas, a few cases of homemade tomato sauce, olive oil, and whatever else you needed to outfit an Italian galley for two months. So Jon and I were delighted when Frank said that he'd seen us anchored near his boat, *Saint Christina*, and invited us to come alongside that evening for a spaghetti dinner.

Jon and I did a little maintenance on our boats until early afternoon, then left *Sounion* on the hook and took Jon's boat to visit another friend or two who were anchored nearby. After you pulled alongside and tied up to somebody for a short visit, someone would pull out some beer and smoked salmon, or maybe make a pot of coffee. Lounging around on the boats, you could share gossip about last period's fishing, strengthen alliances with people you wanted to keep in touch with on the grounds, and settle in to appreciating the spectacular beauty of the harbor. From certain places you could see Mt. Illiamna not far away to the southwest or Mt. Redoubt just to the north. And you could almost touch a nearby waterfall that fell to the beach from the high end of the island. Just to be swinging on the anchor near one of those waterfalls, the sound of it mixed with the cry of gulls.

I had time for a short nap when we got back to the boat, and when I got up, an unbelievable aroma was wafting downwind to us from *Saint Christina*. We supplied ourselves the best we could with a few contributions to the party—some plates and silverware, a loaf of bread, a precious six-pack of cheap beer, and part of a fifth of rot-gut whiskey—and started up *Carol Lee*. Frank and his deck hand came up from their cabin to take our lines and tell us dinner was under way. Frank jammed his cigar in his mouth and accepted the things we had brought (though he made us take them back with us when we left that night), and then poured us each a glass of homemade red wine. His deck hand went back down into the cabin to tend the stove, and Frank took us on a quick tour of the boat. It was a huge and certainly not beautiful old wooden boat, about forty feet long by twelve or thirteen. With its high house forward and low working deck, it made a whimsical silhouette that you could spot for miles on the Inlet. *Saint Christina*'s work deck seemed as big as a tennis court, and when Frank lifted the hatch to show us his engine—an enormous rusty old 671—he could hardly contain his pride in packing that kind of diesel power. He could buck tide or tow the net out of a rip. I couldn't believe the size of the hold, which was at least four times as big as *Sounion*'s. The pilot house atop the cabin gave a view that Frank said was better than what you'd get from a flying bridge. It was better than being on a bridge because it was enclosed with big windows and you could always be close to the radio. Frank liked to talk on the radio, and later that year we heard him give some very excited fish calls when he wanted to share his luck with friends. He'd come on the radio and say, "looks like a million dollars!" You loved hearing a report like that, but people on other boats could recognize his excited voice, and anyone could pick out *Saint Christina*'s silhouette in the distance. You'd be lucky to get there in time.

From the wheelhouse he took us down and forward into the cavernous cabin. His deck hand was working at a white porcelain stove that burned propane and looked like it had been salvaged from an apartment. It had an oven and four burners, one of which held a simmering pot of spaghetti sauce with meatballs. A large pot of water sat astride two other burners and seemed about to boil. Frank turned it down and got out some dry salami and Mediterranean olives. Then he motioned us back up on deck, where he topped off our wine and we sat around talking about fish and what kind of season it was going to be. It was after nine o'clock and the sun was still high in the northwest sky. Looking at the thick green world ashore you could almost hear things grow.

When it was time to eat, Jon and I got our plates and silverware from his boat and Frank dished out heaps of spaghetti, meatballs, and sauce. He opened a package of thin breadsticks, put out a shaker of parmesan cheese, and encouraged us to take more wine. Fishermen on other boats anchored nearby must have been enjoying their dinners, as well, I thought, many of them probably having fried up a fresh red. But I couldn't imagine anyone anywhere having a better meal, and certainly not in a more spectacular setting: in that protected harbor, under a snow-capped volcano, within a fleet of anchored fishing boats, along a beach with waterfalls and cliffs alive with seabirds tending their nests. One of us said something like, "This is the life," and Frank and his deck hand raised their glasses. Taking a drink, they both stood up and shouted into the cliffs, "Ngul-a fatica! Ngul-a fatica!" Their voices bounced off the cliffs and some screaming gulls seemed to echo their words. "Ngul-a fatica! Ngul-a fatica!" When Jon and I looked at each other, blankly, Frank took the cigar out of his mouth and gave his big squinty-eyed smile. He thrust his finger to the sky and shouted again, "Ngul-a fatica!" Then, reaching for a bottle of the red wine, he pointed to the homemade label, "Ngul-a Fatica!" and said, "Means somethin' like 'fuck work!'"

"Yeah!" Jon said, and he and I shouted out with them, "Ngul-a fatica!"

Snug Harbor Evening

I knew what they meant. Over the past two days we had made the six-hour run down from Kenai and then fished a twenty-four-hour period. We'd set the net and picked up the net, time after time, getting waterhauls once in a while and only a few fish on other sets. We'd fished all night and had rocked and rolled with the boats as we crossed riptides or rode out sloppy seas. We'd made the long run in to Snug Harbor, fighting to stay awake, then waited in line at the tender, and finally pitched off our fish. We were dead tired. But that's not "work." Work is being on your feet for ten hours a day, six days a week, standing at your place in rain gear, on a concrete floor, tearing the gills out of freshly boiled king crab and throwing the crab onto a conveyor belt in the processing plant, trying to keep up with the crab that flooded up out of a big tube onto the conveyor belt at your station. I had done that.

You're fishing with your partner on a twenty-four-hour period and the wind just keeps blowing a steady twenty knots or more and, with no reel or hydraulic roller to pull in the net, you take turns, each pulling in a shackle of gear, then letting the other guy pull in the next one. Your backs and arms ache, and your hands swell from working with the lines, but you do it again and again, and on the long, cold night sets, you dread putting on your wet gloves and pulling in the net again. But that's not "work." Work is being a gandy dancer on the Alaska Railroad, six tens, day after day digging, prying, filling in, slowly lifting up the tracks along Turnagain Arm on Cook Inlet, where the tracks running from Seward to Anchorage sank below the high-tide line in the Good Friday earthquake of '64. I had done that. Work is spending your weekend reading sets of undergraduate papers, most of which were turned in by students who worked twenty to thirty hours a week at Taco Bell and could barely find time to type a paper, much less research and compose it. And you realize you're spending a lot more time with the bad papers than with the few that are clear and thoughtful—an hour or more each, trying to figure out what the hell they're trying to say and how to respond in some helpful way.

You're on a night set and realize too late that you've been sucked into a dirty rip, and your whole net is an impossible tangle of sticks and kelp, each piece needing to be pulled clear and thrown aboard so it won't get back into the net. Once in a while you come to a big log, heaving and rolling in the water, its projecting limbs playing hell with your net, and you know it'll take you an hour to get it out. But that's not "work." Work is trying to sell men's wear on commission, half-heartedly pushing the guy to buy a new tie to go with the shirt he needs, and matching socks, to boot; or having to look busy straightening stacks of pants or underwear when you know the store manager is watching you from the balcony overlooking the store. Work is having to spend hours with your over-complicated income tax forms, when you know that even the IRS people can't agree on how much you owe and that a lot of millionaires don't pay anything at all. Or spending a few days filling out your annual self-evaluation, evaluations for merit pay that the legislature isn't going to fund anyhow, and that must be submitted to a chair and a dean who have no idea in hell what your research is about, who claim to be able to evaluate your classroom work and rank it meaningfully in relation to your colleagues', who have never distinguished themselves as teachers or produced any significant scholarly work of their own but have risen through the academic ranks by sucking up—and who believe in all this crap.

Or, at the end of a long day of fishing, when you've missed them again and again, you have to spend a couple of hours lying in the bilge as the boat rocks, dead in the water, while you try to get a wrench on a fitting at the bottom of your transmission, and your knuckles are a bloody mess; and then, when you're under way again, you have to buck the tide for three hours before you get to the mouth of the river, where following seas give you a ride for your life and you wrestle the wheel back and forth trying to keep your balance and stay in the channel. But that's not "work." Work is lying on your back all day under somebody else's boat, trying to make a buck by scraping off the old paint, the flakes getting in your mouth, your nostrils, and your sweaty eyes. Or maybe even being a deck hand for somebody who doesn't believe in shares and gives you a hundred bucks for the day—and the net's full, full of *his* fish, and it's only noon with six hours to go. Work is preparing footnotes or a long bibliography, or building an index for a scholarly book, placing every comma and semicolon according to the *Chicago Manual of Style*.

"Ngul-a fatica!"

We had drunk a lot of wine. We had laughed a lot and Frank had gone through at least three cigars. The spaghetti and sauce were out of this world. There was a lull in the gulls' cries and *Saint Christina* swung slowly on the turning tide till she pointed the other way.

Everyone caught lots of fish the next day, and Jon and I met up with Frank at the end of the period. We faced a long run back to Kenai, but we knew we were in luck. It was just after low water and we'd be riding the flood all the way back to the harbor. Even better, it was flat calm, so we could tie up and run in together. We put out bumpers and I tied to one side of *Saint Christina* and Jon tied to the other. Running in, we all gathered in Frank's wheelhouse to talk about how it was, and we saw lots of jumpers along the way. It looked good for the next period. We had another glass of red, and *Saint Christina*'s roaring 671 was doing all the work.

Desdemona Sands

THERE WAS A WEAK RUN in Cook Inlet in 1968, and Fish and Game closed the season early. This left me in a bind, because I couldn't make my boat payment for *Sounion* and I needed more money to finance my next year in graduate school. The National Marine Fisheries Service let me make only half a boat payment for the year, and then my friend Ted helped me find the money I needed for school. He told me about a short gill-netting season that would open soon at Astoria, on the Columbia River, and suggested that I take a shot at it. Like many other Cook Inlet gill-netters, Ted had also fished the Columbia for most of his life. He lived in Vancouver, Washington, and fished that area as well as Astoria, Grays Harbor, and Willapa Bay. If I showed up at Vancouver during the first week of August he'd take me under his wing, lease me a net, find a boat that I could lease for the two-week season, and show me the ropes. I jumped at the chance.

In Vancouver Ted lined me up with a boat that belonged to our mutual friend, Ken, who wasn't fishing that season. It was a conventional Columbia River bowpicker, with no frills such as a depth-finder, and not even a name, but I was happy to have it. Within a few days I was following Ted as we made the day-long run down the river to Astoria, each of us standing outside, at the wheel behind the house. Neither of us had a radio, so once in a while Ted would slow up enough for me to come alongside and then he'd shout something to me about where the channel was or what to look out for on my way back upriver in a couple of weeks.

We saw several ships on their way to or from Portland, and I'd heard a lot about this traffic. You were supposed to stay clear of the shipping lanes when you were on a drift, but it was hard to tell where these were, even in daylight—and Astoria was a night fishery. I'd also heard a lot about the bridge at Astoria, how it was right in the middle of the area where we'd be drifting, and how you had to stay clear of its huge pillars. The fishing boundaries were from about six or seven miles above the bridge to six or seven miles below it—that is, almost to the mouth of the Columbia. The idea was to begin a drift on the flood well below the bridge and then pick up just before you got to the bridge. Then, you would set out above the bridge. On the ebb you would do the same thing, in reverse order, drifting down and picking up before you got to the bridge, and then setting out again below the bridge.

When we finally got to Astoria and passed under the bridge I couldn't imagine how to avoid catching it. The current was racing out just then, and when the tide changed it'd race the other way with equal speed. We'd be out here again in just about six hours, and I was doing my best to get my bearings. So when Ted slowed down again I pulled close enough to hear any advice he might shout to me. We were just below the bridge and he pointed downriver to a stretch of water that looked exactly like the rest. "Over there's Desdemona Sands."

It was just after high water and the river seemed enormous as it widened toward the mouth. We were headed to the little town of Chinook, on the Washington side not far from the mouth, where Ted and his family rented a small cabin each August. We were in a hurry because we wanted to take a short nap before dark, so Ted no longer slowed down to point things out. He just pointed to a rock jetty, or a buoy, or some old pilings, and shouted something that I couldn't hear over the engine noise and propwash. Only once, about halfway from the bridge to Chinook, he slowed down and pointed out a landmark on the north side, a weather-greyed and abandoned old church. "When you're drifting up on the flood, you gotta start picking up here, otherwise you'll catch the bridge." I was happy to have that hint, because it gave me an idea of how fast I'd be drifting; it was two or three miles to the bridge, but I wondered how in hell I could see the old church in the dark. Before long we passed another jetty, rounded a breakwater, and pulled into the small boat harbor at Chinook.

I checked the oil and made sure the net was ready to lay out, and then we walked over to Ted's cabin. His wife Pat and their three kids were already there, and Pat had made us a fine dinner topped off with an unforgettable blackberry cobbler. We had time for about a three-hour nap, but, as usual before a fishing day, I couldn't sleep. I was excited and nervous about fishing in this new place, and was trying to remember the flood of details in Ted's advice. I'd just have to go out, take my chances, and, as much as possible, follow the other boats. That approach had got me through my first years on Cook Inlet, and besides, I knew that the fishing business was half luck, anyhow.

The alarm rang, we grabbed cups of coffee and headed for the harbor. The tide was flooding and, although I followed Ted out of the harbor, I immediately lost sight of him. It was dark as hell and all I could see was a maze of tiny lights, indistinct and blinking, stretching across the water and ending in the distance with the bridge and the twinkling hills of Astoria. There must have been over a hundred gill-netters on the river, some of them with their running lights on, and some already on their first drifts. The ones drifting had turned on their mast lights, and when you got close you could see the faint lights in the cabins. If you looked hard you could also see the tiny blinking light each drifter had on the end of his net. The nets were eighteen hundred feet long, stretching and winding across the surface, and you couldn't see the cork lines until you were within about forty feet of them. I knew I was taking too long to find what I hoped was a safe place for my first drift, but I didn't want to take any chances. When I finally decided that I was far enough from the other boats, I began to set the net, but when I had it about half out I saw another guy's cork line just ahead and had to stop and pull my net back in.

I finally found another place to set out but immediately wondered why the rest of the boats were further out toward the middle of the river. I could see the lights from the bridge and its shadowy form, but I couldn't judge how far away it was or how fast I was drifting that way. Looking ashore I suddenly saw what looked like the old church and realized that I'd already drifted past it. "Christ!" I yelled to myself, "you're gonna wrap the goddamned bridge," and immediately began pulling in the net. I pulled as fast as I could, but I also had to stack it well enough so it wouldn't collapse in a tangled mess. I kept an eye on the bridge, first telling myself, "Maybe the tide's slacking up, you're gonna make it," and then, "Oh, for god's sake, it's getting closer, fast." The net came in quickly because I didn't have any fish to pick, but then I began to pick up some trash from the bottom, and that slowed me down. There was some rusty old metal that tore the net and a few foul-smelling dead crabs that almost made me puke. The dim picking light on the bow illuminated a half circle of about thirty feet in diameter, but I couldn't see any fish in the net until suddenly there was a splash just under the boat and I pulled in a big wad of net with a good-sized fish all balled up in it. It was a chinook of about forty pounds–far bigger than the seven- to eight-pound reds I was used to catching on the Inlet. A few fathoms farther along the net there was another fish tangled near the lead line, and I was picking it when I looked up and saw the bridge. Its huge shape rose way above the boat and was illuminated indirectly by the green lights along the roadway on top. I pulled as fast as I could for the few remaining minutes before I caught one of the huge pillars with the far end of the net. Then the boat swept under the bridge and upstream until the net between the boat and the pillar pulled taut and I just hung there in the current. It was eerily calm and silent under the bridge, despite the noise from the rushing water and the engine idling on. Once in a while I could hear a car or truck speed over the bridge, the lucky bastards. I felt better seeing another boat caught on the next pillar over.

It was easier than I imagined to pull the boat back toward the piling as I brought in the net, and then all I could do was cut off the piece that was hung up on the piling, with the other loose end drifting upstream on the other side of it. The worst of it was that I knew Ted would be pissed. He was leasing me the net for 15 percent of my catch, and it was beginning to look like a losing deal. The rest of the night went more smoothly and I quit as soon as it was light enough to see that other boats were heading in. By the time I delivered my few fish, got back into the harbor at Chinook, and cleaned up the boat, I was beat. At the cabin, Ted had finished lunch and was getting ready to lie down. I was happy to hear that he had had a good night. It seemed to help him laugh off the chunk of net that I'd lost for him.

Over the next two weeks I managed to catch enough fish to make it pay and even to turn a small profit for Ted and Ken, on their leases of the net and boat. I walked away with three thousand dollars, which was enough to help me through the school year ahead. But before it was over I had a wild series of nights—a good taste of nearly everything that can go wrong at Astoria—that made me swear I'd never fish there again and underscored my respect for the Columbia River fishermen. I knew it was different for them. Most of them had grown up fishing on the river. Some of them had slightly bigger boats, and some had deck hands. And since all of them were expert at mending nets, they could handle the inevitable mishaps that made the Astoria fishery a nightmare for greenhorns like myself. Ted tried to show me how to square out a big tear in the net and then sew in a nice patch, but he worked so fast that it just left me baffled.

One night I caught hundreds of big, reddish-brown jellyfish. They hung from the net in globs and I'd lean over the bow to try to get rid of them before they came in with the net. All I could do was grab a bunch of web and beat it against the side of the boat to shake-strain them out. But their goo splattered all over everything, stinging my face and hands, and the globs that unavoidably slipped into the boat oozed under the floorboards and slid into the bilge. Eventually the globs were drawn to the bilge pump and clogged it. On other nights I caught hundreds and hundreds of little flounders that weighed about a pound each. I'm sure each one would have made a fine meal, but at one and a half cents a pound they were worse than worthless; just the right size to stick in the big-mesh nets that gilled the chinook, each one tangled and balled up in the web. Working in the dim light to extract them one at a time, it was almost impossible to avoid getting jabbed again and again by the wicked little barb that each wields to discourage larger fish from swallowing it. I wasted lots of time clearing the jellyfish or flounders, but at least I wasn't in a tight spot, about to catch the bridge or something.

Two nights later I lost half of Ted's net to a freighter, and it happened just the way I'd heard it would. Because I was drifting near some other boats I wasn't worried about the shipping lane. But the channel bends along its way, making it doubly hard to know where you are at night. I was trying to keep track of the other gill-netters' lights but then I saw some faint lights that seemed too high above the water. I couldn't make out the silhouette of a ship but the lights were coming my way. I had already begun to pull in the net when I first saw the high grey shape, but the Columbia River gill nets are too long and deep for even two men to retrieve one in the amount of time I had. Sometimes in such crises on

Cook Inlet, where the nets are shorter and shallower, you can tow the net clear. But with the length of this net and the size of my little engine, that was impossible. And I knew that the freighters on the Columbia can't possibly maneuver around all the gill-netters, even if they could see the nets. The channel's so narrow. All I could do was pull in as much as I could and save time to cut free of it if it looked like the ship was going to run me down. I pulled and pulled until the last minute and then, forgetting the butcher knife, hoped that I had enough of it aboard to tow the rest clear. I gave the little engine all the gas it could take, but there was no way. Even over the scream of my own engine I could hear the rumble of the freighter engines and its propwash, and then the dark mass swept between me and the tiny blinking light on the other end of my net. It passed in a second, its big props shredding the puny net as you might break a cobweb that crossed your trail. All I could do was pull in the rest of it, up to the ragged end, and then spend a few minutes circling around in a futile search for the other piece. Running back in that morning, I again dreaded telling Ted what I'd done with his net. He tried his best to muffle his anger, telling me that he'd lost nets that way before. (And when he told me two days later that it had happened to him again that night, I was embarrassed to feel such relief.)

Instead of getting some rest that morning I borrowed Ted's truck and drove to Vancouver for another net. By the time I made it back to Chinook and loaded the new net, it was getting dark and time to head out again. I caught quite a few fish that night but just a couple of hours before daylight I also caught the net in the propeller—"web in the wheel"— and couldn't cut it free. Dead in the water, all I could do was wait until morning and hope that another gill-netter would see me and tow me back to the harbor. I just hoped that I wouldn't drift out to the mouth or into a jetty or something. There was an old AM radio aboard, and I listened to it while waiting out the night. I picked up some rock and roll music out of Portland that seemed strange out there in the middle of the river, songs like the Stones' "I can't get no satisfaction," and there were some headlines that were mostly preoccupied with news about the Viet Nam war. Casualty reports, talk of "pacification" operations, and so forth. And I picked up the Ira Blue talk show from San Francisco. Angry callers argued what to do about the "pinko" draft dodgers and whether the plan to defoliate the forests over there was a good idea. And there were lots of commercials, one that stuck in my mind from a faint crackley station in Denver for a company called "General Control." They could do about anything for you, it seemed, such as controlling winter itself by selling you paint to keep your lawn green.

Just before daylight a boat drifted close to me and after the two people aboard picked up their net they pulled along side to see if they could help me out. Unbelievably, I knew the guy who was running the boat, Alan Takalo, a fellow fisherman from the cannery in Kenai. He was as surprised to see me as I was to see him. He and his deck hand took me in tow. When I finally made it back to Chinook late in the morning, Ted and Pat met me in the harbor and told me that they were just getting ready to call the Coast Guard. I was touched to hear that they had prayed for me. Pat was wonderful. She baked another blackberry cobbler for me and, after my nap, went down to the harbor with me to help disentangle and patch the net I had cut up. She made us another fine dinner and we all sat around for a while, giving Ted time to hear my story, offer advice, and share some horror tales of his own. It was good to be a part of this family that shared the work of the fishing season—Pat cooking and working on nets, the kids picking berries and running errands, Ted bringing in the fish that kept the enterprise afloat.

But by this time I was getting tired of the Astoria season. It would be nice to be back in school, to have leisurely mornings with coffee and the newspaper. And I still couldn't figure out this whole business. I liked the simplicity of Ted's family operation, their single purpose of catching as many fish as possible during the short season. But they also had a TV set with its commercial blare. There were their mealtime prayers and their having prayed for me, whose faith had dissipated years before. I had trouble abiding Ted's discordant patriotism regarding the war and guns, and I didn't know what to make of his odd enthusiasm for a local healer they knew in Vancouver—a healer who specialized in dental work. They knew people whose teeth he had straightened, or whose cavities would suddenly disappear. And the fishing itself—the age-old method of gill-netting, which retained a degree of primitive simplicity in Cook Inlet: here in the more populated surrounds of Astoria it seemed warped in time. There were all those lights from downtown Astoria and the distant hillside homes, the eerie green-lighted bridge running right through the fishing grounds, and the ocean freighter traffic in and out of Portland. The family seemed to hold it all together so strongly that I wasn't prepared to hear from Ted at the beginning of another season on Cook Inlet a couple of years later that he and Pat had split up.

As much as I wanted to get this season behind me, though, I still had one more night to fish. It turned out to be a drizzly, windy, fog-patched night, and I was thinking of my more orderly existence at the university, browsing in the library, or sitting at my desk with a cup of tea and a collection of essays. I was catching a few fish, though, including a big sturgeon that made me jump when it came in over the roller and dropped at my feet in a bundle of web. I had never seen one, and in this dim light its strange shape and large scales made it look like a creature from the geological past. Then realizing what it was and that it was longer than the legal limit for sturgeon, I slid it back into the murky water and went on to make my last drift on the river. I didn't want to take any chances on this one so I moved out toward the middle, staying clear of other boats, and taking advantage of a clear shot at the incoming fish. Everything seemed to be working fine until I began to notice that the boats inshore from me were drifting faster than I was. When I pulled in a little bit of the net the reason was clear. I was in shallow water with my net aground on Desdemona Sands.

Ever since Ted had pointed and shouted out his warning about Desdemona Sands, the name had stuck in my mind. It was partly just the sound of it—Desde*mona*—and partly what I knew of Desdemona in *Othello*. But my only thought now was that I had to get the hell off the sands. As soon as I brought in a few fathoms of net, though, I was welcomed by a fine catch of the blasted flounders, each tangled in the web and bristling with its wicked little barb.

It was slow going. But I was getting the net in, bit by bit, all the while hoping that the thickening fog would lift long enough for me to get my bearings. All I could tell was that the tide had begun to ebb and that I was still dragging slowly across the Sands. I didn't want the embarrassment of being stuck there in broad daylight, and I didn't like the thought of being stuck out there if the wind began to pick up. It wouldn't take much to roll you over.

After I cleared a couple of hundred flounders, it began to seem that I was drifting off the Sands, and before long I could hear fog horns. Once, for about thirty minutes, I drifted near what I thought was a buoy with a fog horn, but I couldn't see it through the fog and worried that I'd wrap it with the net. And I had no way of knowing what it marked. A rock? A jetty? At last it seemed that I was drifting past it, and, since I was still in fairly shallow water, I wasn't worried about being in the shipping lane. Then, along with the endless supply of flounders, I began to bring in jellyfish. I worked like mad to bash them out of the net before they came into the boat and oozed between the floorboards, toward the pump. With all the water that comes in with the net, I knew I couldn't handle a clogged bilge pump. And now I began to worry because the wind had picked up and the foghorns seemed farther away. The seas had built enough for me to see whitecaps around the boat, and I had to take more frequent breaks from picking jellyfish and flounders in order to run into the cabin and clear jellyfish from the bilge pump below the engine. Sometimes the water was already over the floorboards.

When I could finally see the end of the net I pulled harder and faster, wanting to get the hell out of there. There wasn't a salmon in the whole net, nothing but flounders and jellyfish, and when I had only about ten fathoms to go, the picking light dimmed and flickered out, leaving me completely in the dark. I felt my way back to the cabin, which was all steamed up because the pump was clogged and the rising water was deep enough for a belt to pick it up and spray it over the hot engine. I couldn't clear the pump and the only thing I could think to do was to loosen the belt that was driving it and picking up the water. The pump wasn't doing any good anyhow, and I had to keep the water from spraying over the engine and shorting out the whole electrical system. I didn't like working so close to the belt and pulley—it would be easy to catch a sleeve or finger—but I finally got the bolts loose enough to let the belt go slack and stop throwing water. I rushed back to the bow and brought in the last few fathoms of net, flounders and all, and began the run to Chinook.

For the last few hours I'd worried about drifting out to the mouth. I'd heard enough stories about the Columbia River bar and didn't want to mess with it even in broad daylight and calm weather. But in the foggy dark I couldn't tell how far out I'd drifted, whether I was on the bar or not, or even which direction to steer for the harbor. All I could do was run with the seas pushing into the mouth. The boat was heavy with sloshing bilge, but I was lucky to have only a few fish aboard. From where I stood at the wheel right behind the cabin, the following seas seemed about to wash in over the stern, but the light from the low whitecaps helped me see which way to steer. So I dovetailed on toward the harbor.

It was beginning to get light, but I still had no visibility in the fog. Before too long, though, the seas began to get smaller and finally stopped capping, and not long after that I began to hear the foghorns again. If I just kept going with the swells I'd get close enough to shore to see buildings or trees or maybe even lights from another boat. At last I began to break out of the fog and then it cleared well enough for me to see some buildings I recognized from just below the harbor at Chinook. It was still early morning when I got there, but Ted and the other fishermen had already delivered their fish and tied up their boats. Pat and Ted had been praying for me again, and when I told them about drifting over Desdemona Sands and out toward the mouth they seemed assured that their prayers had worked and someone had watched over me. I didn't know how to respond, except to hug them and try to thank them for their hospitality and concern.

Ted helped me get through graduate school that year, and over the next twenty years when we fished in the same group on Cook Inlet, he helped me more. I've never been able to thank him enough, and the last time I talked with him I didn't even try. I called him the day before he went in for open-heart surgery. We both knew it'd be a tough one, and the last lesson he taught me was how to keep a steady hand on the wheel when things look bad.

Sounion and *Scrivener*

DURING OUR THIRD SEASON on *Margaret*, in 1965, Dick and I talked about dissolving our partnership and getting boats of our own. Not that our friendship was at all bruised from the years of fishing together. I can't imagine a better partnership, not even the one between John and Mike that impressed me so much a few years later. They'd started as partners fishing one of CWF's conversions, and then graduated to more impressive old cannery boats. They, too, moved beyond their partnership after a few years, each getting his own boat. But, working together, they'd devised a method of sharing command that still amuses me. It could have worked only for two people who were such good friends, each with a playful sense of humor. Every day at midnight they changed command, John being the captain one day and Mike the next. On their small scale, they'd found a perfect solution to the old problem of how a captain should wield his authority. They realized that in fishing you couldn't have a debate about whether to set the net here or there, or to run east or west. And each was relieved to let the other guy take responsibility. When I stopped to talk with them on the water, I could never tell who was captain that day. Only sometimes I'd catch a trace of sweet smoke that lingered in the air and seemed to contribute to their good humor. Dick and I didn't have such a system but managed to share the work and responsibility in as good-natured a way as I can imagine. It's just that we both realized that we'd get a lot further by not splitting our earnings fifty-fifty.

I looked at several used boats that were for sale in Kenai and finally fixed my attention on one called *Kaye Lynn*, a thirty-footer that a fisherman from the Columbia River had recently brought to Columbia Wards. Although it wasn't much larger than *Margaret*, it seemed to me like a powerful and glamorous vessel, with a big Chrysler V-8. It had twin carburetors and a wet exhaust system that made a wonderful low-pitched rumble. And with its small forward cabin and a chain-driven reel, it promised to be a boat that I could live on and operate alone. Word got around that it had won the Columbia River fishing boat race, as a bowpicker, before being rebuilt as a sternpicker for the Inlet fishery. Much of the attraction was that the owner, Danny, was a true highliner both in Kenai and on the Columbia River. Again and again that summer I watched him bring in as many fish as the boat would carry. Dick bought my half of *Margaret* for $1,250 and fished it for another year before selling it and getting his own larger boat. I paid Danny his asking price of $6,500, though that was a lot of money from my point of view. I could swing it with a low-interest loan from the National Marine Fisheries Service.

I was slow getting to Kenai the first summer I owned it and found that, because its position on the ways had been blocking other boats, the cannery crew had already launched it. But in launching it, the beach gang hadn't taken the necessary precautions and it quickly sank in the river. The boat was made of Port Orford cedar, which is notorious for drying out over the winter. The dry planks spread at the seam but swell tight after a few days in the water. Other fishermen knew to spray the planks with water for a few days before launching. But *Kaye Lynn* went in dry, began to take on water, listed to the unplugged scuppers, and sank. When I got there the inside of the cabin was still a mess from the Kenai silt, but the cannery's mechanics had cleaned up the engine and changed the oil several times. I was pissed that they'd sunk it before I even had a chance to take it for a spin, but I also knew how those mechanics could keep the old cannery boats going and quickly got over it. Later that week I finished renaming the boat by tacking on new plastic letters, *Sounion*, and this caught the attention of a man whose boat I'd almost bought instead, one named *Shag Two*. He wondered where I got the name, but mainly warned, "Hey, don't you know it's bad luck to change a boat's name?" I never had any unusual bad luck with *Sounion*, and when I bought another used boat several years later I changed its name as well. In the meantime *Shag Two*'s former owner died of cancer. I've never been afraid to whistle on the boat or to bring bananas aboard.

Sounion proved to be a good little boat. Like many other fishermen on Cook Inlet at that time, I fished alone for most of the seven years I owned her. Few things will shore up your self-confidence as much as owning and

Author Aboard *Sounion*

running your own boat. But during my first few years with *Sounion*, I spent a lot of time each winter trying to anticipate what I'd need for the following summer, things that I might not be able to find in Kenai. If I were in Seattle I'd haunt the fishing-supplies and marine-hardware stores, looking for gear or gadgets that I might need. When I flew into Kenai each June my bags would be stuffed with everything from spare parts to tubes of sealant or liquid weld that just might get you out of a tight spot if you broke a fitting or sprang a leak. Dwayne, one of the mechanics at CWF, told me that he'd never be without a tube of liquid weld, either when trying to keep his truck running on the Al-Can Highway or to keep a rusty old marine engine chugging along. As a very inexperienced mechanic with a touchy high-powered engine, I believed in liquid weld, though I can't remember ever using it.

I haven't seen *Sounion* for many years now and wonder where it ended up. The last time I saw it, at a boat yard in Homer sometime in the eighties, it looked old and battered. It reminded me of *Margaret* and the other Bristol Bay conversions that by then seemed to belong in a maritime museum. I was struck with that sense one night in the summer of 1969, when I was running *Sounion* up the Inlet toward Kenai after a long period. It was calm on the Inlet that night, the twentieth of July, and an unforgettable full moon rose and shimmered in the wake. I couldn't keep my eyes off it because earlier that day someone had reported over the marine-band radio that Apollo 11 had landed on the moon. I tuned into the scratchy local AM station and got the excited reports, and as I watched the full moon rise in my wake it was hard to comprehend. My Chrysler V-8 was purring along quite nicely, but here I was out near the middle rip, on an old wooden boat, catching fish using an ancient technique—and Neil Armstrong was walking around on the moon.

I earned enough with *Sounion* to get me through graduate school. But it had a cramped little cabin, the big V-8 burned more gas than I could carry (causing me to get towed in several times), and you could barely squeeze a thousand or eleven hundred fish into the hold. This last limitation cost me a fair amount of fishing time over the years; I'd fill the hold early in the day, run to a tender, unload, and then try to get on the fish once again. The cramped cabin and the limited hold were particularly troublesome one summer when my then-wife, Roberta, fished with me for part of the season. Despite the unhappiness that led to our divorce, I still admire her courage and the hard work she put in with me that summer. She put up with a fair amount of seasickness, which was harder to deal with in a cramped little cabin than in more comfortable quarters. *Sounion*'s huge gas engine protruded into the little cabin, roaring and pounding away only a few feet from the head of the bunk. She did less well in putting up with some of my friends—Ted, for example. When he was anchored up with us one night at the north end of Kalgin Island, he put out a line and caught a two-hundred-pound halibut, but couldn't get it aboard without first shooting it in the head with a 22. Although that is a common and absolutely necessary practice, in those years of violence in Viet Nam, not to mention the string of tragic assassinations in America, Roberta was shocked when Ted shot the halibut and could never abide his presence after that.

I give her a lot of credit, though, for hanging in there with me on one rough day, in particular, when we were in danger of overloading the boat and maybe even going down with it. We were on a very good set and worked like mad to pick two thirds of the net in the sloppy weather. Roberta held tough, and we finally avoided either overloading the boat or cutting off the last third of the net. Another fisherman, Roy, answered our call and came over to pick up the last, heavy piece of net. It was a good deal for Roy, as well, because he hadn't been able to find the fish that day. As we agreed, he sold the fish he picked out of the net, but he returned our net the next day, along with a nice bottle of wine to show his thanks. Even with experiences like this on *Sounion*, though, Roberta fumed when I decided to get a larger boat a few years later.

Besides being too little to pack enough fish, *Sounion* was like nearly every other boat of its size at that time in lacking the luxury of a head. By the 1960s most new gill-netters sported heads, and beginning in the 70s some gill-netters even had heads that were enclosed in watertight closets with a shower and drain, using fresh water heated by the engine. But *Sounion* had only the dependable but quite uncomfortable deck bucket. This method has worked quite well for hundreds of years, but I grew tired of it in rough seas. There were no porta-potties in those days, and even if there were *Sounion*'s tiny cabin wouldn't have accommodated one. But I found a suitable solution in a little camp toilet with a seat that was fixed to fold-up legs. You could attach a plastic bag beneath the toilet seat and thus *sit* there in relative luxury. I know it isn't polite to speak of such matters in writing of the sea. Only a few writers have described the heads on sailing vessels, even in the muted ways that Felix Riesenberg does in *Mother Sea*, or Patrick O'Brian in *Master and Commander*. And it's hardly necessary to describe such things any longer, now that nearly all gill-netters are equipped with a comfortable head, some even with showers. But I neglected to use proper caution when I first made use of my new fold-up device on *Sounion*. You never want to relax too much when running a boat, and there's little risk of that where the deck bucket is concerned. I wanted to make a night set that night somewhere in the middle of the Inlet above the mouth of the Kenai, and was probably in too much of a hurry to pick a safe spot. I wanted to stay away from other boats and certainly far away from a rip, so ran several minutes toward the west and then ran twice as far back to the east. Then, finding no sign of debris from a rip, I headed a short way back to the west and strung out the net. I watched the bit of it that I could see from the stern and then went into the cabin to enjoy my new device.

Such luxury and comfort.

But at once I began to hear a faint rushing sound coming through the porthole, and, quickly investigating, discovered that my net had been drawn into the edge of a rip. Unfortunately, my runs to the east and west didn't allow for the way that the rips don't always run north and south and sometimes meander to the east or west. I had set out right next to one and spent the rest of the night and nearly till noon the next day bringing in the net and clearing it of driftwood and kelp.

Even on *Sounion*, which had no through-hull fittings for either a head or a depth-finder, there were six such fittings that kept you aware of how fast you could take on water if something went wrong. Three of these were especially important: an intake for salt water to cool the wet exhaust, and two outlets for the wet exhaust, one on either side of the engine and exiting just slightly above the water line. The wet exhaust did a fine job of muffling the engine noise and saving deck space that a conventional exhaust stack would have taken. But I always worried that if the engine coughed or backfired in rough water, just when one of the exhaust outlets dipped beneath the water, it might suck enough sea water back into the exhaust to crack a manifold and probably the block as well. Two more through-hull fittings were required for the keel cooler, and these were convenient to inspect from the engine compartment. The sixth fitting was easy to forget because it was out of sight and seldom used. Being an old Columbia River gill-netter, *Sounion* had a fitting beneath the deck, next to the rudder post, that provided access to the wheel in case you got web in the wheel. You got to it through a hatch cover on the rear deck, beneath which a pipe of about eight inches in diameter was fitted to the bottom and rose inside the boat to a height just below the deck but above water level. The pipe had a screw-on cap that could be removed, thus allowing you in calm weather to stick your hand and arm through the pipe and down beneath the boat if you needed to clear web or other obstructions from the wheel. I once used this access port to cut web out of the wheel and appreciated how useful it could be.

One day toward the end of my second season on *Sounion* I was steering from atop the cabin, a kind of poor man's flying bridge that I'd arranged in order to get better visibility. From the low wheelhouse it was hard to spot distant boats or jumpers, so I'd cut a hatch in the ceiling, directly above the wheel and throttle control. On days like this, sunny and flat calm, I could see forever, and I needed to. It had been a very slow day, but now I was running south to check out a fish report. The prospect of finally getting on the fish is enough of a lift, especially if you think you can outrace the other boats headed that way, and perched on my "bridge" I was enjoying the added thrill, as though I were driving a convertible. The wind was blowing in my hair and my kind of hot-rod V-8 was pushing me along at about fifteen knots to the accompaniment of the wet exhaust's throaty throb. Fish or no fish, it was great to be cruising around on the Inlet on such a day, with Mt. Redoubt and Mt. Iliamna towering in the distance. So I hardly took notice when the boat began to feel a little sluggish. The engine wasn't missing a beat, but the boat slowed down just a tad and seemed oddly heavy. The stern normally sat down a little at high speed, but now it seemed a bit lower in the water.

I throttled back, quickly slipped down into the wheelhouse to check things out, and the first thing I did was open the engine cover. I hadn't hit anything in the water, but there was water well above the stringers and the belts were picking up spray from the bilge. I checked the through-hull fittings but saw no water gushing in, yet it was rising so fast that I knew I was going to sink. I got to the radio and gave a "Mayday" before the water got to the batteries. My voice was shakier that I wanted it to be, but I gave my position—just below Humpy Point and about five miles out—then threw down the mike and raced to look into the hold. If I'd somehow sprung a plank maybe I could stuff something into the hole and stay afloat. The hold was a quarter full of water, but I couldn't see a leak. Then I thought about the hatch cover in the stern and scrambled toward it. When I took off the cover, there it was. The screw-on cap had vibrated lose and come completely off the eight-inch pipe, which was now nothing but a huge gusher because the top was well below the water line. I'd been running fast enough to make the stern sit down, and the top of the pipe had sunk below the water line. It took only a second to find the cap and screw it back on. This stopped the gusher but now the water was so high in the boat that the higher and usually dry planks were letting water in at the seams. Now the engine was dead, the radio was shorted out, and there wasn't anything to do but grab the deck bucket and begin to bail.

I was luckier than hell with the calm weather and perfect visibility, and not long after I started bailing I saw a boat headed my way. It was Poopdeck, pushing *Hummingbird* for all it was worth, black smoke pouring from the stack. As soon as we tied him alongside, Poopdeck started his pump and threw the intake hose into my hold. It was a small pump but I knew that, tied to his boat, I wouldn't sink. Poopdeck took a call from another guy, Waldo, who was headed toward us on his gill-netter *Lion*, which had a two-inch pump. After Waldo arrived, I told both of them what had happened, more than a little red-faced to have given the panicky call and to have let the situation develop in the first place. They were both cool, understanding how things like that can happen so quickly, and relieved to know that things weren't any worse. With Waldo's pump making quick work of it, Poopdeck wished me good luck and headed off toward another boat that had found some fish. Waldo radioed the CWF tender, *Beaver*, who was already headed that way, and stayed with me till they were close at hand. *Beaver* quickly got a line on me, towed me around for the rest of the period, and then dropped me off at the cannery dock.

That ended the season for me. One of the cannery's mechanics rebuilt my engine over that winter, and *Sounion* served me well over the next five years. I loved the boat and would have kept it if I hadn't begun to feel the competitive pressure in the Inlet fishery. Because of *Sounion*'s small hold, I'd frequently have a full load by mid-morning and then have to leave the grounds to deliver. That took a lot of time, and it was hard to find the fish again. There was also the risk of overloading the boat in dangerous situations. Many boats have sunk in this way, and often not because the captain was simply too greedy for his own good. One incident in particular convinced me that I needed a bigger, safer boat. By then my former partner Dick had bought a thirty-two-foot boat called *Tula*, and one day he found a lot of fish in the middle rip off the north end of Kalgin Island. He gave me a call and I managed to find him. He was getting hits all along his net, but the rip was so snotty that I couldn't risk making a set. *Sounion* was low in the stern, even without a load, and I was afraid that if I tried picking up a loaded net in that slop I couldn't avoid taking a wave. It would take just one. Because *Tula* had lots of freeboard, a big hold, and a powerful engine, Dick had one of his best days ever, and I began to look seriously for a larger boat. I found one and had the pleasure of selling *Sounion* to my good friend, Mike, who fished it for another few years before passing it along to someone else. And when I retired from fishing some twenty years later, Mike surprised me with a gift that I'll lug around with me to the last, a piece of deck beam that he'd had cut away many years earlier when he installed a new engine in *Sounion*.

The new boat, *Surf*, was an aluminum thirty-two-footer—one of the disparaged "tin cans" that had begun to show up in the Inlet by the early sixties. They were fast, efficient, and seemingly indestructible, but owners of wooden boats hated them. Fishermen on the tin cans would sometimes tie up to you and not bother to put out bumpers. Worse, if you were coming back into the Kenai at the end of a period, you'd often see the faster aluminum boats already tied up waiting in line to unload at Kenai Packers. They seemed to fish in packs and they'd often be low in the water.

"Damned tin cans," you'd say to yourself and to friends who shared your disdain. Though the tin cans had good lines, they lacked the beauty of wooden boats, and they were also cold, loud, and uncomfortable. The cabins weren't insulated and so reverberated with engine noise and the noise of crashing water, and each boat was a network of unforgiving sharp metal edges that took their toll on knuckles, elbows, shins, and knees. Also, as they were susceptible to electrolysis, you needed to inspect the hull and replace the zincs frequently.

Despite these several limitations, though, the tin cans were almost perfect fishing machines. They would take a beating, didn't need painting or caulking, and were easy to keep clean. So, after ten years of maintaining wooden boats and leaving them to weather on the ways for nine or ten months a year, I began to see the appeal of aluminum boats and made a deal on *Surf*. At twenty-five thousand dollars it was a stretch, but CWF's superintendent agreed to help me finance the boat with an interest-free loan like those they offered other fishermen. Such loans were good for both the fisherman, who could make annual payments based on a percentage of his season's catch, and the cannery, who thus guaranteed itself a supply of fish.

When I took possession of the new boat I wanted to rename it, partly to distinguish myself from the previous owner, and partly to honor my favorite author, Herman Melville. I chose the unlikely name *Scrivener* from his great story, "Bartleby the Scrivener," even though there's little in that story to suggest that it could have been written by the author of *Moby-Dick*. Set in Wall Street, the story has but one image from the sea, Melville's description of Bartleby as "a bit of wreck in the mid Atlantic." Unlike poor Bartleby, *Scrivener* was a sturdy and efficient workboat and never refused a command the way Bartleby does with his repeated, "I prefer not to."

I was never foolish enough to think of any vessel as unsinkable, but *Scrivener* was tough and seaworthy enough to get me beyond the kind of vague insecurity I'd felt in fishing either *Margaret* or *Sounion*. I no longer lay awake on windy nights before a fishing period, dreading the thought of heading out into the Inlet on a rough day. The aluminum hull with its much greater freeboard eased my mind. Besides, the engine was almost new, a little six-cylinder Chevrolet that gave me all the power I needed. Its 165 horsepower was far less than what I had had in *Sounion*'s big V-8, but it was quieter, burned only half the fuel, never missed a beat, and, with only a single carburetor, was far easier to keep in tune.

Still, while I developed a lot of respect and appreciation for *Scrivener*, it was never a boat you could love or romanticize. It's easier to feel that way for a wooden boat, whose planks and ribs somehow live in the imagination as other materials do not: aluminum, steel, ferro cement, even plywood or fiberglass. For such reasons, it seems, I saved no photographs of *Scrivener* and have only indistinct recollections of being on the boat. It served me well and I earned a lot of money with it. But in thinking of *Scrivener* now, I feel something like the laboratory monkeys who rejected surrogate "mothers" constructed of wire. Even though the "moms" nursed them with bottled milk, the babies would cling to them only if the wire figures were covered with terry cloth. The cold metal. For similar reasons, when I try to imagine the fishing life as I first knew it on Cook Inlet, there are only boats made of wood.

Yet one memory of *Scrivener* floats on a strange sense of security I once felt aboard it in Snug Harbor. I was spending a three-day closure there over the Fourth of July in 1976, and Roberta flew there to meet me, bringing our seven-month-old baby, Todd, and her good friend Deborah. *Scrivener*'s cabin could accommodate the four of us comfortably for that time. A friend, Dick Moll, owned a floatplane for charter, so picked them up from the cannery dock in Kenai for the flight across the Inlet. I was anchored in front of the cannery when Dick circled and prepared to land. The tide was flooding pretty hard as he taxied up even with my stern, stepped out onto a pontoon, and threw me a line. It was easy enough to secure the plane and for Roberta and Deborah to step along the pontoons and climb aboard the boat. Dick helped them and then went back into the cockpit to take Todd in his arms. As he walked along the pontoon toward the boat, preparing to hand Todd to me, I knew and certainly Dick did that if either of us slipped or lost his grip the tide would have its way. Dick held onto a strut with one hand and passed Todd to me with the other. I'm sure I was shaking when I took Todd in my hands and placed him in his mother's arms. I was grateful for Dick's steady hand in it all, and for

Scrivener's sturdy hull. I never saw Dick again, but I'll never forget his smile when he gave me a thumbs up and headed back to the cockpit—nor what I felt a few years later when I heard the news. He and a few other floatplanes were spotting herring for some seiners in Chinitna Bay and began circling a ball of fish that they'd spotted. He collided with another plane and both went down in flames.

We had some very good years on the Inlet in the middle seventies, and like other fishermen I needed to decide whether to pay lots of tax on my fishing earnings or take advantage of incentives offered by the IRS to invest in newer equipment. And as the pressure to reinvest encouraged my boat-owner's natural lust for better gear and more gadgets, I began to think I needed a more suitable boat. I shared other fishermen's wariness of gasoline engines, with their risk of fire, and thought it would be good to have the safety and economy of a diesel. And, hell, I couldn't keep up with the competition if I didn't have radar, for example. So, at the beginning of the season in 1977, my friend Jon and I began to talk about building new boats. He had already built up a Cook Inlet gill-netter from a smaller boat that he'd fished in Puget Sound, and he'd settled on a particular kind of boat that both of us thought perfect for the Inlet. We could buy bare hulls from the factory in Port Townsend and then finish them ourselves, using Jon's house in Port Townsend as our base. This required a considerable leap of faith for both of us that season, as we had to sell our old boats in order to finance the new ones, and we had to put down quite a sum to make sure the hulls would be ready for us late that fall. If we sold our present boats and then couldn't finish the new ones in time, we'd be out of business for the season in 1978 and possibly thereafter.

I placed an ad in the *Anchorage Times* and by the middle of July had an offer to buy *Scrivener* for my asking price of twenty-five thousand dollars. Other fishermen around the state were also apparently intent on upgrading their investments. I accepted the earnest money and agreed to deliver the boat to Seldovia in early August. So, after my last day of fishing, I left the grounds and headed for Seldovia to hand over the keys to the boat. But I began to experience the anxiety that pleasure-boat owners and fishermen alike feel in being without a boat. On the eight-hour run I even began to feel a kind of love for the old tin can, and asked myself again and again,

"What's wrong with *Scrivener*? Do you really need another boat?" And, "Are you really up to building a new boat? You've never done anything like that!"

After almost fifteen years of fishing in Cook Inlet, I had never been in Seldovia. I've grown to love that little town and harbor, but that day it was so gloomy and unwelcoming that I thought I'd never return. I felt my way up the channel early that morning through fog and light rain, barely able to stay awake after the previous day's fishing and the long run. I tried to cheer myself by thinking that I might be broke next year but I'd at least have radar to make it through this kind of murk. I finally spotted the breakwater and made it in to the harbor, tied up the boat, had a drink, and went to bed. When I got up early that afternoon, a few hours before the buyer was due, I walked up the ramp to look around town. I'd heard that the earthquake of '64 had wiped out most of the boardwalks, robbing the town of its full charm. But with the lingering fog and rain all I could think was how dismal the place must be in the winter. Walking past the harbormaster's office I made my way to the bar I'd seen from the boat harbor, a place called the Linwood. There were quite a few people sitting at the bar, smoking and drinking in the dim light. It was even more depressing inside than it was outside in the fog and rain. But I ordered a beer and sat looking out over the harbor. I could make out the gray shape of *Scrivener*, half dissolved in the fog, yet looking better than ever.

It was still an hour or so before the buyer would show up. He said he'd have a certified check with him, but he'd never seen the boat, only pictures and my description of it. I began to feel a little relief in thinking the deal might fall through. It was a good boat, and if I kept it I wouldn't have the risk and labor of building a new one. I felt restless, decided to walk around a bit, and began to look at notices on a bulletin board just inside the door at the Linwood. Boats for sale, some really junky ones, outdated notices from a few people who were looking for jobs on boats, other things wanted or for sale. And I noticed a note pinned to the board along with a very tattered and crumpled dollar bill. The note said only, "Dirty John's last dollar." It touched me and I began to imagine a story about old John that reflected my own mood. The guy was down and out, maybe got drunk last winter and then stumbled out into the snow. On his way back to his cabin he toppled over, and when they finally discovered the poor old guy all they found on him was this last crumpled dollar. Poor old son of a bitch. I couldn't stop thinking about him and so went back to the bar and ordered another beer. When the bartender brought my beer, I asked, "What's the story about Dirty John? I saw that notice on the bulletin board. What happened to him?"

"Oh, that." Then, seeing that I was prepared to hear a sad story, he smiled and said, "Ah, that's just somebody ribbing old John. He comes in here all the time and never buys a drink for anybody else—always says he's on his last dollar."

Ishmael

AFTER I GAVE *SCRIVENER'S* KEYS to the new owner that day, I felt a little like Ishmael in "Loomings." It was only August and not November, but it was a damp, drizzly day in Seldovia and in my "soul." As soon as the plane back to Homer rose above the fog bank, though, I could see forever—the glaciers pouring into Kachemak Bay, the wide Inlet to the north and west, with Mt. Iliamna and Mt. Redoubt glowing high and white on the other side, and the Homer Spit just across the Bay. The way ahead seemed clear. Jon and I would put down our money and place our orders for the new hulls. They would be ready for us in Port Townsend by late December. In the meantime I would return to my academic life in Arizona, where I was beginning my first sabbatical leave. I had applied for and received a full year's leave, based on my proposal to research and write three essays, one on Hemingway's great story, "The Short Happy Life of Francis Macomber," and two on *Moby-Dick*. During the previous school year I had completed the research on Hemingway. Then, after the end of the spring semester and before leaving for Cook Inlet in late June, I wrote "Margot Macomber's Gimlet." Now I had to immerse myself in the great, intimidating book and write two essays between mid August and late December. After submitting them for publication, I'd drive to Port Townsend and spend the second half of my sabbatical year building the boat, running it from Puget Sound up the Inside Passage and across the Gulf of Alaska, and fishing the Cook Inlet season.

I'd need a lot of luck to pull it off, especially at the end. It would take lots of fish to pay all the bills. In opting for the full year's leave, I had happily given up 40 percent of my normal salary. But, realizing that few college deans are blessed with lively imaginations, I hadn't mentioned in my sabbatical proposal that I also planned to build a boat. I'd found that many academics resemble the landsmen Ishmael describes at the beginning of *Moby-Dick*—hopelessly "pent up in lath and plaster—tied to counters, nailed to benches, clinched to desks."

In my main essay on *Moby-Dick* I wanted to weigh the book as a whole. I set out to find its center of gravity and explain, if I could, what Melville gave us. No one has ever succeeded in so ambitious a project, of course, but I attempted it and ultimately described *Moby-Dick* as America's great lyrical novel. It is a celebration of life—"the ungraspable phantom of life," Ishmael calls it—in which Melville proclaimed his faith in Genesis and in what he believed were the Christian-democratic values of the young United States. He wrote his great book at the same time that Wallace and Darwin were building on the new sense of geological time and would soon formulate the revolutionary theory of natural selection. But Melville defended his faith in the Biblical whale by clinging to the ill-fated biology of that time, natural theology. Similarly, he wrote as a common sailor to celebrate the Christian-democratic values that he believed would preserve the nation from the threats of civil war and deranged autocrats like Captain Ahab.

As I immersed myself in the novel that fall, my plans for the two essays took shape, and I also found a name for my new boat. Reading and re-reading the novel, I kept hearing, "Call me Ishmael." I couldn't help loving a character who can joke of working sailors who pass wind from the forecastle and leave it for their unwitting officers to breathe; who can declare it better to "sleep with a sober cannibal than a drunken Christian" and then share his bed with his new-found "fellow man" and "bossom friend" Queequeg; who can sing of the great "Spirit of Equality," the democratic "dignity" he sees "shining in the arm that wields a pick or drives a spike"; who can imagine the Nantucket whaler in the middle of the ocean as he "furls his sails, and lays him to his rest, while under his very pillow rush herds of walruses and whales"; and who all the while acknowledges "the full awfulness of the sea . . . whose creatures prey upon each other, carrying on eternal war since the world began."

At about the time I fixed on the name *Ishmael*, I had to set my writing aside for a week and fly to Seattle for the annual Fish Expo, a trade show for the commercial fishing industry. Fishermen from all over the West Coast gather there to see new products on display, from nets to diesel engines and radar sets. It's something like the huge book displays at the Modern Languages Association convention, except that the products displayed at the Expo have the appeal of concrete reality that you can appreciate in a survival suit but maybe not in a new volume on Derrida. By that time Jon and I had been joined by our old friend Thor, an architect and long-time commercial fisherman, who had also decided to build a new boat. We had all ordered the same kind of bare, fiberglass hulls from a factory in Port Townsend, and we planned to meet there in early January. The hulls would be done and we would begin work on them in a makeshift shop adjacent to Jon's house. We'd use the same plans for all three boats and, though each of us would build his own boat and stamp it with his own identity, we could save a lot of money on equipment and materials by ordering three of everything at once.

When we met at the Expo, our main problem was to choose a diesel engine that would give us the power, economy, and durability that we wanted, and we made a deal for three Detroit 671s, a long-time workhorse in the industry. And, writing checks like mad, we ordered other equipment that we would need for our projects, from hydraulic motors and reels for bringing in the net to radar sets, radios, survival suits, and anchors. When I returned to Arizona I couldn't stop thinking about the boat, doubting that I had the skills to actually do the work and worrying how I could pay for it all. But somehow, keeping my focus on Ishmael the character as that seemed to merge with *Ishmael* the boat, and knowing that I had to finish the sabbatical project before I could concentrate my energies on building the boat, I finished my main essay on *Moby-Dick* and another less ambitious one on Melville's cetology. By Christmas I had submitted both essays to scholarly journals and was buoyed by news that the essay on Hemingway had already been accepted. A few days later I headed north in a pickup truck full of tools and gear for the project, and with plans to meet Roberta and Todd at the Seattle airport in two weeks.

Jon and his wife Heidi had found a little house for us to rent in Port Townsend, perched on the very edge of a high bluff overlooking the Strait of Juan de Fuca, and just a few hundred yards up the road from their house and our boat-building shop. During my first week there, before

Roberta and Todd arrived from Phoenix and while Jon, Thor, and I were getting geared up for the project, I could linger with my morning coffee at the picture window overlooking the Strait. Watching the constant traffic of ocean-going vessels on their way to or from Seattle or Vancouver, in the ever-changing weather, I eased into the work that lay ahead—yet also dreamt that *this* might be the good life: fishing in these waters. Jon told me of a friend who lived in Port Townsend and earned his living as a gill-netter in Puget Sound. One night when drifting right out here in the Strait, he picked up his net and found a large, well-wrapped bundle of high-grade marijuana from Thailand. Someone had dumped it overboard when the Coast Guard was closing in. The lucky fisherman saved out a bit for himself and then sold his catch for a very high price. Hell, I dreamed, fishing these waters might be the way to go. No academic politics, no huge risk of building a boat and running it to Alaska, a couple of metropolitan centers not far away for concerts or plays. Just a simple life fishing the Strait or Puget Sound, always close to home.

That fantasy passed quickly and the reality of what lay ahead set in with the winter rain and my first few days' experience with fiberglass. The fibers work into your clothes, the abrasive dust from the grinder powders your hair and fills your nostrils. You can't get away from the fiberglass itch or the noxious fumes from the resin and acetone. Barely sheltered from the rain in our plastic-sheeted shop, we kept a fire going to keep things warm enough for the resin to kick, and did our best to retain our belief in this remarkable material. Our hulls came from the factory's mold for a thirty-four-foot boat, but we cut off the transoms and patched in four-foot-long extensions to make boats that were thirty-eight feet long. Each of us had fished boats of only thirty or thirty-two feet and now wanted more deck room, larger holds, and more comfortable cabins. Even though we hired an experienced man to help us with these extensions, it took a leap of faith to believe that the end of your boat wouldn't just fall off in a pounding sea.

We also hired a couple of local shipwrights to help us build the bulkheads, decks, and cabins. Then we glassed over the marine-plywood construction and after a month or so each of us began to feel confident that these boats were not only going to work but that they were going to be damned fine-looking boats. We loved the hulls, which had been designed by a well-known marine architect in Seattle named Munk. But none of us liked the cabins that the local manufacturer could have provided along with our hulls. Instead of their high, box-like design, we wanted low cabins that would complement the hull's classic lines. So Thor, an architect, and Jon, with a BA in art, collaborated in designing a cabin that pleased us all. Throughout the fall we had sent preliminary drawings back and forth through the mail, and Thor had said repeatedly, "I want these boats to sing." They finally did, largely because of his skill in fine-tuning the "tumble home" in our cabins' design. The cabin walls slope inward from deck to roof at the exact degree that brings the cabin into organic harmony with the vessel's other lines. Framing in the cabins, we almost sang along, though in a different key from the rock and roll that blasted from the radio inside our shed. The pleasure we took in all this not only helped us contend with the fiberglass itch, the bloodied knuckles, and the long hours of work. It bound us together in the joint venture of our lives.

I often felt that I had little to contribute to our shared project—nothing of Thor's architectural brilliance or Jon's eye for design and his experience in rebuilding other fiberglass boats. But I did introduce several practical ideas gleaned from my own experience. I wanted a large hatch to the fish hold, even though that would take up valuable deck space. You need room for shoulders, elbows, and equipment in loading gear and offloading fish, and I wanted an engine room large enough for you to work on the engine without tying yourself in knots. But my main contribution was to keep us on track. I could see farther ahead than either Jon or Thor and kept pushing us to stay on schedule. We had to finish the boats in time to head north by early June, and I kept reminding the others that we had to order this or that by a certain date, that we had to install the engines on schedule, or the fuel tanks. I'm sure that Jon and Thor dreaded to hear my concerns about our schedule, but for the most part we worked together as shipmates and ended feeling far more affection and respect for each other than might seem possible under such stress.

With each of us working on his own boat, we were set up for what could have been an atmosphere of strained competition. Each of us had a long history of competing in the fishery, and before that each of us had excelled as athletes. Sometimes, when we broke for lunch, we did compete in play, shooting baskets or vying to see who could jump the highest or farthest. I was forty and Jon and Thor were barely thirty, but in some ways we were all still adolescent males. Nevertheless we were committed to each other's success, and if one of us figured out the best way to install a pump, say, we shared the idea, as we borrowed each other's tools or helped each other when a particular job required two or three strong backs.

Not that we didn't get on each other's nerves from time to time or have some tense moments in figuring out how to split some bills. Jon and Heidi were under particular strain from having the noisy, fume-and-dust-laden shop butt right up to their house, and from having all of us and other workers tromp through their kitchen to use the john. Heidi managed to keep cool and made me and Thor feel part of their large family. Meanwhile, just up the road in my own home, the project was adding to the strain of an already rocky marriage, particularly when my mother wanted to take advantage of our being so close to her home in Seattle and visit us. She and Roberta had never been on good terms. And sometimes tension developed between Jon, Thor, and myself over insignificant matters like who should be responsible for buying a vacuum cleaner that we all needed for the shop. Jon and I concluded that it was Thor's turn to buy an item like this, so I bought one and then let Thor know that he should pay for it. It embarrasses me to remember my part in that petty disagreement. We felt its irritation right up through the end of the fishing season that August, when we settled up with each other. The machine ended up on Thor's boat, and when I wrote to him explaining why I expected him to pay for the stupid thing, I quipped that even nature abhors a vacuum, and he was a good enough sport to let it pass. But as we worked together for those six months in Port Townsend and finally ran north together, tempers never flared. Nearly thirty years later, we're still good friends and greet each other not with handshakes but hugs.

From the beginning we had planned to reward ourselves for the long months of boat building by taking three or four weeks to run north. It would be both a pleasure cruise and a shakedown cruise, and we'd stop along the way whenever we found an inviting bay. Catch some fish. Dig some clams. Anchor up early each evening and save time to play around in Ketchikan or Petersburg or other little harbors along the way. We could make it work if we left Port Townsend by the first of June, at the latest. Inevitably, though, we fell behind and the last weeks of finishing the boats required nonstop work and brought countless frustrating problems with batteries, radar sets, or equipment that didn't arrive on time. Because of the delay, two old friends, Roger Murray and Tony Angell, had to cancel their plans to accompany me on the trip north. I didn't blame Roberta for declining to make the run with Todd aboard. They would fly to meet me in Kenai a few weeks later, but that left me to find whatever crew was available in Port Townsend. They were two workers we'd hired to help with last-minute projects, and they proved to be reliable companions along the way. Another crew member was our Australian Shepherd named Kate C (for a favorite author, Kate Chopin), who spent much of the trip walking around and around the outside of the cabin or, in rough weather, crawling as far forward as she could get in the foot of my bunk. Finally, on Sunday, June 18, 1978, I made my first entry in *Ishmael*'s log: "After 5 long months, the last two of which were hard and hassled, we left Port Townsend at 8 p.m. Arrived, after a beautiful calm sunset and nearly full moon sail across the Strait of Juan de Fuca at Friday Harbor, on San Juan Island, about 10:30. A good shakedown for us all. The only hitch, a small oil leak for Jon."

After that, we did have a fine but rushed trip up the Inside Passage, beginning with the run inside Vancouver Island up the Strait of Georgia, on into Discovery Passage and through the legendary Seymour Narrows. My entry for the Narrows indicates that we timed it well and entered at close to slack water; so we saw no whirlpools and only "a few ripples at Ripple Rock, nothing serious," as I logged it. "I can see how it could be terrible." Running on through Johnstone Strait and by places with unforgettable names such as Whirlpool Rapids, Alert Bay, God's Pocket, and the Storm Islands, we anchored by nine or ten each night and pulled away by seven or eight. Heading on more quickly than we had wished, we crossed Milbanke Sound and ran through some "beautiful water, Finlayson Channel, Tolmie Channel, Graham Reach–wonderful narrow deep channels, killer whales, eagles" and on into a deserted old cannery in Princess Royal Channel called Butedale. Leaving there we allowed ourselves the luxury of detouring from our main route for a run into Ursula Channel, where we made our way to a place well known to people who cruise the Inside Passage, the hot springs at Bishop Bay. After a few days on the boats, it was good to relax and clean up, and we were also lucky enough to meet other visitors there who gave us three small spring chinook, enough for welcome meals on each of the boats.

After our leisurely baths, we pressed on, knowing that our own fishing grounds lay many miles and several days to the north, beyond Prince Rupert, Ketchikan, Wrangell, and Petersburg–on through Icy Strait and out into the Gulf of Alaska. We were all nervous about crossing the Gulf. Along the way we made a few quick stops for minor repairs and modifications. Thor had found that trimming two inches off the trailing edge of *Cheryl Lynn*'s rudder made the boat steer more easily; so Jon and I went on the grid in Ketchikan and made the same changes to *Nuliak* and *Ishmael*. When we finally left Cape Spencer we were all relieved to find the Gulf in one of its good moods. Besides running into a little slop around Kayak Island, we had a break in the weather and enjoyed an easy crossing that took a day and a half.

My log for Thursday, the 29th reads: "11:30 a.m. passing through Hinchinbrook Entrance . . . It's nice to be across the Gulf. The last 6 hours have taken us across the water where Uncle Bert was lost." (The sailboat he was on five years earlier had disappeared, and his body later washed up on Kayak Island.) After we arrived in the Seward small boat harbor later that day, I wrote, "Entering Resurrection Bay was like sailing into heaven. I've never imagined it to be so beautiful out there." Our final leg—rounding the end of the Kenai Peninsula and running on up Cook Inlet—took us to the Kenai River. We had missed the first slow days of the season, along with the opportunity to take our time in learning how to fish the new boats, but the season lay ahead of us with all the promise of a new, unopened book. My log entry for Monday, July 3, reads: "2:10 a.m. Left Kenai to fish!" It would be a disappointing season, and a strange one that turned my career in a new direction, as I explain in the following chapter.

Our cooperation in building the three boats, the shared labor, risks, and adventure—all this drew us together. Our new boats were sister ships, and we were half-brothers. For this reason alone the project was one of the best experiences of my life. I would never have attempted to build my boat alone. I might have gone into greater debt and simply ordered one from an established builder. That would have been a lot easier, and I probably would have loved the boat. You tend to love your boat, no matter what, as long as it keeps you afloat. But beyond the camaraderie I enjoyed in the boat-building venture, it was one of the best experiences of my life because it gave me self-confidence that I can't imagine acquiring in any other way. Not that there's anything unique about building your own boat. I've known many fishermen who did that, and many who did it all alone, from designing it to laying up the hull and finishing it off. It's just that I share with these others the feelings of security and self-confidence you gain when you've done it all or mostly by yourself. You know the boat, where everything is, and how everything works or is supposed to work.

People who build their own houses can also gain such feelings of security and self-confidence. My friend Roger built his house alone, a beautiful nest of a house, with nothing more than a skill saw, and he knows exactly how it grips the earth and how all the systems interconnect to give it life. It's like that with a boat, except that you *always* know how quickly it can sink, how much your life depends on it. If you're proud that you built it, proud that you know it inside and out, that it's a good-looking boat that keeps you afloat and takes you through some rough weather, your pride and self-confidence are more vital because they are tempered with gratitude. I'm sure that building *Ishmael* made me a better fisherman. When you know your boat intimately, and are confident in what you can do with it and what it can do for you, you can concentrate on the fish. More than that, my confidence running *Ishmael* extended to the larger questions that I think Hemingway had in mind in arranging for his sea-going hero Harry Morgan's words, "You got to have confidence steering" (in *To Have and Have Not*). Harry says that while at the wheel of his boat one night; but, as was often the case, Hemingway was getting at his submerged idea about Harry's navigating the darkness of his *life*. Writing this in 1936, Hemingway was confronting the darkness in his own life—

not long after his father's suicide—while also giving us the troubled main characters in "The Short Happy Life of Francis Macomber" and "The Snows of Kilimanjaro." You have to keep yourself together. In fact, I took Harry Morgan's words as my motto, writing them on the first page of *Ishmael*'s log, and including them as an epigraph in my first book, *Sea-Brothers*. Unexpectedly, I found that the self-confidence gained from boat building also made me a better scholar.

This might seem odd to people unfamiliar with academic life. But those who have experienced it can appreciate how academic training is a constant assault on a candidate's self-confidence. This isn't *all* bad. But after years of taking exams and learning how to survive graduate school by deferring to your various professors' sometimes eccentric views and writing papers that safely adhere to the favored theory of the moment, you might become a teaching assistant and, if you haven't offended your dissertation committee, even earn the degree. Then, if you're lucky enough to avoid being exploited as a part-time instructor and actually land a regular position, you are faced with the seven-year period of academic probation that lies between you and a secure position. On this treacherous pathway to tenure, you learn more about the monastic academy and refine your skills in how to please deans and department chairs and how to avoid offending students whose negative evaluations could also wreck a career. And, concentrating your energies on producing an acceptable number of publications by the tenure deadline, you learn to play it safe and key in to the prevailing critical conversation wherever you can. Throughout the probationary period you sense that you're barely making it, and are required in annual evaluations to justify your academic existence. Along the way to tenure your confidence might be battered even more when colleagues who seemed sure of getting tenure are suddenly fired.

All this plays hell with your confidence. And I'm sure that many academics have experienced the kind of insecurity and anxiety I did as the tenure decision neared. In a frequent sweaty dream, I'd learned that the registrar was questioning my degree because I'd never taken Sociology 100. Trying to remedy the problem, I'd enrolled in Sociology 100, a section that was being taught by a senior colleague. I had actually worked quite amicably with this man on a university committee. I admired him and knew that he liked and respected me. But in the dream, it is now final exams week, and I've never talked with the professor, bought the text, or attended one class. The exam is about to begin and the dream ends. After receiving tenure I never had the dream again.

As far as my self-confidence was concerned, I was one of academe's walking wounded. I was awarded tenure just the year before I built my boat, but building the boat did more to restore my self-confidence than did getting tenure. I felt this immediately on returning to the university after the 1978 fishing season. I had previously opposed deans and department chairs, once successfully leading a tiny revolution among assistant professors of English to stop the chair from removing our telephones. But far less willing now to put up with administrative incompetence, I questioned authority on many occasions. Once, for example, I fought a long losing battle in the Faculty Senate to limit the numbers of students in writing classes, and in another battle, successful this time, worked to win the faculty's right to vote on whom they would recommend in searches for Department Chairs. I had developed a much stronger and healthier conviction that, despite their artificial, institutional power, deans, department chairs, and senior faculty were not always impressive figures in what I conceived to be the real world. Stripped of their academic regalia they were no more than the pathetic "unaccommodated" human beings we all are, in King Lear's enlightened view—the "poor, bare, forked animal." Not that I imagined my academic superiors naked, god forbid, but perhaps as trying to make it through a storm on a small boat in the Gulf of Alaska.

More important, I noted that not all of my senior colleagues seemed very daring in their academic publications. A number of deans and department chairs had risen in the academic ranks by accumulating a good many publications that avoided controversy and lacked originality. But I didn't want to play it safe and so began to move beyond my recent work on Melville to learn what Melville and subsequent American writers drew from the sea after *Moby-Dick* appeared in 1851. Existing literary history proclaimed that there *was* no significant American sea fiction after *Moby-Dick* because the sailing ships had given way to steam and because the cowboy had displaced the sailor as a compelling figure in the American imagination. Actually, there is a very rich and extensive literature of the sea in the United States after Melville, with commendable works by several unknown writers and many by well-known writers such as Stephen Crane, Jack London, Hemingway, and Peter Matthiessen. A key element in this sea fiction is the new, Darwinian view of the sea as the cradle of life on earth. From this angle, many writers dispelled the mystery that Melville had celebrated as "the ungraspable phantom of life." I don't think I would have been drawn to this study in the first place if I hadn't experienced something of the ocean reality on my own, including the struggle for existence as a commercial fisherman. And I doubt very much that I would have dared to begin rewriting a century of literary history if I hadn't learned, through building and fishing *Ishmael*, the truth of Harry Morgan's words, "you got to have confidence steering."

Having built *Ishmael* before I built a book, I imagined that there is a similarity between these two projects, and I now believe that it might well be as hard to build a substantial boat as it is to build a substantial book, or perhaps harder. I decided that if I were going to write books, I wanted to write books that would not only float in the sea of thought, but pack a load. I expected rough going. Even now, eighty years after the Scopes Trial, vast numbers of Americans either ignore or deny Darwin's theory of evolution. Creationists have resurrected the old idea of "intelligent design" that emerged shortly after the *Origin of Species*, when a book called *The Genesis of Species* focused on the eye or wing and denied that such complex organs could evolve through natural selection. And even now, over a hundred years after *The Descent of Man*, an American president denies Darwinian evolution and with it the related ecological thought that warns of global warming. And the ivory towers are filled with literary scholars who have never thought about the theory of sexual selection but nevertheless resist the idea that writers such as Henry James, Kate Chopin, Edith Wharton, F. Scott Fitzgerald, or W. E. B. Dubois turned to Darwin as the essential guide in their own studies of human nature.

Revenge

 THE TWO HUNDRED REDS we caught on our first day's fishing with *Ishmael* helped ease the stress of boat building and missing the first days of the season. The weather was perfect, the boat and all the new equipment ran well, and John was much stronger and more self-confident in this second year as deck hand than I would have thought possible. We ran in to Snug Harbor to deliver our fish and planned to hole up there for the next two periods. Joining with other friends, we had another fine Fourth of July barbecue on the beach, feasting on fresh-dug razor clams, halibut, and of course a red. The next period's fishing was even better, and when we delivered our seven hundred reds to a tender in Snug, we shared other fishermen's optimism for the season ahead. But the next day we learned that Fish and Game was alarmed by the fleet's unexpectedly good catches for so early in the season. They had projected a rather weak run and now needed to insure that enough fish would ultimately escape into the spawning grounds. Few fishermen argued with Fish and Game's decision to close fishing until they could develop a clearer picture of the run's actual strength. But we were all uneasy as we headed back to Kenai to wait it out, especially because another uncertainty was now causing much confusion throughout the Inlet fishery. A new market for frozen salmon had developed in Japan, and most of the canneries had responded by setting up large freezer operations. But Columbia Wards had dragged its feet and set up only a very small freezing operation. Still committed to the market for canned salmon, they couldn't buy fish at the prices the freezing plants now offered. A number of Columbia Wards' fishermen began to sell their fish elsewhere.

It was a tough time for Columbia Wards, and for fishermen like myself. We valued our old ties with the company but had to pay our own bills. Now the season was looking iffy and I needed to make payments on the new boat. My added bind was that just a few months before this I had borrowed eight thousand dollars from Columbia Wards to finish building *Ishmael*. They'd offered me the same very favorable terms that they'd long offered other fishermen, including myself, when they helped me purchase *Scrivener*. There would be no interest, and annual payments would be calculated on a percentage of my season's catch. And of course they rightfully expected me to sell them all my fish, as they did in providing free winter storage for my boat.

But I now began to realize that, interest-free loan or not, I couldn't afford to sell my fish for much less than the going rate, and I wondered whether, in extending the loan, Columbia Wards had foreseen the year's developing market conditions. To make matters worse, Columbia Wards had not kept up with other processors in the Inlet in compliance with the new state regulation requiring that fish be bought by the pound, instead of by the number of fish. Other processors had set up scales to weigh the fish as they were off-loaded, but Columbia Wards continued to count the fish and then convert the number of fish to pounds, using a complicated formula that aroused many fishermen's suspicions. You'd deliver your fish and then have to wait several days to learn their final value. I joined a number of my friends in selling fish elsewhere, and tried at first to deliver some to other processors for the higher price, and some to Columbia Wards for the lower price. I hoped that Columbia Wards would meet the competition.

I'd been associated with Columbia Wards for sixteen years and wanted to continue what had been a very happy relationship, but I was feeling the squeeze and I soon learned that Columbia Wards felt it too. One day when I was especially worried about the price, and after I had delivered only a partial load to Columbia Wards, the superintendent, Ray, looked me up on the docks. He didn't mention my having "sold down river"—that is, to one of the competing processors that were located near the mouth of the river. Instead, Ray began to talk with me about *Ishmael*'s length. "You know, Bert," he said, "we've been looking at that new boat of yours, and we think it might be too long for the ways. We might not be able to put it up this winter."

It was clear what he was getting at, and clear to both of us that this was a somewhat friendly but absurd way to tell me that if I continued to sell down river I'd have to move on. Thor's new boat, *Cheryl Lynn*, was identical to *Ishmael*, and the cannery would have room for it and several other boats that were as long or longer. I was polite enough, saying only, "Well, I was wondering about that, Ray. It's a damned shame. Guess I'll have to look around." We didn't discuss it further, and although I hated the thought of leaving the cannery, which had become a kind of home to me over the years, I knew that it was time to make a move. Other friends who'd fished there for years had already moved on, and it was easy enough to do. Different processors were looking for their own supplies of fish, and if you were known to be a good producer, they'd welcome you with open arms. So I moved on to establish a similar relationship with a newer company near the mouth of the river, Salamatof Seafoods. A freezing operation, they paid the more competitive price for fish and also agreed to store *Ishmael* over the winters. When I went to the office at Columbia Wards to settle up at the end of the season, I paid off the loan, took the little money that remained from the fish I'd delivered, and thanked them again for having backed me. It was a clean break but for several years I missed the cannery community as you might miss former relatives after a divorce.

But the day Ray talked with me and I made my decision to move on, I was feeling in no mood to sell my fish for anything less than they were worth. We had fished a six-hour period the previous day, just half of a normal twelve-hour opening—and this after we had sweated out a four-day closure during the time when we should have been making our biggest catches of the season. It was a cool gray morning, with a diffuse haze that made you worry about fog. But shortly after the fleet left the river there were reports of jumpers being sighted over a wide area. The fish had schooled up over the closure and it looked like we'd have quite a day. Boats began to maneuver, staking out places for their opening drifts, and too many concentrated in the small area where the jumpers seemed heaviest. I eyed all this and wanted to play it safe, wanted to move away from the boats and avoid getting tangled with others or getting involved in ugly confrontations with other fishermen. At opening time there'd be a race to throw out your buoy and lay claim to a spot, and some fishermen always put out their nets ahead of time. I decided it'd be better to find a few jumpers in open water away from the crowd. At least I'd be able to stay on our first drift for as long as it seemed worthwhile.

I moved a little north and just before opening time found a nice show of jumpers. "Good move," I thought. We were well away from other boats, and when we began setting the net we started getting hits right away, all along the corkline. John had never seen anything like it, and we were both going a little crazy. This would make our season. But I immediately began to worry that we might be getting *too* many, more than the net could keep afloat. Fishermen dream about drifts like that, where you sink your net and hope that you can somehow get it back. Sometimes, if your reel is powerful enough, you can slowly winch it in, picking fish for all you're worth and finally getting the whole thing in. But sometimes the fish are so heavy in the net that the whole thing will go straight down and be impossible to budge, or the loaded web will just tear away from the cork line and sink. If you think you're catching too many, you have to start picking it up right away, and hope for the best. Or, you can take time to let go of the net and then run slowly along the length of the cork line to clip on extra buoys that might keep it afloat. As I was trying to decide whether to pick it up or buoy it, a friend came by on another boat. He saw all the hits in our net and I yelled, "Don't put it all out, Tom! You'll sink your gear!" He waved and ran on for a half mile or so and then set out. Years later he told me that he should have taken the advice. He ended up sinking and losing most of his gear.

Just as Tom pulled away I decided we didn't have time to clip on the buoys so we started bringing it in. But before we got through the first five fathoms of it, another boat moved in and made a set only a few hundred yards away from us. I didn't like him being that close, but it looked like we might have enough room, so we just kept picking fish and throwing them into the hold. There were already low spots in the net, but in this first serious test of the new reel I was relieved to see that we had plenty of power. We just kept picking, but when I looked up, the other boat was closer. This was well above the mouth of the Kenai River, where the Inlet begins to narrow, but the tide was already picking up speed and creating great swirls along the rip. Luckily, there wasn't much debris in the water, but the rip was drawing us closer to the other boat.

Sometimes in situations like that, boats can tow their nets away from each other and avoid the tangled mess you get when fish in one net also gill in the other, sewing the two together. You don't like to tow on the net unless you have to, because it mangles the fish, causes many to drop out and sink, and tears hell out of the web. But it was now time for both of us to tow. John and I tied off the net and I ran up to the bridge, where I motioned and yelled to the other boat to begin towing away. I started to tow on ours and, seeing it begin to move, was happy as hell to have all this new power with *Ishmael*'s 671. We couldn't have budged the thing with *Scrivener*'s little six-cylinder Chevy. But when I looked over to the other guy, he wasn't towing at all. He and his deck hand were in the stern just picking fish, and would only pause briefly to look up when I whistled to get their attention. Our nets were even closer together, but he still wouldn't tow. Almost all of our net was still out, and it was really heavy, but I kept towing and after about fifteen minutes it looked like we were beginning to slip by the other net. I knew I was tearing up the net and losing lots of fish, but there was no way around it. And that other jerk just ignored it all. I didn't know who he was, just that he was fishing one of Kenai Packer's aluminum boats, and I thought he might be new in the Inlet. Anyone with experience here would have towed his net to help us both avoid a huge mess.

As soon as I thought we'd towed far enough away from the other net I took the boat out of gear and we began picking again. The net was full, and as we picked we could hear radio reports that everybody was catching fish and that a number of boats were getting sucked into the rip and tangling with other gear. We picked nonstop, wading in fish till we could take time to throw them into the hold and for me to clean my glasses. The splattered blood and fish scales made it hard to keep track of the other boat. I thought we'd drifted away from their net, but with so much of our cork line sunk, we couldn't see the far end of our own gear. Then, after about an hour of furious picking, we reeled in some more and suddenly came to the end. "What the hell?" I yelled. "We're not even half way through the net!" And then I saw that the end of the cork line had been cut. It was definitely a clean cut, with no frayed edges to show it had broken under the strain of towing. I couldn't see the rest of the net anywhere, even from on top of the bridge. All I could do was to circle back to where the net should have been, going slowly to avoid running over it. It could have been half sunken, just below the surface.

We crisscrossed the whole area and couldn't find a trace of it, and then I ran over to the other boat. The two of them were in the stern, picking fish and not looking up to see me as I approached. I pulled within about thirty feet of them and yelled, "Hey, man! For Christ's sake! Why the hell'd you cut our net? Did you see where it drifted?" They kept their heads down and continued to pick fish. Then I pulled a little closer and yelled out, "God damn it! Why'd you cut our net? You got a bunch of buoys there, why didn't you at least buoy it off so I'd have a chance to find it?"

The older one yelled back, "Fuck off, man! We never saw your damned net," and then he bent back to his picking. I yelled some more, but they just ignored us, so I pulled away and continued looking for our gear. It wasn't tangled with his and it didn't look as though they'd taken any of our gear aboard. All I could do was hope to come across part of it that still floated close enough to the surface to be visible. We went back and forth, around in big circles. Nothing. Not a sign of the damned thing. And I began to calculate. It was brand new gear, and with all the fish in it I guessed that we'd just lost about eight or nine thousand dollars. Besides, all those fish just sank to the bottom, where they would rot, and the net would be there for a long time, fouling the place.

I gave up trying to find it and decided we had to do the best we could, fishing with half a net for the rest of the period. We did catch a few more, but, as is often the case on such days, the fish either sounded or moved off. If you don't get them on the first drift, you probably won't get them at all. At the end, we had about nine hundred fish, less than half of what we'd actually caught, and on the way in I decided to sell about three-fourths of them to the freezer operation, for the higher price, and then sell the other fourth to Columbia Wards. When Ray talked with me the next day to tell me that I couldn't keep the boat there that winter, I was on my way to the web loft to get a new piece of gear, thinking that I'd damned sure sue the bastard who'd cut off my net.

We were just in the middle of the season, though, with another period the next day, so I had to shelve the idea of finding a lawyer and just get on with fishing. But I was fuming and it didn't help that fishing began to taper off. We knew that we'd had our one big day. We caught about five hundred the next period, and a day after that Fish and Game thought the run was about over so gave us an unusual twenty-four-hour period. About six hours into that period, we developed a problem with the engine that cost us another twelve hours. Just after we'd picked up a set and started heading for another drift, the engine raced out of control. We could run wide open, the engine screaming like mad, or not at all. I shut it down and realized at once that the governor had gone out, but I had no idea how to fix it. All I could do was call the marine operator and try to get through to the company in Anchorage that sold me the engine. I was lucky to get through to them right away, but when I described the problem they said I couldn't fix it myself. At that point we were well south of the Kasilof River, so we agreed that they'd fly a mechanic to Kenai. He'd then drive to meet us on the dock at Kasilof, and maybe I could limp in to the river if I took off the valve cover and bypassed the governor by pushing the rack back and forth to speed up or slow down. We tried that, and it worked, after a fashion. We opened the engine cover inside the cabin, and one of us leaned over the hot, roaring machine, holding the rack in position while the other steered and signaled for more or less speed. We were OK running it this way until we got into the Kasilof and had to maneuver. There are easier ways to dock a boat. John couldn't take the lines because he had to manipulate the rack. We were both almost deaf from the engine noise and John was covered in the hot oil that sprayed everywhere. But in less than an hour after we shut it down, the mechanic appeared on the dock.

The guy fixed us up in a hurry, but when we finally made it back out to the grounds for a night set and the next morning's fishing, there was little to be found. We had about two hundred fish for the twenty-four-hour period. Two days later Fish and Game opened it again, this time for sixteen hours, and, even though we had another mishap, we added about two hundred more to what was now becoming a poor season's catch. I was sweating out the weak season and the upcoming boat payments, and still fuming about the eight or nine thousand dollars we'd lost in the net incident. For whatever reason I let myself get distracted long enough to catch our web in the wheel. We were on a drift somewhere out in the middle on a breezy day with big swells, and as I was trying to pull away from the net I cut it too close and suddenly heard the sickening sound of the cork line thumping the bottom of the hull and the wheel lugging down to a stop, choked with a wad of line and nylon web. I tried jamming into reverse and then forward and then reverse, hoping to spit it out, as you sometimes can, but we were dead in the water with a serious mess. It was either call someone to try to get a long tow in or go over the side to cut it out. At least we were far enough south to be in clear water, but it was a little uncomfortable being under the boat in swells that size, cutting away at it with a butcher knife, coming up for air and then going back under to cut some more. I finally freed the wheel enough for us to make it back to the river at about half speed. Along the way I had plenty of time to kick my butt for not paying attention, to check the tide book to see when and where I'd be able to put it on the beach and cut out the rest of the web, and time enough also to tie myself in even tighter knots over how to get even with the bastard who cut off my net.

There was no fishing over the next few days so I approached my old friend John, a fellow fisherman who also practiced law, and he agreed to take my case. He wasn't hopeful, but he shared my anger that somebody would pull a stunt like that on the fishing grounds, and I think he sympathized with me for taking that kind of a loss in a year when you needed everything you could get. I know he wasn't trying to make anything on it himself. In fact, he finally gave up his law practice mostly because he was uncomfortable billing people for the work he did. I've always loved him for that. But in about a week we learned that the guy had hired his own lawyer, and not just any lawyer but the Anchorage lawyer Helen Simpson, wife of the old friend who had convinced me and Dick to get into fishing. Herb had died by then, and I hadn't seen Helen for years, but I hated the idea of fighting with *her* about my lost net. And within a few days, I began to realize, with John's advice, that it would be impossible to prove. I hadn't actually seen the guy cut off my net. And there was no one else in that area who could have seen it. Maybe I could have nailed him if I'd taken a picture of him in the act, but all I had was my log entry describing the incident, my deck hand's testimony, and the end of a piece of cork line that had clearly been cut with a knife. In my anger and frustration it took me a few days to let John's advice sink in.

"There's no way to prove it, Bert. The jerk deserves to be tried and convicted. He's an asshole, period. But you can't touch him. I'm willing to go ahead with it if you want to. But, really, the best advice I can give you is to forget about taking him to court. Forget the suit and just get revenge."

John gave me this excellent advice with a smile and a jocular tone of voice meant mainly to share my outrage and exasperation. He sure as hell wasn't inciting me to assault the guy, but it was clear that I could never win in court. Revenge sounded good. I went by his boat when he wasn't there and imagined taking it out on his boat or gear, maybe putting sugar in his fuel tank or throwing battery acid on his net. Sometimes I'd imagine coming upon him in serious trouble on the grounds, where I'd remind him of the day he cut off my net and then just pull away, leaving him to deal with it alone and even sink. When I'd see him in the distance at one of the stores in Kenai, I'd think about catching up with him and having it out. And when I realized that he'd left Kenai to return to his home in Astoria, I fantasized about stopping in Astoria some time, finding out where he lived, and doing something to mess up his car or his boat.

These and other embarrassing fantasies eased the knot of anger—more, I'm sure, than a legal battle would have, or some physical act of retaliation. I've heard that some people can rise above such ugly obsessions through prayer or forgiveness, or perhaps through meditation. The closest I came to this kind of resolution was to remember the character in Poe's story, "The Cask of Amontillado," where the narrator gets his delicious revenge but loses his mind. Poe's irony helped me see the humor of my own situation. Even better, when I think about the incident now I sometimes smile, knowing that my old enemy is long dead and that I can't even remember his name or the name of his boat. All I can see is his gray-white hair, his face, and the way he walked. Still, just recalling the incident as I write causes a tightness in my back. It's been there for three or four days, like a muscle about to spasm. After almost three decades the old outrage and anger are still there, physically imprinted in my mind and body, in the same way recalled images of fish hitting the net affect my blood. I'm familiar with Darwin's analysis of this sort of thing in *The Expression of the Emotions in Man and Animals* and believe that there must be some kind of survival value in it all.

When the old anger rises in me again I imagine I'm walking the docks in Astoria and there he is, just stepping off his boat. I walk right up to him, shove my chest as close to his as I can get it, and tell him right to his startled, questioning face, "You know damned well who I am, you bastard! For Christ sake, why'd you cut off my net that day?" We both blink, and I think, now isn't it funny how that knot in my back has begun to ease.

Moontide

 MY DECK HAND JOHN AND I were waiting at the dock for a skiff ride out to our friends' boat. About half the fleet had already quit for the season, but there were still quite a few boats in the Kenai. We began to notice several boats scattered across the river, barely moving against the tide, and three or four skiffs that were nosing along the far bank. Just when we realized that something was up, a cannery worker came up to us and said, "If you're lookin' for a ride to your boat, you'll have to wait a while. Everybody's out there lookin' for that kid that fell in."

"Somebody fell in? Where?" I asked.

"Up there at one of them canneries around the bend. Didn' ya hear the sirens a while ago?"

"Yeah, I heard a siren, but it sounded pretty far away, over toward town."

"Nope. It was over there alright, across the river."

John asked, "Who was it?" and I looked out toward the boats. Some were checking along the bank, and a few zigzagged slowly across the river. Two or three boats were way out toward the mouth, probably hoping to catch sight of whoever it was before the tide sucked him out into the Inlet.

"Ya got me. All I know is it was some guy that fishes for one of the canneries over there. Somebody said it was one of those boats out there by the mouth."

The boats were too far away to tell which ones they were, but one of them made me think of *Dancer*. I knew the people on it and hoped they weren't the ones. The guy had a couple of his kids aboard, and he fished for one of the canneries up river. "John, can you tell if one of those is *Dancer*?" I asked.

"Can't tell." He strained to see something distinctive about the boats' silhouettes.

"Jesus!" I said. "Right here in the harbor."
"Yeah, and after the season's all over."

The season had ended for us about an hour before. The boat was out of the water, keel-blocked and propped up with old fifty-five-gallon oil drums. All wrapped up for the winter—antifreeze for forty below, pumps drained, stack covered, tanks topped off. It was always a job getting it ready, but it was a relief to do it this year, our worst season for a decade. The fish just weren't there. I drank the last beer we had on board—it would just freeze over the winter—and we checked to make sure we hadn't forgotten anything. We'd lived on the boat for a couple of days after being lifted out of the water, while it was in its awkward winter posture—bow-down and a little off keel. I could tell John was anxious to get off it for the last time that season. Maybe he sensed that kind of dead feeling the boat gets when it's not afloat, like being stuck on a sand bar. But he probably just wanted to be home. There had been some scented blue letters for him that year. He'd watched the mail pretty closely and put whatever he got on his pillow. When he had a few minutes to himself he'd go down to his bunk and I could hear him open the blue letter.

I double-checked a few more things. Then, satisfied it was all buttoned up for the winter, we swung over the stern and jumped to the ground. All we had to do was shower and then head out to Jon's and Heidi's boat for dinner. They wanted to say goodbye to John before I took him to the airport that night. This was his fourth summer on the boat. The first year he wasn't even big enough to carry five gallons of water without his knees buckling. Now he was sixteen, an inch taller than I was, and able to do nearly anything without supervision, from hanging and handling the net to running the boat when I needed some sleep. That was the first year I paid him the deck hand's regular share of 15 percent. Everybody told me I was lucky as hell to have such a good kid for a deck hand, and, living and working with him on the boat, I'd grown to like him a lot.

It was good to have a hot shower, even in the cannery's cramped, grubby shower room, to get rid of a season's fish gurry, battery acid, and diesel oil. John was scrubbed pink, had on clean underwear, deodorant, and the city clothes he had packed away since the trip up, already transformed again into a sophisticated college-town teen. By the time we got down to the dock to catch a skiff ride out to Jon's and Heidi's boat, we were both so set on having finished the season that we hesitated to climb down the ladder to the floating dock. The tide was running like mad and the bar in the middle of the river was already showing. On a big ebb like that it's a long way down the ladder to the water, and the usual debris had caught on the ladder and the steel pilings—limbs and roots washed down from upstream, stringy white fish guts from the canneries. The gulls usually clean up the guts and fish heads, but a lot of the rotten stuff hangs around for weeks. John seemed reluctant to get his good clothes dirty. Besides, with the tide running hard like that, you can't stand on the floating dock without getting your feet wet. So we stayed up on the permanent dock, where we'd have a better chance to see the skiff and wave it in.

<hr>

"And the season's over," John said.

"Yeah, but you never can tell," I said. "I remember when Vince Miller's kid slipped off a dock down on the Columbia River. Just a quiet splash and he was gone, and there were a lot of people around, too. Didn't have a life jacket on. Went right down and never even bobbed to the surface. Vince said the tide was running pretty hard."

Pretty soon a boat out in the river untied from its buoy and pulled over to the dock for fuel. We talked to the guy when he tied up and started pumping diesel. He didn't know any more about the kid than we did, but he said he'd give us a ride out to Jon's boat after he fueled up. When we jumped aboard their boat, Jon and Heidi wanted to know what we'd heard. They had seen us waiting on the dock but couldn't come in to pick us up because Jon was working on his starter. They'd yelled to one of the search boats as it passed by, and heard that the deck hand on *Rachel* had fallen overboard—a high school kid from Oregon. John and I were relieved to know it wasn't our friends' boat. Some boats had been anchored together out in front of one of the canneries, and someone heard a splash. They looked around to see what it was and then somebody on another boat yelled that he'd seen the kid slip and fall between a couple of boats. Nobody saw him come to the surface and they thought he might have hit his head going over.

We stood on deck looking around and talking about it for a few minutes and then went inside. It was warm, and whatever Heidi had cooked was smelling good. Nobody seemed hungry right then, but we sat down and tried to carry on some kind of end-of-the-season celebration. Heidi poured some wine and we sipped at it while we talked and kept looking out over the river.

John and Shane, Heidi's son, went out on deck to talk about their girl friends, we supposed, and to arrange for a possible visit over the winter. They seemed less concerned about the missing kid than we were.

Thinking of my own five-year-old son, I said, "God! The kid must not have been wearing a life jacket."

"But, hell," Jon said, "you can't wear the damned things all the time, especially when you're not even fishing. I hardly ever wear mine. John and Shane are out on deck right now and they don't have 'em on either. It's just one of those things."

"Yeah, I guess you're right."

Heidi hoped he wasn't wearing his rain gear. We didn't think he would have been, because he would have cleaned up the boat a few days before, after the last period. But lots of people wear their rubber boots all the time, and we didn't like the thought of that.

"Boy," I said, "I'll never forget the time I fell in with my gear on, boots and all."

"When was that?"

"Seven or eight years ago, when I still had *Sounion*. I was fishing alone and was tied up to the *Whale*, delivering fish. I'd just finished pitching my fish and stepped aboard the tender to get their wash-down hose. The deck was covered with fish slime, and the next thing I knew I was gasping in the water. I went clear under, and my boots were heavy as hell. It was late in the season, dark as could be, and the tide was ebbing like mad. I still can't believe how lucky I was. I'd just untied my stern line from the tender's cleat, trying to get at their hose, and I still had hold of the line when I fell in. All I remember is gasping and being under for about a second before I jerked on the line and came up to see their blurry deck lights. Thank god for adrenalin. I still don't know where I got the strength to pull myself up that high, with all that weight and the tide running like that. Nobody'd seen me, either. If I'd hit my head going over or if I wouldn't have had that line in my hand," I snapped my finger, "that would have been it."

"You were one lucky son of a bitch!" Jon said. "Even if you saw somebody go over at night like that, and with the tide running very hard, you'd have a hell of a time getting to 'em. I mean, by the time you could get a boat untied and under way, the guy'd be gone. Can you imagine trying to find somebody in that kind of current at night? Hell, we don't even have a spot light."

"Yeah, and can you imagine how you'd feel if your own kid went over?"

"Oh, Christ! But how'd you like to be the guy on *Rachel* and have to call the kid's folks and tell 'em what happened?"

"Shit! Believe me, I've thought about it. The first few years he was up here I made him keep his life jacket on all the time. Just seems like too much trouble now. He's so big."

"We're the same way with Shane," Heidi said, "and sometimes I get scared to death when we're out there and it's a little rough, maybe, and I look around and can't see him right away. You know, like maybe he's on the bridge or something, and when I look back to the stern no one's there."

"Yeah. I can't imagine what I'd say to his folks. Especially right here at the end of the season, when they're about ready to go to the airport to pick him up."

Heidi opened the cabin door and yelled for the boys to come in to dinner. We didn't have long before we had to head to the airport. Heidi's dinner was great and would have been a regular feast at any other time— baked halibut and some crab legs. John and Shane dug in pretty well, but the rest of us sort of picked at it. About half way through it, I caught sight of something in the water just up ahead of us and jumped up, knocking over the wine on my way to the door. It was floating fast and coming close by. "Hey, that's a hat!" I yelled, but we were too slow with the pike pole and the hat swept on by.

"Do you think that was his?" Jon yelled. "See anything else?" We looked and looked, but that was it. Some guys in one of the skiffs saw us yelling and pointing on deck, and they pulled over right away to see what was up. We told them about the hat, but they said somebody else had seen it, too, and it wasn't the kid's. "They don't think he had a hat on. Even if he did, it would've gone by here a long time ago. We just hope he might have come up under a boat and got hung up on somebody's rudder or something. Maybe he'll drift loose. Keep your eyes peeled."

"For sure!" we shouted back, and they pulled away.

When we got back to the table Heidi had cleaned up the spilled wine, and Jon got out a fifth of V.O. He poured us each a shot, and by the time we finished it and another one it was time for us to head to the airport. We waved over another boat that was heading in to the dock. While we were waiting for him to come alongside, *Rachel* passed close by us on its way back up the river. The owner was alone at the wheel on the bridge. Moving slowly against the tide, he stood leaning forward with clinched jaws and a grim white face, looking, looking.

Our ride came alongside and, as John and I jumped aboard, Heidi yelled at us to be careful going up the ladder. We helped the guy tie up at the dock and then I sent John up the ladder ahead of me. We made it to the airport in plenty of time to check his bags and watch for the plane to land. It was one of those little ones that make you nervous when it flies over Turnagain Arm on the way into Anchorage. After the passengers from Homer got off and the attendant announced it was time for the Anchorage passengers to board, we stood up to get in line. Again, I had waited until the last minute to tell John how much I appreciated his good work. I took his hand and said, "Thanks for the good help again, John. I really counted on you." He mumbled something about his luck in being on a good boat, and I thought I might have seen his eye glisten a little. Probably not, but the first couple of years he'd had tears in his eyes when I put him on the plane. I used to give him a hug goodbye. "Maybe we'll have a better season next year," I said, knowing that Fish and Game had already predicted a poor return.

"For sure," he said. Then he got his things together and we exchanged a "Take care" as he moved toward the door. He went out to the little plane, and it seemed that the pilot took a long time to test the engine and taxi away. I waved as it went out of sight.

It was starting to get dark when I headed out the door of the airport. John's plane had come back down the runway and the pilot throttled up as it strained to lift off. I turned to catch sight of it and waved again. Then, when I turned back toward the parking lot, I stopped in my tracks. I couldn't believe my eyes. A full moon had risen right in front of me, brilliant and enormous the way it always is when it just breaks over the horizon. It was just above a low hill, where the tips of some birch and black spruce seemed to reach for it. It had something to do with the big tide that day, and I knew it must be about dead low water right now. Maybe that kid's body had already washed up on the beach out toward the mouth. I imagined a form slumped there in the grey silt, and hoped that he hadn't been sucked way out on the ebb, out toward the middle. He'd eventually end up in one of the rips. Everything collects out there. I saw a brown bear out there a long time ago, probably shot by a beach fisherman. It floated head down in a slow swirl of driftwood, kelp, and gull feathers. About a week later I saw it again. Way out there in the middle rip. I wondered how long it had been there, how many times it had drifted up and down with the tide. By then it was really foul, and somebody else had found it and cut off the claws. Everything out there just drifts up and down the Inlet, churning till it sinks or falls apart.

I stood there at least a minute, just staring at the moon. Then I jumped into the truck and headed back to the cannery as fast as I could. I wanted to get a picture of the moon before it got too high and began to seem smaller. I made it just in time. A few small clouds drifted in front of it and their silver-lighted edges emphasized its size. It was huge, just above some scraggly tops of black spruce. I grabbed my old 35 mm camera and got four good shots. I was using color film and tried shots at different speeds, wanting to make sure. I leaned against the truck to try a longer exposure and heard the long bzzzzzzz . . . until the shutter clicked. I'd set it on "infinity," too, but when the slides came back they were all blurred and out of focus. I must have moved.

Sea-Brothers

 IF YOU WERE THE ONLY GILL-NETTER in Cook Inlet you wouldn't have any competition. You'd have all those reds to yourself! But you'd probably end up running a long way to find them. You'd realize how big the Inlet is, and if you broke down you'd wish you weren't out there alone. When you're out there but not catching much, it's always good to spot a group of boats on the horizon. It might be a good idea to head that way and see what's going on. Even if you took a chance and ended up doing pretty well way south of the fleet, you can't help wondering how the other boats are doing up north. It's part of the natural history of fishing to want both things at once—to have the fish all to yourself, and when that's not working out, to have a little help from your friends. You learn right away that it's nice to be in a group, to be able to talk with friends on other boats, to help each other even if you're also trying to out-fish them. You love being high boat in the group or catching even just a few more than a particular friend you've been running neck and neck with all season. The competitive spirit is real and undeniable in all of us, I'm afraid. I like the way Hemingway dealt with it in *Green Hills of Africa*, where he confessed to the embarrassing bitter sense of competition he felt when a hunting partner bested him. The guide, "Pop," finally puts things in perspective when he says, "We have very primitive emotions. . . . It's impossible not to be competitive. Spoils everything, though."

The really good fishermen or "highliners" muster enough quiet modesty to conceal their pride at being high boat, but you don't get to be a highliner without a lot of drive. In the old days when fishermen would gather at mug-up to tell stories about how it had gone the day before, to find out how others had done and where the best catches had been made, you could tell by the way people stood around and glanced at each other who'd done well and who hadn't. The highliners knew for damned sure who their competition was. Among the fishermen I've known, the competitive drive seems reflected in their athletic careers. Jon was an All-American halfback at a Los Angeles high school, before an injury sidelined him in his first year of college. Mike was a Big Ten end at Michigan, and John a Big Ten wrestler at Iowa. Thor was a brilliant high-school and small-college basketball player and decathalete. I set school and stadium records in the shot put at Washington, and Tim, the new owner of *Ishmael*, was a high-school track star. But even with all this competitive edge in the fishing life, you also want a group of friends you can count on to help you get on the fish when you're drawing a blank, and you want to do the same for them.

It's complicated, though, because, for one thing, every group has one or two people known for giving excited calls on the radio that never seem to pay off for their friends. Somebody might see a few fresh hits and want to pass on the good news. If he can put you on the fish, maybe you'll reciprocate. Or there are fishermen in the group that you suspect might get on the radio to give good reports—but only after they've been seeing good hits for quite a while. They might want to help their friends, but they don't want everybody to show up too soon and ruin their good set. You get to know whose calls are most important and how to read the emotion in a friend's voice.

The dynamics of the group raises the old question about cooperation (or mutual aid) and self-interested competition. I think most fishermen realize that it's not either or, but both things at once, something like reciprocal altruism. And I wonder how much different we are from other fish hunters like the whales. Of course the orcas (which are actually dolphins) hunt together, sometimes in horrific feeding frenzies, when they've been known to attack small pods of sperm whales. But I think it's odd that until recently even biologists believed that some of the baleen whales hunted more or less as automatons, swimming straight ahead with their mouths open to skim the surface for plankton and such. Now we know that the humpbacks fish together, surrounding schools of fish with great "nets" of bubbles that they blow into the water, making something like a big seine. Then, when the fish are gathered in a ball, single whales rush up through the mass and take the fish in great gulps. We might not be quite that advanced in setting our own nets or in our cooperative behavior, but the groups of Cook Inlet gill-netters I've known bear a certain resemblance to the humpbacks—even in what biologists have recently identified as the humpbacks' "summer feeding song." At the end of one really good day on the Inlet in the late eighties, when people in our group were talking on the radio as we made the long run back to Kenai or Kasilof, one of the guys held our attention for a few minutes by keying the mike and singing a rousing old whaling song, one with a haunting Scandinavian air. The humpbacks, the drifters, and certainly the fish: we're all in this together.

Who cares if it's "only" reciprocal altruism? and I do believe it is. One time in 1983 I learned how good that can be. We were expecting a strong return that year, so I had done a few things on the boat to be as ready as I could, including having the prop repitched. I had taken out an inch of pitch in order to gain a couple hundred more rpm from the 671, and it did the trick. We could now turn 2200. The boat was running well and the fishing season started off so well that Fish and Game decided to let us have a number of unscheduled openings.

The good fishing continued right through the middle of July (we caught about nineteen hundred fish on the 15th, with over ten thousand pounds of reds), to the point that the processors were getting plugged and some had to put their boats on limit. And things started out very well for us on the 20th, when we had good weather and good fishing off the North end of Kalgin. We were fishing close to a rip and decided to cut loose from the net, go to the other end, and try to tow away from the rip before we got sucked into the driftwood and trash. Maneuvering to pick up the other end of the net, I shifted into reverse, heard a sudden clunk, and immediately lost power. I looked over the stern and could see just a bit of our prop, spun off the shaft but wedged between the rudder and shoe. Fuck! I'd rather have web in the wheel than this. Here we were, untied to the net, and drifting away from it while the other end was getting drawn into the rip. And other guys in the group were reporting good hits not far south of us.

It wasn't a "Mayday!" situation, but we were in a mess that could get much worse. There weren't any tenders patrolling the grounds in those days, looking to take fish or assist boats in distress. But I did spot one of the boats in our group, *Kuro*, which has a distinctive silhouette, and as soon as I gave him a call, Mike came back and asked how I was. I'd hesitated to call because, when fishing is hot, you can't expect your friends to drop everything and give you a hand. But as soon as I told him what was going on, Mike said, "Hold on. I see where you are and I'll be right up there." I told him we were OK and that I didn't want him to leave a good set, but he said they were just picking up their net and getting ready to make a move anyhow. "We'll be right there." I watched them through the binoculars, and before long saw a black puff of smoke as they got under way and turned in our direction. Mike is a strong, stocky man, maybe five seven or eight. But standing at the wheel on his bridge as he pulled up to us, wearing his usual crumpled, wide-brimmed hat, he looked like he was about six feet six. He blew it off when I thanked him for giving us a hand, and in a second his deck hand threw us a line. Mike towed us back to our net, stood by while we picked up the end of it, and then towed us far enough off the rip to give us chance to pick it up in a hurry if we got sucked back in. All the while we were getting a few hits. I waved to Mike and gave a thumbs up, so he could get on the way to his own set. He waved back and yelled, "Give us a call if something happens. I don't think we're gonna have to run too far." Then, flashing his big smile, he turned the boat and headed south.

We couldn't go anywhere, but we were catching some fish. The engine was running fine and we could pick up the net whenever we needed to. Others in the group had followed our story on the radio, and before long I got a faint call from Jon, who was almost out of range of the VHF, maybe fifteen or twenty miles to the south. Fishing was very good down there, but he'd been thinking about us. He was wondering about our wheel, and I told him it was still jammed between the rudder and the shoe. He answered, "The nuts are gone, though, right?" These were the big nut that held the shaft in place and a thinner lock nut. Then he said, "You know, I've been looking around here and I've got the spare nuts we bought for those shafts. Maybe I can get them up to you." When we were building the boats, he, Thor, and I got shafts with a special taper at the ends that required custom-machined nuts, and we had a spare pair made as well. Jon didn't want to make the long run himself, of course.

He was catching good fish, and anyhow, even if I had the nuts, I'd have to get the boat out of the water. Maybe I'd get lucky and find somebody to tow me onto a sandy beach at high water somewhere, where I could let it go dry and then get under the boat to work on it. That was such a remote possibility that I hadn't even thought to check the tide book. "We gotta pick the net," he said. "I'll think about it and get back to you later."

It was getting late in the afternoon, but we were still OK. It wasn't a very big tide that day so the rip wasn't sucking us in. We just hung onto the net and continued to get a few hits once in a while. Somebody came on the radio and said that Fish and Game had extended the period through the following day. They were afraid of letting too many fish up the river. This was great news for everybody else, but I just gritted my teeth. We were not only missing the best fishing today, but we'd miss out on this rare opportunity to stay on them for an added day. This late in July you couldn't tell whether we'd get another chance at them. But just after we heard the news about the added opening, there was a lot of talk on the radio about processors who were already plugged. They couldn't handle all the fish and were putting their fishermen on limit. They'd take only a thousand fish per boat.

Not long after that we got a call from John on *Dancer*. "Hey, Bert, how's it going?" I told him we were OK. Dead in the water, just drifting around, but catching a few. "Yeah, that's what I thought. I think I see you up above me, toward the north end of Kalgin. We just picked up and I'm headed to the north end to deliver. Thought we'd better get ready for tomorrow. How about if I tow you in there?"

"That'd be great!" I said. "But maybe you should just get on up there. There'll be lines to deliver."

"Ah, what the hell. Won't slow us down that much. You got your net in?"

"No. Not yet. But we can pick it up in a hurry. How far are you, anyhow?"

"Two or three miles, I think. Maybe you can see me if you look towards Humpy Point."

"Yeah, I think I see you down there, John. I'll hang up and get this thing in, OK? Really appreciate it, man."

"No problem. We're not going very fast. See you in about twenty minutes."

We got right on it and picked like mad. There were quite a few fish, but by the time John was pulling up and getting ready to throw us a line, we almost had it in. I was pissed that we made him wait around for a few minutes, so we busted our butts and then round-hauled the last few fathoms. He didn't seem to mind, though. They'd had a good day and were pretty low in the water. As we were taking the line and getting ready to go he asked me if my processor, Salamatof, would have a tender at the north end. I didn't know. John delivered to another outfit, Whitney Fidalgo, and he knew they'd have a tender at the north end later that day. He'd also heard that Whitney had put its boats on a thousand-fish limit. While John had us under tow, I radioed Salamatof and found out that they couldn't free up a tender to take fish at Kalgin. John had heard my call, and right after I signed off he called me on our group's frequency and said not to worry. We could still work it out. When he got to Kalgin he'd talk to the Whitney skipper and see if he'd take my fish too. If one of your fishermen comes in with a boat in tow, you can't just tell him to cut it loose.

When we pulled in to the north end, John got in line at the tender and went aboard to talk to the captain, telling my sad story and hoping the guy would help me out. Of course I was tickled when John came back and said it'd be OK. I'd at least be able to salvage this much of the deal, selling the seven or eight hundred fish we had aboard. I could drop the hook here at the anchorage and worry about getting towed back to Kenai after the period tomorrow.

But just before it was my turn to deliver, Jon came on the radio and said that he was running into Kasilof to deliver, but he'd managed to pass off the spare nuts for my shaft to a tender that was headed up this way. Also, he said, another guy in our group, Bill, on *Whalesong*, was heading to the north end and should be there later that night. I should give him a call, because Jon had talked with him, and Bill had diving gear aboard—a tank and a wet suit. He was sure Bill could get under the boat and put my wheel back on, if it was still wedged there on the shoe. This sounded too good to be true, but things were going my way. I thanked Jon and signed off, and before I could call Bill, he called me. The group keeps in touch. I told him the wheel was still there and the nuts were on the way. I'd sure appreciate it if he could help me out. "Oh, yeah, no big deal," he said. "I've got the tank and wet suit and we're headed up that way." He had a full load, though, and the boat was pretty slow, but he thought he might show up in two or three hours, about midnight or one. He'd be delivering to the same Whitney tender. If I'd tie off their stern, he'd see me later that night.

When we tied up to deliver our fish, I told the skipper how much I appreciated his helping us out. I knew the boats were on limit. "That's OK. I understand, man. Happy to do it. Good luck with your wheel." While we were delivering our fish, the other tender pulled in alongside and passed us the nuts that Jon had sent along. When I yelled "Thanks," he yelled back, "You bet. Hope it works out," and then pulled away to get on with his own work. We finished unloading our fish, then washed down, tied off on the tender's stern, grabbed a bite to eat, and had time to sack out for a while. In about a minute, it seemed, I heard some noise alongside, and there was *Whalesong*, looking as beautiful as its name, even in the glare of the tender's decklights. Bill had joined our group just that year, and I had never seen him up close, only when we waved from boat to boat on the grounds. Everybody in the group was happy to have him with us because he was a good fisherman. He's a native who lives in Homer, and he knows his way around the Inlet. *Whalesong* was a thirty-two-footer, a double-ender with classic lines and every sign of having been treated with much respect. All of us missed it when Bill sold it a few years later and built a bigger, faster boat.

Bill had a place in line, but there was plenty of time before his turn to deliver. I knew he had to be tired. They'd had a good day of heavy fishing and then the long run, but after we chatted a bit, he said, "Well, whatta we got? Did you get the nuts?"and he began to get his stuff together. A lot of guys keep a wet suit aboard, because you never know when you might get web in the wheel, but only a few carry diving gear as well. I don't think anyone with just a wet suit could have stayed under long enough to get the wheel back on. We had a pretty good flashlight and Bill asked us to wrap it tightly in a couple of clear plastic bags. And when he went under to take a look everything seemed OK. All we needed was something to take the place of the big cotter key for the slotted jam nut, and we found a good sized nail that might do the trick. I could see Bill working away down there in the murky light, and I knew it was heavy work to unwedge the wheel and wrestle it onto the shaft without dropping it. I heard him slip it onto the shaft, and in a second he came up to rest and get the nuts. When he went back under I could see his dark shape move around in the light and hear him working away. Before long he came up again to get the nail-key and a pair of vice grips and a hammer. He went under again and I heard him pound the nail through the hole and bend it over so it wouldn't slip out. When he came up for the last time he said, "Well, it's not perfect, but it oughta hold till you get a chance to put it on the beach and finish it off right."

How can you thank somebody for that kind of help? Bill wouldn't take any money, of course, though I would have happily paid him five hundred dollars or so and still felt that he had done us a huge favor. I remember feeling stupid but still asking if I could at least pay him for a new tank of air or something, but he waved that off too. We were in the same group, but I think he would have done it for me anyhow. The best I could do was ask what he liked to drink and finally left a good bottle of cognac aboard his boat at the end of the season. It helped that right after he got out of the water and got his gear put away, it was his turn to deliver, and we had to pull away. When I eased it into gear, everything held, and we had power again. It was 2 a.m., and we had another full day's shot at it. The weather was perfect and we got into the fish right away off the north end of the island. We stayed on them most of the day, ebbing down to well below the island, and finally making it back into the Kenai early the next morning. We did as well as anybody that day, getting eighty-five hundred pounds of reds. Over the closure I beached the boat and got the wheel on securely. We had a few more half-decent days for that late in July and even did pretty well during the first week of August. The price was up, too. I can't remember what reds were worth that year, but all that other stuff is something else.

Sign of Wind

IN A BAD YEAR—like '81 on Cook Inlet—you get more keyed in to signs, any sign that could explain a poor run or foretell a change, if only in the weather. I think most fishermen are this way. Who—except maybe athletes before competition—outdoes our nervous and sometimes superstitious attention to the swirl of details? You know, the lucky pair of socks, say, or the birds you see on the water way over there to the east. The way the boat came through the winter and the way things seem to go either right or wrong as you launch it and yourself into the new season. It comes from being on the water. We watch the clouds, the surface of the water, and we *will* take a silent warning if it's red in the morning. It's a sure sign of a sou'wester if Mt. Redoubt has a cloud cap with its bill trailing up the Inlet. And it comes from years of not being able to figure out the fish. If at the beginning of the season you hear they showed up early at Cordova or in the Bay, you're damned sure to be out there ready for them on the first day. Or if at the end of the season you pick up a few bright fish in a set, you're a sucker for the inevitable rumor that somebody spotted a school of jumpers down off Augustine.

I'm not talking about the technical things you come to know about fishing—the way you've learned to hang or set your gear just the way you want it, or how to drift a certain beach without getting hung up on the rocks. You can't beat experience. But you can't always count on it either, even though you're sure about the color of your web, say—that certain shade you use early in the season in the clear water; or even though you think you'll find the fish at the same spot and at the same stage of the tide where you slugged them in '77. And you know something about luck. Like your friend's, when he picks up a couple hundred on a drift less than a net-length from where you get seventeen, and you were there first. Within the cycles of strong and weak runs, we all have our lucky and unlucky years. Some years you're always on the fish and other years everything you touch turns to shit.

I felt lucky in June of '81. Everybody expected a good return. The boat had made it through the winter with no problems. The engine kicked over at the first touch of the button. The gear was in good shape. The weather looked great, and like most people who made it out for the first couple of periods, I thought there was a promising early show. After the two worst years in a decade, this looked like the one we were waiting for, and even the price for reds had pushed back up toward where it had been in '78.

I can't remember exactly when the season started falling apart, but it was around the time *Lucky Lady* almost sank after being hit by a tanker. I'd followed her out of the river that morning. It was a clear day with only a light breeze; so like everybody else who listened to the Mayday on the VHF, I couldn't figure out how it happened. *Lucky Lady* is a pretty good-sized boat, a limit seiner—how could the skipper on the other rig not have seen her? Was he asleep? I never heard the explanation but watched from a couple of miles away as the Coast Guard plane out of Kodiak flew over *Lucky Lady* several times to drop pumps. I could hear their talk on channel 16 and knew the plane had dropped a few pumps right on target, but for some reason the guys on the boat couldn't get them to work. *Lucky Lady* and her crew made it in OK, but by the middle of the day the wind had picked up a lot, and before the day was over most of us had run for cover. The Coast Guard had seven separate distress calls that day, and from then until the end of the season it blew almost every day we fished.

It was about this time that I stopped listening to a tape I had aboard, one by the Grateful Dead. I'd played it almost nonstop since the season began. One of the cuts caught my attention and kept catching it, probably because of the way the season was shaping up: "I Need a Miracle Every Day." It's rousing rock and roll, for one thing, but I sure as hell knew I needed a good season. I couldn't get the refrain out of my mind. "I need a miracle every day." And another line amused me: "It takes dynamite to get me high. Too much of everything is just enough." (Only years later did I learn from a student who had been a Grateful Dead groupie what the "miracle" is—a syringe full of heroin.) You can't really appreciate the words without the music, but yes, too many reds would have been just enough. Anyhow, I played the tape enough to drive John my deck hand batty, and then finally turned it off. It was superstitious of me, I know, but I began to worry about the words. Maybe I was asking too much—I mean, a miracle *every* day? You shouldn't offend the gods.

As the season went on, I began to wonder if I hadn't already done that. But it wasn't just me. Nobody was catching much. The fish weren't showing up the way we expected them, and when a few did show, so did the wind. Then I lost a couple of fishing days right when the red run finally peaked. Fueling up at the cannery, I'd taken on a load of watery diesel. There was more water than my filter could handle, and before I discovered it I had cracked the head and blown the injectors on my 671. The situation developed into a nightmare, involving the usual problems you have when you try to beat the clock, locating parts and flying them in—anything to get things fixed up so you can make it out to fish the next period. The worst of it was that, at one in the morning before a six o'clock opening, I managed to drop the head into the Kenai River. It (the rectangular top of the engine that bolts on to the block) weighs about two hundred fifty pounds. We'd found a new head and got it ready at a diesel shop in Kenai. The mechanics and I were beat. It was raining when we got the head down into a skiff and ran it out to the middle of the river where *Ishmael* was anchored. By mid-July it's dark as hell at that time of night. And the ebb was running hard. We pulled alongside *Ishmael*, tied off the bow of the skiff, and, standing in a couple of inches of water, began to lift the head out of the skiff. We wanted to set it up on the rail where some other guys could reach it and lift it onto the deck. We were stretching up on our tip toes and leaning out . . . when the stern of the skiff began to drift away from the boat, just a little. Straining like hell, our hands more than full, we finally got a corner of the head up onto the rail, but that only nudged the stern a little further from the boat and the head slipped out of our hands. Straight down. Sploosh. Gone! It disappeared in the murky tide stream so easily, so quickly, so quietly that we just stood there staring at nothing. After a few seconds somebody gasped, "A diver. We gotta get a diver!"

The incredible part is that we did find a diver, a guy named Ivan who was asleep on another boat just up the river. He took a minute to rub the sleep out of his eyes and listen to our story. Then he put on his wet suit, quickly got his tanks and gear together, and headed with us back to *Ishmael*. We had been smart enough to drop an anchor at the place where we'd lost the head, and he groped his way down along that line. He felt around in the silty dark, and finally touched a piece of the cardboard that we'd tied around the head in order to keep the rain off it. He managed to get a line on the head, and we had it up and into the skiff within an hour after we'd dropped it. That was a little after 2 a.m. We got it back to the shop, cleaned it up, soaked it in hot oil, hauled it back out to the boat, and installed it. By early afternoon I was underway again, but neither I nor anyone else could find the fish. That's when I threw away my tape of the Grateful Dead.

By then Fish and Game was worried that too few fish would escape into the spawning grounds and so they closed the Inlet for a week. There was a steady wind from the southwest throughout the closure, and we watched nervously from our anchored boats as more and more reds made their way up to the spawning grounds. When we fished again and tried to find them where they should have been at that time of the year, somewhere between Kenai and the middle of Kalgin Island, the whole fleet drew a blank. There was rampant speculation. It was just a late run and they were still on their way. No, they were already up the river and gone. No, if you just looked at the eggs you could see they weren't ready to spawn yet. Or, those southwest winds we had during the long closure pushed them up the Inlet beyond the boundary, and we'd still get our shot at them. And then the Fish and Game test-fishing boat made some unexpected good catches along the southern boundary line, and people began to think that the main run had finally arrived. It was late, all right, but they'd be so thick that we'd risk sinking our nets. When we fished again, though, we caught next to nothing, and the season dragged into August.

I began to hear of boats and permits for sale, and stories circulated about guys who were going to lose their big, new, heavily mortgaged boats. For two years we had smiled at the names of some of the newer boats—like *Mastercharge*, *Costa Lotta*, and *Mutoa* ("mortgaged up to our ass")—but the humor had blackened. The fleet thinned noticeably. The cannery beach gangs worked overtime as fishermen gave up on '81, pulled their boats for the winter, and headed into crabbing or back to the Columbia River or Puget Sound, or to the bars.

I decided to hang it up, too, after just one more day. I'd try it below Kalgin Island, where I and a few other boats had picked up some dogs the period before. The red run was already up the river. But maybe a few fresh ones would trickle into the Inlet, and maybe I'd be lucky and pick up a few hundred mixed fish along the rip. I felt lucky, somehow, told myself and John, what the hell, we'd give it one more try. Make this last one kind of a pleasure cruise. Let it blow, even—we'd have the last wild rodeo ride of the season. We'd leave the river the night before and anchor at North Kalgin, have kind of a picnic of it, and maybe even see the walrus that we heard was hanging out on the northwest corner this year. In the morning we'd drop down below the island, drift south on the ebb, and ride the flood back up toward the river at the end of the day.

When we got to the dock with our groceries and waited for the skiff to take us out to the boat, a couple of guys were standing around bitching about some bastard from Kenai Packers who was running his boat around the river, kicking up a wake. A guy trying to fuel up was getting bounced around a little and yelled, "What's the matter with that son of a bitch? Fucker's responsible for his own wake!" Then my friend Heidi, who was standing next to me on the dock watching it all, said, "That's the thing. This *is* a wake. Did you hear about the guy on *Pisces*? He got killed in a car wreck yesterday. That's his boat. Some friends of his are giving it a last run."

The wake wasn't really causing any damage, and you couldn't help being touched to see *Pisces* make its run alone up and down and back and forth across the river, then out toward the mouth. I didn't know the guy. He was just a fisherman I had seen around, and I'd admired his boat, a damned good-looking one that he must have been proud of. As it made its turns alone out toward the mouth and back, I was glad his buddies had done it. At the Kenai Packers dock the crane waited to pick her out of the water for the last time.

I had already psyched myself into a positive mood, trying to make the most of my last day of the season and to have fun doing it, to the point that even the *Pisces* ceremony gave me a lift. It seemed like a good sign. So as I climbed down the ladder to the floating dock, I was ready to go, the way you aren't, always, not just confident that we'd have a good day, but anxious to get out there. The weather looked great, and I knew right where I wanted to be in the morning; there was none of the uncertainty you have sometimes when you're heading out and don't know whether to go north or south.

Waiting on the floating dock for the skiff, I'll be damned if I didn't see a mouse duck behind a tiedown cleat. There wasn't any way for the furry little bastard to climb up the steel pilings to land, and I wondered how he got there. Before the skiff arrived, I managed to catch him in a bucket and let him loose higher on the dock, where a beam gave him a path to land. The miniature rescue further buoyed my spirits. Later, on our way out to the mouth, we passed *Pisces* on its way back to the dock, and it was a beautiful calm evening as we headed out into and across the Inlet to Kalgin Island. I was sure we'd have a good day tomorrow.

As we crossed into the sunset a breath of northerly breeze barely disturbed the surface. When we got to the island we looked for the walrus on his favorite rock at the northwest corner, but he wasn't there. We looked for him on our way down the back side of the island to the next little point south, but he wasn't there, either. But that was a good place to drop the hook, because we'd get some protection in case the breeze picked up out of the north.

Of course, it did. So after a rolling sleepless night, resetting the anchor once, we bucked the last of the flood down to the end of the island and below, off the east edge of the Kalgin bar, where we made our opening set. Damned if we didn't pick up a few right away, even a couple of reds. Even better, some of our friends above us weren't doing as well. The run south had paid off! It was a little sloppy, though. The wind had picked up, and the seas seemed to swell after low water. The slop kicked up more water in my tanks, and I had to drain the filters again and again; I didn't want to mess with any more fouled injectors. Then, almost simultaneously, I heard two reports on the VHF: a vague report about *Winter Wind*, somewhere southeast of us, as far as I could tell. She was in some kind of trouble. And, a single clipped report from Eric telling someone that Tucker had picked up eight hundred on his first set, way north of us.

Well, the wind picked up, helping the big ebb suck us further south. The seas built, and the fish disappeared. The sketchy reports about *Winter Wind* got worse. It sounded like it was caught on the cable between a tug and barge, and the skipper on the tug sounded helpless. The report from way north was true. The damned dogs *were* up there. A few boats coming out of the river late had run across them, and others had been close enough to run for it and make it pay. One guy picked up a thousand on one drift! I tried bucking the seas and tide but barely inched my way up toward the bottom of Kalgin Island.

I was beat and pissed when we finally got into the river that night with our ninety-four fish. Some of the boats were already in from up north, and they were loaded. I saw *Pisces* still on the dock at Kenai Packers, where some people were working around the keel. I heard later that the crane had dropped her after picking her out of the river the night before. And we heard that *Winter Wind* went down.

Judith on the Bluff

ON THE BLUFF ABOVE THE MOUTH of the Kenai River you can look down the Inlet to the southwest. If the weather's decent you can see Chisik Island, over fifty miles away, and beyond that, Mt. Iliamna, out toward the beginning of the Aleutian Range on the Alaska Peninsula. From the other direction, on a boat out in the Inlet, you can see the bluff from about twenty miles away. It's an especially welcome landmark if you're bucking an ebb and trying to get in across the bar before low water. When you approach the mouth and catch sight of the buoy outside the entrance, you can line it up with the marker high on the bluff and stay in the channel. From the road out to the bluff you can check out the weather and see what's happening in the mouth. There might be boats heading out or coming in, or beluga. It's a good place to watch for jumpers late in the season as the sockeye sweep in toward the spawning grounds. From this vantage point the local Indians must have watched in amazement on the morning of May 30, 1778, when Captain Cook passed by the river without realizing it was there. His vessels anchored between the river and the East Foreland, to wait for the flood. Later that day two single-manned canoes rowed out to visit Cook, and he wrote in his journal that "one of [the natives] talked a great deal to no purpose for we did not understand a word he said; he kept pointing to the shore and we guess'd he wanted us to go there."

The Indians undoubtedly watched from the bluff again when Vancouver made his way up the Inlet in 1794, and after that early white settlers recorded their own interest in the few sailing ships that ventured that far. An old log cabin that was once located near the bluff was moved into the center of Kenai in the early 1980s, as part of the tourist center, and on one of the outside walls there is a small weathered picture of a sailing ship carved by one of the early inhabitants. In more recent times wives, friends, or family members drive to the bluff after the end of a commercial fishing period to watch as the drift fleet makes its way back into the harbor. If you're waiting to catch sight of the boat that drew you there, you might be able to spot it with binoculars when it's a few miles out, and when it passes in under the bluff you can exchange waves with the people aboard. You can also get a rough sense of how your boat fared that day, judging from how low it rides in the water. Coming into the river on *Ishmael*—no matter what kind of day we'd had—we watched for Judith on the bluff. On July 10 of 1992, for example, I wrote in the log that we'd had a very good opening set of a thousand or eleven hundred, and another good set off the Sisters late in the afternoon. Then: "Arrived Kenai–to see Judith waving from the bluff–at 9:30 PM. 1921 fish (1894 reds)."

We didn't always get to see Judith waving to us from the bluff, because her legal career in Phoenix limited the time she could spend with us in Kenai. She, too, loved this other way of life that the Cook Inlet fishery gave us. Escaping not only the Phoenix heat and embattled freeways but the stress of preparing briefs to meet court deadlines, she yielded to the saner rhythms of the long Alaskan days and deadlines according to the tide book. She spent her most adventurous days alone on the inside beach of Chisik Island, at Snug Harbor. Sometimes when we holed up there early in the season, we'd put her ashore at three in the morning before we left for a fishing period. She preferred her solitude there near the waterfalls and among the nesting eider ducks and other migrating birds to the clamor and discomfort of a rough day's fishing on the Inlet. Building a fire to keep warm and make a pot of tea, she always enjoyed the company of a good book. It was a relief to catch sight of her along the beach at the end of those fishing days, to know that she'd avoided an unpleasant encounter with the bears that work that beach, black bear and sometimes brown bear.

More often, though, she would remain in Kenai, at the Inlet Salmon cannery, about two miles upstream and on the south bank of the river. There she would spend her days supporting our fishing operation or fixing up the thirty-foot trailer that was our home off the boat. It stood just at the edge of the river, which came within two feet of the trailer on very high tides, and looked out over the river to a tidal flat that teemed with nesting gulls along with occasional sandhill cranes. Between fishing periods *Ishmael* swung on its anchor in the channel about two hundred feet from the trailer. Judith was our only net mender and sometimes worked at that while we were out fishing, or she would do the laundry, run errands, or cook.

On fishing days I'd leave the trailer at two or three in the morning, and catch a skiff ride out to the boat. When I let go of the buoy and began to head down the river, Judith would signal by turning the trailer lights off and on, and I'd answer by switching the running lights off and on. I'd then begin the day's entry in the log book, secure the coffee pot between the sea rails, and settle in at the wheel with the first welcome cup of coffee, hoping to find moderate winds and easy going in the mouth and calculating where to run for the first set.

Judith would try to get back to sleep, maybe reading a while, and then organize her day according to whatever needed to be done. She might mend a piece of net, or take the truck into town to pick up a part for the boat. On days when I thought we'd come back to the river after the period, she shopped for whatever groceries we needed on the boat and what she needed for our dinner for that night. She couldn't tell when to expect us for sure. That depended on the weather, on how far south we had to run that day, where we ended up at closing time, whether we had to buck the ebb or ride the flood on the way back in, and sometimes on what kind of announcements Fish and Game might issue late in the day—extending the period, perhaps, or opening a limited area for the next morning. We had no cell phones in those days, nor were we able talk by radio between the boat and the trailer. But by sometime in the middle of the afternoon, Judith could ask around at the cannery and get a pretty good idea of where the fleet was concentrated that day and what kind of announcements Fish and Game might have issued. She could then make a rough calculation about when we might be getting in. Once in a while, if we were fishing lower in the Inlet and decided to save time between periods by delivering our fish in the Kasilof River instead of the Kenai, we could radio a message to her through the cannery office and she'd drive the truck to Kasilof, greeting us with a homemade dinner. The truck was a tough but rusted 1969 Dodge with a stick shift on the floor, and she drove it with authority.

Knowing that we'd be tired and hungry when we got back, she considered it her main job to prepare a big meal that she could quickly warm up when we arrived. In our normal way of sharing the domestic work at home in Arizona, I did the shopping and cooking, and Judith did the cleaning and laundry. But she is an excellent cook, and she always greeted us with a fine, hearty meal—maybe a huge pot of meaty chili or something from her favorite cookbook, the *Moosewood Cookbook*. Though *Moosewood* was not infallible (Judith's marginal note in the recipe for mushroom curry is "not good," and the book includes a misguided epigraph by William Blake: "All wholesome food is caught without a net or a trap"), she found a number of excellent dishes there that made feasts of our homecomings, even if we were depressed and frustrated after a disappointing day on the water. Mushroom moussaka was a favorite, when modified according to Judith's marginal notes ("cut down by 1/3" or "make runnier"), and she would always have an appetizing dessert, all prepared to perfection in the trailer's cramped kitchen.

At some point in the afternoon she might take time for a walk on the beach below the mouth of the river, where she could get a feel for what kind of weather we were having on the water, or pick a few wild flowers, lupine in June or by mid July, fireweed. Then, perhaps, after writing a few cards and letters or attending to some chores, she would make the last-minute preparations for the meal and calculate the time that *Ishmael* might get back to the river. Wanting to arrive at the bluff an hour or so before we could arrive at the mouth, she'd drive the eight miles or so out Cannery Road to Kalifornsky Road and then across the bridge to Kenai. She'd take a novel, a pair of binoculars to keep watch for us, and often a bunch of grapes to snack on in the truck while waiting for us to appear on the horizon. She enjoyed those times.

Meanwhile, on the boat, we'd begin picking up the last set of the day, just before the 7 p.m. deadline. After we got it aboard, we'd do a quick wash-down, get out of our rain gear, point the boat toward the river, and maybe drink a beer. I'd estimate how long a run we had ahead of us, and if it was going to be a long one, we'd have a sandwich or something to tide us over until dinner. Mike, my deck hand from the late eighties on, would take the wheel while I took a nap, our routine being that I drove out in the mornings, while Mike slept, and he ran it in at the end of the day. Unless we'd had a really bad, frustrating day, or a mishap of some kind, I could easily fall asleep to the sound of *Ishmael* cutting through the water and the muffled throb of the engine. It was a restful but shallow sleep, and I'd always wake up as we neared or entered the channel at Kenai. As the fleet converged on the mouth, we'd take the controls on the bridge. From there we had a better view of the boats ahead, alongside, or behind us, and could better contend with the maneuvering at close quarters in the confusion of wakes and following seas. On the bridge we could also judge not only how the others had done that day but which boats we'd be competing with in the race for a place in line to deliver our fish. Missing a place in line could cost you a couple of hours' wait, and our unspoken code was that it was OK to pass slower boats in the channel, but not after we got around the first bend and headed further up to the plant.

But also from the bridge we could get a better view of the bluff. By the time we passed the buoy and if there was still enough light, we could scan the bluff with binoculars and try to see whether the old green and white pickup was parked there. Others would be waiting there and you could never tell for sure until you got almost into the mouth. By the time we could identify the truck, Judith would already be tracking us, standing outside the truck and waving to us with both arms. Whoever saw her first would yell out, "There's Judith!" If it was getting dark she'd flash the headlights and we'd answer by turning the running lights off and on. If others were on board with us, they'd come out on deck and join in the celebration. We would have been gone only a day or two at the most, and there probably hadn't been any real danger or cause for concern, but it was always a celebration.

After we passed under the bluff Judith would jump in the truck for the eight-mile drive back through town, across the bridge, and out Cannery Road. Unless we were riding a strong flood, she could finish that trip before we could run the two miles around the bend and upriver to the cannery. By the time we could get in line to deliver, she'd be back in the trailer and warming up the dinner she had prepared. It would be late at night. We'd button things up on the boat, call for a skiff ride ashore, and head in to have dinner before it was our turn to deliver. Tired and hungry, we'd wash up and sit right down to eat, beginning at once to exchange our news of the day. Maybe we were high boat in the group, or maybe we had about the same as the other guys. Or, it had been rough heading out that morning, but the wind had died down after our second set and it turned out to be a beautiful day. We'd have a glass or two of wine and second helpings of the moussaka, all of us agreeing that it was the best meal yet. And we'd demolish the creamy dessert. After Mike had had his fill and checked to see whether he had any mail, he'd head back out to *Ishmael*, oversee the delivery, and then hit the sack in his bunk on the boat. I'd visit the cannery's dank shower room for fishermen and cannery workers, still swaying from the roll of the boat. Heading back to the trailer all tingling clean and dead tired I'd find Judith almost done with cleaning up the mess. First in bed, I could look out the window to the boat, checking to see if the cannery workers had started unloading our fish, and, beginning to go under, see vivid hits along the cork line. She would crawl into bed beside me, and I'd not fall too quickly asleep with Judith in my arms.

A Mouthful of Sand

 ON SEPTEMBER 23, 1976, my cousin Suzanne called my office at the university to tell me she was worried about her dad, my Uncle Bert. He had flown to Alaska from his home in Seattle for a sailing adventure with his old friends Don and Cathy Lowcock. On September 4 the three had set out from Seward on the Lowcocks' sailboat *Tiger Lil*, bound for Seattle. The Lowcocks would sail on alone to Hawaii. Now they were overdue in Ketchikan, and the Coast Guard had begun an air search. Suzanne was scared and wondered what I thought about it. I told her not to worry. They hadn't been gone all that long and had probably run into some bad weather, maybe ducked into a little bay somewhere to wait it out. I didn't mention the Gulf.

I learned later that *Tiger Lil* was a good-sized boat, roughly the dimensions of *Ishmael*, a thirty-eight-footer with an eleven-foot beam. It was well-equipped for blue water sailing, with radar, loran, a depth-finder, at least one emergency beacon, and three radios—a VHF set, a citizens' band set, and a Ham radio. Don Lowcock had equipped it with two self-inflating life rafts in addition to an Avon inflatable dinghy, and they carried more than enough life jackets and survival suits to satisfy Coast Guard regulations. He had extensive experience with small boats in Southeastern Alaska and around Kachemak Bay and had taken a class in small-boat sailing before sailing *Tiger Lil* to Alaska the previous spring. Their Gulf crossing on that trip had been pleasant and uneventful, and Don's main concern on this trip was that he wanted to reach Seattle in time to catch favorable winds from there to Hawaii.

By the time that Suzanne called me, the Coast Guard had begun checking harbors in communities between Prince William Sound and Seattle, and they had received reports from people who believed they'd sighted *Tiger Lil* near Sitka on September 10, and near Ketchikan on the fifteenth. There were later reports, one from a man in Sitka saying that he'd heard a Mayday on his citizens band radio at about 3 p.m. on the twenty-first, but he hadn't caught the vessel's name or position. And on the twenty-fourth someone near Cordova heard an indistinct "Mayday!" and "Going down!" but again there was no vessel name or position. On the same day the Coast Guard began a shoreline search by helicopter out of Ketchikan, from Sitka north to Yakutat, and another one out of Kodiak from Seward south to Sitka.

Early in the afternoon on the twenty-fourth the Coast Guard helicopter out of Kodiak spotted debris on the Gulf side of Montague Island, and by 3:30 had recovered two large battered pieces of fiberglass and a clear plastic skylight hatch, all thought to be from a sailboat. After flying the debris to Seward they determined that one piece with rectangular windows was from a cabin, and measured 12 feet 7 inches by 4 feet 2 inches. One of the windows was crushed inward. The other piece was from a boat deck and measured 7 feet 9 inches by 2 feet 2 inches. Both pieces had ragged edges. By the next day people who knew the boat identified the debris as belonging to *Tiger Lil*.

On September 28, two members of a maintenance and repair team arrived at Kayak Island to inspect the light station at Cape St. Elias and found my uncle's body washed ashore. Partly covered by sea weed, badly decomposed and showing considerable "animal damage" (as the autopsy reports), he was wearing long underpants, two pair of socks, and only the neck ring of a cotton tee shirt. A short distance away they found a pair of trousers with a wallet that contained his driver's license. Further along the beach they found a torn and deflated life raft under some logs, but there was no way to identify it as *Tiger Lil*'s. The Coast Guard picked up the body and flew it to Cordova, where an autopsy showed that my uncle had not drowned but had died of a crushed chest.

The Coast Guard suspended its active air search on October 1, and on the tenth a man walking the beach on the Gulf side of Montague Island found a life ring from *Tiger Lil*. On the twenty-fourth someone found a scuba tank with Lowcock's name on it at the eastern end of Hinchinbrook Island. And on November 16 two Coast Guardsmen walking the eastern shore of Kayak Island a mile or so from the light station found a yellow life vest with Cathy's name and *"Tiger Lil"* written on it. The vest was still zipped up but one side of the zipper had been ripped from the vest. A couple of miles further along the beach they found a plaid vest in good condition and marked with Don's name and *"Tiger Lil."*

These facts are from the Coast Guard's preliminary and final reports on the incident, which conclude only that *"Tiger Lil* was lost at sea due to unknown circumstances." But, given the condition of the retrieved debris and the fact that my uncle died of a crushed chest, the report suggests that "whatever happened was of a rapid and violent nature." The two most likely scenarios, in the Coast Guard's view, were either that the boat was caught in a storm and thrown onto a reef near Middleton Island, or that, perhaps "in the darkness of night," *Tiger Lil* "was struck by a larger vessel." Weather records showed that a storm began on the night of September 6, when the weather station on Middleton Island recorded southeast winds of twenty knots with gusts to twenty-five. By noon the next day it was blowing at thirty-six knots with gusts to fifty.

My aunt wrote to me shortly after my uncle's body was recovered and a few days before they buried him in Seattle, telling me how he had looked forward to the adventure. When the Lowcocks were purchasing and fitting out *Tiger Lil* in Seattle the previous spring, he had haunted the docks. Other family plans had prevented him from joining them on their maiden voyage to Alaska, but he had hoped they would ask him to fly there and accompany them on this first leg of their planned voyage to Hawaii. When they did, he was beside himself in anticipating the adventure, and I believe that he also hoped they would invite him to sail on to Hawaii. Although he had very little experience on the ocean, and none on a sailboat, he had always dreamed of such an adventure. My aunt wrote that, preparing for the Alaska trip, he bought a new watch cap and wore it constantly in and around the house, sometimes making fun of himself as the ancient mariner and yet with teary eyes. The day before he left he told a neighbor how much he was looking forward to the trip but also admitted that he wished it would have been a few weeks earlier, in advance of the bad weather associated with the equinox. Later, I learned that a friend of mine, a Cook Inlet gill-netter named Quentin Johnson, had met my uncle and the Lowcocks at the dock in Seward, where they talked about their plans to cross the gulf. Quentin left Seward on his boat *Iliamna* just hours before *Tiger Lil* did and, with more speed, made it safely into Yakutat ahead of the storm. My brother, who was living temporarily in Anchorage, also visited my uncle and the Lowcocks at the dock in Seward. He told how my uncle displayed a bottle of whiskey and danced a jig on deck, with uncharacteristic boyish exuberance. At about this same time, my aunt wrote, she dreamed she would never see him again.

My uncle's death wasn't as terrible a blow to me as it was to my mother (his sister) and his three surviving brothers, or especially to my aunt and their two daughters. Because we had lived so far apart when I was growing up, I never got to enjoy his companionship in the outdoors or to realize what he might have given me as a close link to my grandpa. He looked more like my grandpa than his brothers did. But I was named after him, and I never would have made my way to Alaska if I hadn't known of his earlier experience there and if he hadn't nudged me in that direction. I've been troubled by his death for nearly thirty years, and still can't stop wondering how it happened. Only now have I tried to imagine it.

My uncle and the Lowcocks were in high spirits that night. They were fueled up and everything was in order for their departure the next morning, the fourth of September. The weather looked good, and they had chanced to talk with my friend Quentin, who would also leave for Seattle the next day. The boats wouldn't be running together, but, like any one about to cross the Gulf in a small boat, both Johnson and Lowcock were glad to know that someone else was headed the same way. There was a high wind that night but it lay down by morning. Iliamna had already left the harbor. Cathy whipped up a hearty breakfast to get them started, and while they finished breakfast and enjoyed a second cup of coffee, Don said that they could take their time crossing Prince William Sound. It was a beautiful stretch of water that my uncle had never seen, and if they passed close to the beaches along Montague and Hinchinbrook Islands, they'd have a good chance of spotting some brown bear. My uncle was tickled at the chance to see bear, and Lowcock was happy to have a day or two in protected waters to shake things down and to check out my uncle's sea legs before they nosed out into the Gulf.

As they got under way my uncle took pride in his work as deck hand, helping pick up the anchor and coiling the lines. They left the harbor towing the dinghy, counting on calm weather in the Sound and leaving themselves a chance to go ashore on one of the islands if they saw something of interest. My uncle wasn't a religious man, but he felt tears come as he stood on deck and watched Resurrection Bay open up before his eyes. He wondered how the bay got its name and admitted to himself that its sheer beauty, especially around the islands and the tip of the peninsula, was almost enough to make you believe in something. By mid morning, not long after they were well out into that little corner of the Gulf and headed toward the backside of Montague, Don gave him the wheel for the first time and he felt like a kid. A gentle ocean swell kicked up a little spray, adding to the thrill and assuring him that he wasn't going to be embarrassed by getting seasick. There wasn't enough wind to try out the sails—they could do that if conditions were right when they started across in a day or so. For now, they just enjoyed the ride and shouted to each other if someone spotted a whale. They saw several spouts, and when they were about ten miles off Montague, one breached within a hundred yards of them.

Running along the island they stayed just close enough to scan the beach with binoculars. The sun was out and Cathy prepared a fine late lunch that they ate in the cockpit while watching for bear. My uncle spotted a sow and two cubs, but they were a long way off. They didn't see another one all afternoon, but with the whales and the three bear, it was a memorable day, and my uncle smiled to himself in thinking how he would tell his grand kids. As they passed Green Island and came to the east end of Montague that evening, they saw Iliamna anchored in Rocky Bay. Don thought about going in to say hello and check things out, but there was still enough light for them to head on to Hinchinbrook, where they could anchor for the night and then have a full day to look for bear and possibly go ashore for a walk on the beach.

It was a peaceful anchorage. The bottom was good, and the anchor set on the first try. While Cathy cooked dinner and Don put out a halibut line, my uncle unpacked his bottle of whiskey and made drinks for the three of them. A drink at the end of the day, and just one, made a fitting celebration for the first fine day of this adventure. They toasted to their further good fortune and enjoyed their first opportunity to sit back and talk as shipmates. They had known each other for years, and Don and my uncle had grown especially close on hunting trips for moose and mountain sheep. They respected and trusted each other, but they had never known the kind of companionship that began to develop now in their small shared space inside the cabin and nestled in the cove.

When Don checked the halibut line in the morning there was nothing on it but the bait was gone. They were all looking forward to some fresh fish on this first leg, something to tide them over until they would have another chance to fish after crossing the Gulf. But Don was sure they could easily catch some rockfish or cod as they played around that day. It was another clear day, and after breakfast they got under way, their plan being to run along Hinchinbrook and watch for bear. Also, Don wanted to find a good place to go ashore in the dinghy, to give them a little practice with it as well as to give them a chance to stretch their legs. Tonight they would bring the dinghy aboard and lash it down for the crossing. They'd get an early start, and Don said that, weather permitting, they could shoot straight across and make it into Elfin Cove without running in to Yakutat. They were packing enough fuel and should make it to Elfin Cove in three days. My uncle sensed that Don was just a little on edge about the Gulf, not from anything he said but the way he busied himself checking and double checking some fittings, the EPIRB, and the two life raft canisters.

Before long they were absorbed in checking out the beach along Hinchinbrook. Don had been ashore on Montague a couple of times to hunt deer, but not on Hinchinbrook, which he knew was out of the way for most hunting traffic. It had the excitement of new country and, sure enough, they quickly spotted a good-sized brown bear. That was the only one they saw that day, but looking through the glasses my uncle thought it was a monster compared to the grizzlies he had seen around Denali and on his sheep hunts in the Wrangell Mountains. They nosed their way along shore toward the north end of the island, seeing a few whales and porpoises along the way, and by noon pulled into a little cove with a protected sandy beach just across from Hawkins Island. It was a good place to have lunch and then take the dinghy ashore for their walk. So they dropped the hook, and by the time Cathy had lunch ready, my uncle had caught two nice cod, enough for two or three good meals, and enough to whet his appetite for the more serious halibut fishing they were sure to have in Southeast. After lunch he filleted and iced the cod before they went ashore. Don was relieved to see how easily they were able to get in and out of the dinghy and land it on the beach without any mishaps. They weren't spring chickens, after all, my uncle being the oldest at 68. He was fit but sometimes short of breath with emphysema from years of smoking.

It was good to stretch their legs along the short beach, though Cathy wished that they could have walked an outside beach instead, where the beachcombing was far better and where she might have found another Japanese glass float for her collection. At least they saw some huge bear tracks. But it was now the middle of the afternoon and they wanted to get back aboard, lash down the dinghy, and motor back around the island to somewhere near Hinchinbrook Entrance. By late afternoon Don had picked out his anchorage, just inside the entrance. As they were dropping the hook they saw the only other vessel they'd spotted all day, a tanker headed out from Valdez and probably on its way to Seattle. While Cathy cooked dinner, Don checked the oil and asked my uncle to see whether the running lights and mast light came on when he threw the switches. Everything was in order, and once again they sat down to relax over their pre-dinner drink while keeping an eye out along the beach and waiting for the potatoes to boil. When Cathy served them up with a small salad and the fresh-baked cod, seasoned with one of the few lemons they'd been lucky enough to find in Seward, my uncle wondered how good can it get?

Before they went to bed Don listened to the weather report on the VHF. As often, though, it seemed ambiguously normal—forecasting SE winds of 10 to 15 through the sixth. But a single long high cloud just before dark was enough to arouse the slight nervousness he often felt the night before a trip. It wasn't worth mentioning, and besides, he didn't want Cathy and my uncle to lose any sleep. He would be up off and on all night, checking the anchor and taking a leak, but they could get a good rest. He knew he shouldn't worry too much before these trips. Before crossing the Gulf last spring he lay awake all night at the dock in Elfin Cove listening for wind, and when they got outside it was almost flat calm. The worst they had was a half day of big swells out around Kayak Island, and from then on there wasn't enough breeze to put up the sail even if he had wanted to. The blow they'd had crossing Queen Charlotte Sound was bad enough to keep Cathy in the bunk and make them wary of the Gulf, but it turned out to be a piece of cake. Before he went to bed that night my uncle stepped out on deck to have a cigarette and look at the amazing stars.

The next morning my uncle was already awake when Don turned on the cabin lights. He'd just come in from peeing and checking out the weather and said, "time to get up, Bert. Looks like we got a good one."

"I'm with you," my uncle said, putting on another pair of socks and stuffing a few things into his duffle bag before stowing it at the foot of his bunk. Cathy was even more chipper than usual and quickly put on the coffee. They had agreed last night that she would get a simple, light breakfast and that they would get things buttoned up for a quick departure. They were all excited about this big day, their first venture into the open ocean. There was a little chill in the cabin, and when Don and Cathy hugged each other to signal the beginning of their long-awaited voyage to Hawaii, my uncle joked that by the time they got to Seattle it might be hard to get him off the boat. As they were finishing their instant oatmeal and second cups of coffee, Don started the engine. It was still dark when he and my uncle went out to pick up the hook, dark enough for my uncle to pause in coiling the line to take in the astonishing sweep of stars as Don maneuvered Tiger Lil out of the anchorage into Hinchinbrook Entrance.

The sun rose in a cloudless pink sky just a little before they were far enough out to feel the first Gulf swells rolling in from the southeast. Don set his course for just outside Cape St. Elias, heading right into the sun. "It's a little under 80 miles to the Cape," he said, "and if we just poke along at our normal 6, we oughta be there in twelve or thirteen hours."

"Sounds good," my uncle said. "That'll be just about dark, right?"

"Should be," Don said. "Might be able to pick up the light at Cape St. Elias by around dinner time."

My uncle bent over the chart again. He knew there was nothing else out there between them and the Cape, on Kayak Island, but he wondered about Middleton Island. "What about Middleton Island?" he asked. "Looks like we'll pass north of it by about 30 miles. Think we'll be able to see it from that far?"

"Don't think so. We never saw it when we came up last spring. It's awful low, you know. No, that's about all we'll be seeing all day," he said, pointing to the empty horizon ahead. The sun was well up now and you couldn't tell whether those were low clouds way ahead or just the ocean mist. The weather guy had it about right. There was just a little southerly breeze of 10 or 15, and so Don

*and my uncle put on their rain jackets and went aft to steer from the cockpit.
You could hardly hear the engine back there, only the propwash and water
slapping along the sides. Whenever Don steered from there he seemed more
relaxed and talkative, as though the water and open air aroused something in
him. My uncle was the same, and Don thought that sitting there in his watch
cap and with that turtleneck sweater under his rain gear, Bert looked like
the guy in the Old Spice commercials, only with the stubble of a day's growth.
Don caught himself as he was about to whistle the catchy tune, not that he
was all that superstitious about whistling or bringing bananas aboard. My
uncle looked back at the wake, noting how Montague and Hinchinbrook had
receded and begun to merge. The snowy mountains on the southern half of
Montague would be visible for quite a while, but Hinchinbrook Entrance was
already closed.*

*Don asked my uncle to take the wheel for a while–he wanted to check on
Cathy, who wasn't yet adjusted to the way the boat rolled or rose and fell on
the swells. She liked it better when they were under sail. Don wanted to give
my uncle a good stint at the wheel so stayed inside for a while. He put on some
water for more coffee, made an entry in the log, and checked some papers he
had on the EPIRB and the inflatable rafts. Every now and then he glanced
astern to check the wake and was relieved to see that his old friend could steer
a straight course. My uncle seemed like he was in heaven, but he was just
enough on edge having it all to himself that he bent down out of the breeze to
light a cigarette.*

*By noon the mountains on Montague slid below the horizon and there was
no land in sight. Even though the wind had picked up just a little, Cathy was
feeling better and came out to say that she had some sandwiches ready. "Do
you want them out here?" she asked, and Don said, "Why not? We might take
a little spray but I'd rather duck it than be in the house." She brought them
out and watched my uncle, knowing he would go a little nuts over them—
sandwiches from the last of the sausage they'd had made from the moose Don
got last season. She'd packed enough for them to enjoy once in a while on their
way to Hawaii, but she wanted some today because she knew my uncle hadn't
had this treat for years, and it seemed like a good way to celebrate their first
real day on the ocean.*

"Good god, Cathy," he said. "Fresh cod one day and moose sausage the next!" As they ate the sandwiches Don told him about the moose hunt last fall. It was just a medium-size bull, but he shot him before the rut and couldn't remember ever having such tender roasts. Just then he put down his paper plate in order to get his other hand on the wheel. He steered into a swell that was a little bigger than the rest, and as he did a gust of wind swept his plate and the last half of his sandwich astern. "Damn it!" he said. "I was enjoying that. And I hate like hell to leave even a paper plate out here." When Cathy got up to get him another sandwich, he said, "Well, maybe I should just eat it at the wheel inside." The clouds to the southeast had been getting a little closer all morning, and the breeze freshened. My uncle stayed to take the wheel while Don and Cathy went inside. When Don waved to signal that he had the wheel, my uncle remained outside to have a cigarette. He smiled to himself a little guiltily, thinking how my aunt would be pissed to know he was smoking so much, but, ducking down out of the wind to light up, he thought, "What the hell. After a lunch like that? and out here in the middle of all this?"

There were more whitecaps now, and toward twilight, at around 5 o'clock, it was clear that the forecast for southeast winds of 10 to 15 should be bumped up a notch. Don figured it was close to 20 and turned on the VHF weather channel to see what was going on. He put his ear close to the radio and barely caught the faint signal. They were still calling for winds out of the southeast, but now they were talking 20 to 25, with 8 foot seas. "Not too bad," he said to the others. "It'll probably pick up a little, but you can't expect much better in the Gulf. Might have to throttle back a bit before long. But," he patted the top of the instrument panel, "Lil's made for a lot worse stuff than this." That sounded about right to my uncle. "Besides," he thought to himself, "I've been wanting a little more of a ride than this, anyhow."

"So," Don said, pointing a little more east than south, "if we keep looking out over that way, we might be able to pick up the Saint Elias light before long." It was dark now, the cloud cover blocking out the stars and leaving only the light of breaking seas. The seas had grown large enough to convince Don to throttle back a bit, to about 3/4. Bucking the wind and now running a little slower into the seas, Don realized that the crossing was going to take longer than he had figured. He asked my uncle to take the wheel and began *going over his charts to recalculate his plan. He had been thinking for some time that he'd better forget about heading straight for Cape Spencer and Elfin Cove. That was going to be a long run in this slop and in the dark. So he told the others that it might be best to get around Cape St. Elias and then head for Yakutat. Even that would be a long run at the speed they were making now, and it would be a different ride. They'd have to quarter the seas and might be in the trough at times. He wasn't happy about that, especially running at night, but if they just kept poking ahead they might make it into Yakutat by late tomorrow afternoon. My uncle nodded in agreement but didn't like the idea of maneuvering in this kind of water with no visibility. The boat was plunging a bit now and then and taking a lot more spray. You couldn't keep the windshield from fogging up, and all you could do was hope you didn't hit a floating log or something. Still, he was enjoying the action and preferred being at the wheel and feeling their way along to just trying to hold on to his seat.*

It wasn't a good time to cook so Cathy made tuna fish sandwiches for dinner and my uncle was happy to spell Don at the wheel. Don kept checking their position on the loran, not wanting to get too close to Cape St. Elias but still wanting to catch sight of the light. He listened to the VHF and the CB but didn't pick up anything that he could really make out, and every now and then he went outside to get a better look to the east, hoping to see the light. Coming inside one time to dry his face and wipe the spray from his glasses, he told my uncle to put on his life jacket and be careful if he went on deck. He couldn't tell for sure, but he might have seen the light once. He went outside again and in a few minutes came back in with the news that he was sure he could see it coming in and out of view from behind the seas. "The loran's right on," he said. "That's good to know, but now let's stay a little further off, about ten degrees." He looked over my uncle's shoulder to watch the compass as it turned and said, "Yeah, right there. This'll put us just below Yakutat and compensate for the wind pushing us north. Whataya think? Are you OK with that? If you're doing OK I'll just lie down for a while. We'll need to spell each other til it gets light, at least."

"Sure, no problem," my uncle said. "Get off your feet for a while, and I'll give you a shout if anything comes up."

"Good enough. Can I get you a cup of coffee before I go?"

"No thanks. I'm wide awake. Go on and get some rest."

My uncle knew it was going to be a long night, but that was OK. This was what it was all about. He wasn't looking for a cruise on the Alaska Ferry, and he appreciated it when Don gave him a pat on the back before he went to lie down. He had the hang of it now, anticipating the way he wanted to head up and then compensating at the wheel to stay on course. Knowing for sure now that the compass was right no matter what it felt like as you steered through the dark and the boat moved. The little diesel was purring along just fine, and it was good to know that Don trusted him and respected his judgment.

In just an hour or so Don got up and asked how it was going. He hadn't slept but felt rested. He put on his rain gear and stepped outside to look around and pee. When he came back in he cleaned off his glasses and checked the loran. "Well, we're plugging along, making a little headway. Get myself a cup of coffee and then take it for a while, OK?"

"Good enough," my uncle said. In a minute Don put his coffee cup in the holder, patted my uncle on the back again and said, "OK, I got it. Try to get a nap. I'll take it for a couple hours and then give you a shout." My uncle stepped away from the wheel after Don took it, then stretched his back. He asked if Don wanted anything and then put on his rain coat and life jacket.

"Just gonna step outside for a smoke, OK?"

"Sure. Just keep a good hold, though. Right?"

"For damn sure," he said, and then went outside. It was blowing harder than before and, ducking right behind the house he could barely light the cigarette. He coughed but it did him good, easing the tension he'd built up at the wheel. And it was wonderful being out in the midst of it on deck. The wash, the wind and spray, plunging ahead in the dark and realizing more immediately how alone they were out there, how big it was. He wasn't afraid. The boat was running fine and Don knew what he was doing. But when he finished his cigarette it was good to get back inside, and Don was relieved to see him come back in.

"OK, Don, I'll just lie down a while. Yell if there's anything I can do."

"You bet. Try to get a few winks."

The boat was pounding and rolling quite a bit more when my uncle suddenly opened his eyes, awaking from a dream about his daughters, Suzanne and Joanne, and the grandkids. They had come to him out in his work shop to tell him that dinner was ready and grandma wanted him to wash up and come slice the turkey. He glanced at his watch and it was a little before 3 a.m. He'd slept longer than he wanted to and sat up quickly, slipped on his shoes without tying them and steadied himself as he got over to the wheel. "Damn it, Don, slept longer than I intended. How's it going?"

"Not too bad. Glad you went under. It's been picking up quite a bit. Had to throttle back some about an hour ago, but we're doing pretty good. Be glad when we get some light—about five more hours, I guess. Would you take a peek at Cathy? I think she's been sleeping through it, but I hope she's not sick."

My uncle looked down into the forward bunk, and it looked like Cathy was curled up asleep. Coming back up to the wheel he said, "Sound asleep. Hold on just a second and I'll take it if you want." He wanted to look around outside and see if he could light a cigarette. He started to put on the rain jacket and life vest, and, seeing him, Don said, "Be careful if you go out there! Some big seas now and we been rockin and rollin pretty good."

"I'll watch it. Just be a second," he said, putting on his watch cap and pushing open the door just a bit. It was blowing a lot harder now, and he almost ducked back in. But he wanted to see what it was really like in a blow like this. He tucked the cigarette into a pocket so he could hold on better, then stepped out into the crashing noise, turning around quickly to shut the door and grab the hand hold. He pulled himself close in to the house to keep out of the wind and spray, and when he had his balance turned around into the engulfing blackness overboard and astern. In the same instant he felt and heard a vast low rumble and then a bolt of adrenalin that made him gasp and piss his pants. The crashing high blasts of white water and the black hulk above. He turned, grabbing for the door, banging his head and knocking off his watch cap, flinging it open and screaming, "Hard over, Don! There's a ship!"

Don turned to look, cried out "What the . . .?" hit the throttle, jammed the wheel hard over, and yelled, "Cathy!"

Tiger Lil began her turn to the starboard, wallowing and dropping into the trough, making an even better target to receive the tanker's crushing blow. Still holding on at the door, my uncle turned to see it rise above them. He braced himself to take it, only clinching his jaw to mouth the words, "Wasn't that damn bad."

A blast of light and nothing.

His body crushed in the chaotic swirl, down. Down. Driven deeper now by the great churning wheels. Chunks of Tiger Lil *surface in the tanker's wake and are swept by the still-building seas across the hundred miles toward Montague. The tanker crashes ahead, laboring a bit against the storm but oblivious to the brief thump that only caused the man on watch to cock his head and then resume his place in his engrossing thriller.*

Days later, the broken body floats to the surface. The storm has passed, and a southerly breeze pushes it toward the light. Washing, awash, awash, the blessed dissolution begun. A single gull descends, then a quarrel of screeching gulls. Kayak Island. Washing. Washing, to the abrasive shore. Tangled sea weed and crabs at low water. More gulls, a sniffing fox. Lifted higher on the flood and tucked beneath the ledge. Seaweed. Flies. The mouth full of sand. Sun. Rain. Cold wind.

❊

I recently saw something along the Big Sur coast that stays with me. It caught the stark simplicity of sea death and reminded me of Peter Matthiessen's vivid image in *Far Tortuga* of a fisherman who "got a mouthful of sand, as de old people say." He had been swept overboard and drowned because the steersman had nodded off. In the Big Sur scene a bloated sea lion floated just offshore in a bed of kelp, possessed by a lone vulture standing atop it to feed. A hundred yards away other sea lions clamored along the rocky beach while their pups frolicked in the surf. We watched, quieted, then got back into the car.

Among fictional sea deaths, those by Stephen Crane and Jack London impress me most. At the end of "The Open Boat," Billy the oiler drowns in the surf, he who had worked hardest and most deserved to live, and who, being the strongest and most experienced surfman, *should* have survived. The meaninglessness and injustice of this death evokes Crane's image of a "high cold star on a winter's night" and reveals "the pathos" of the human situation. Even more coldly, London describes how Martin Eden drowns himself. Disillusioned about love, what it means to be a best-selling writer, and the ideal of a socialist brotherhood, Eden forces his way through a porthole. When "a bonita struck at his white body," he laughed. It "reminded him of why he was there" and he then battled the "automatic instinct to live," swimming deeper and deeper until "colors and radiances surrounded him and bathed him and pervaded him" and a final "flashing, bright white light" in his brain blinked out and "he fell into darkness."

But I can't draw even this much meaning from my uncle's death, and certainly not the kind of spiritual possibility that the young Melville offered in commemorating the dead sailor Shenly in *White-Jacket*. As his body sinks in the sea, Melville's democratic hero Jack Chase whispers, "Look aloft . . . see that bird! it is the spirit of Shenly." Still, I believe my uncle's sea death was ideal. I imagine that he saw it coming for an agonizing moment, but whether he did or not, he had the great fortune to die instantly. He didn't flail in the water or suck it in and choke for air. He escaped the dismal misery of wallowing in the seas and confronting the inevitable slow surrender to hypothermia. He was embarked on an adventure of a lifetime into the fresh blue-gray-green world of ocean and islands, and at age sixty-eight he avoided the demoralizing slow death from emphysema that certainly awaited him. The autopsy found little remaining tissue from the right lung, but an examination of the left lung revealed it to be "markedly emphysematous and anthracotic and . . . highly autolytic." I imagine that when my uncle saw it coming he had a split second to realize that that way to death wasn't all that damn bad.

About a year ago I dreamt of my uncle. We were glad to see each other. I don't remember our ever having hugged. He was not as openly affectionate as Grandpa or the other sons, Charles and Frank. But in the dream we gave each other a great "bear hug," like the ones Grandpa gave so often. It was a vivid dream, and I awoke in tears. I never saw him again.

But I conjure another visit. He looks exactly as he did when I last saw him, at about the age I am now. I must be much younger. He looks at me knowingly, but warmly. He seems as leery of this meeting as I am, and he looks at me as though he knows what I've been writing. He is silent.

Finally I ask, "do you believe in the soul?" He says nothing, but I see a faint smile in his eyes. Unnerved by his silence, I blurt, "Well, I don't, really. Only that there's a kind of glow. This throbbing bit of moist earth that holds together for a while and glows inside."

He seems unimpressed, but his kind and gentle look calms me.

I ask, "Remember when you were in Alaska and we lived in your house? I used to practice shot-putting in your back yard. I never said anything about all those holes I made in the cement wall next to the alley, and you never mentioned it. I'm sorry. Remember when you came back to Seattle and found that I'd left my car in your garage? That old 1937 Plymouth coupe that wouldn't run because the transmission was out? You took out the transmission, rebuilt it, and then drove the car over to our new house. I know you must have been pissed, but you never showed it. I was just a kid in college. You pretended it wasn't anything. I'm sorry."

He still doesn't say anything, but again I see the faint smile around his eyes and think it's all right.

"You never got to see *Ishmael*," I say to break the silence. "How about if we go down to the harbor, head out and see if we can catch some fish?"

Exxon Valdez

IN LATE MARCH OF 1989 the thick citrus scent and a dusting of snow on Four Peaks could almost make you forget about the Phoenix smog. Besides, the foothills of the Superstition Mountains were still water colored with lupine and poppies, and we were on the homestretch in the academic year. There were only six more weeks of class and final exams, and then I'd have a month of free time to finish my academic research and writing for the year. By mid-June I'd be back in Kenai, on the water and out of the Phoenix heat.

I had been thinking about *Ishmael* and the Inlet all winter. I'd had my best season ever in '88, in gross earnings though not in pounds of fish, and Fish and Game was projecting another good run for '89. Wanting to reinvest some of last season's earnings, I had ordered new web and three new helm pumps to replace the ones I had been fighting with for ten years, and put more money into other improvements to the boat. The biggest investment was for new aluminum rails from the cabin back, to give us more freeboard. I'd started thinking about building up the rails a couple of years before, after a day when we caught about thirty-three hundred fish. The hold was so full we could hardly get the hatch covers on and we had to deck-load fish as far forward as possible, with even a hundred or so on the bow. Jon helped me sketch out a design that fit with *Ishmael's* low lines. A shop in Soldotna fabricated them over the winter, and they'd be ready for me to install before I launched the boat in June. So, by late March, I'd already been "on" the boat for quite a while.

1988 and the first part of '89 had been good for me in other ways, as well. My book *Sea-Brothers* was getting good reviews and the press was thinking about a paperback edition. And over the two years since I finished that project, I had moved on to related work that was full of promise. Having discovered how Darwin's view of life had helped change American sea fiction after *Moby-Dick*, I began to realize how deeply he

224

had affected many other writers who were far removed from the sea. Yet critics and literary historians had never imagined that writers such as Henry James, Edith Wharton, or Kate Chopin could have found much of interest in Darwinian evolution. It appeared that critics and literary historians had never read *The Descent of Man, and Selection in Relation to Sex.* They never mentioned Darwin's theory of sexual selection, with its powerful role in shaping human nature and human behavior, especially in courtship and marriage. Although biographers had long known that James had met Darwin, that his brother William had produced the first great work in Darwinian psychology, that Wharton had actually titled a book of stories *The Descent of Man,* and that Chopin had revered Darwin, none of the biographers guessed that these writers' interest in Darwin was of much note. Judging from the biographers and critics, Darwin's theory of human nature was irrelevant to the art of fiction. By the end of March I was just completing my first essay in this new project, an analysis of Chopin's meditation on "love" and sexual selection in her great novel, *The Awakening.*

It had been a good year at home, as well. Judith, Todd, and I were all in good health. At age fifty-one I was absorbed in both my careers, Judith was engrossed in new work on streambed law, a field that combined her legal training with her prior interest in the history of the American West, and Todd was finishing junior high, toying with the idea of making a career in music. He played both the alto sax and the bassoon, and he liked the idea of becoming a high-school band director.

Probably because things were going so well for us then, the news of March 24 jolted me but left me hoping for the best. Shortly after midnight an oil tanker leaving Valdez with a full load of North Slope crude oil had run aground in Prince William Sound. It had already spilled about ten million gallons and there was much more aboard. Early reports described it as the largest oil spill ever, anywhere in the world. Christ! I thought, that's a hell of a lot more than we had in Cook Inlet two years before, after the *Glacier Bay* spill. Running *Ishmael* from Kenai to Chisik Island, we'd spotted *Glacier Bay* soon after it happened, and there was oil everywhere. I began to hope that the *Exxon Valdez* crude wouldn't be as hard to deal with as the stuff *Glacier Bay* had lost, but my main, selfish, thought was that Prince William Sound was a long way from Cook Inlet. With any luck they could clean it up and keep it in the Sound. Maybe it wouldn't sweep around the Kenai Peninsula and up into the Inlet.

The news got worse. This was looking like the biggest environmental disaster ever, and just two days after the accident, when they were trying to get a handle on the cleanup, a big storm moved in and was sweeping the oil out into the Gulf of Alaska. We began to see the first pictures of dead, oil-coated sea otters and birds.

It would take years before I or anyone could begin to appreciate what actually happened that day. Not until sixteen years after the spill was Riki Ott able to produce her remarkable assessment of the spill's actual damage. Both a marine biologist and a gill-netter for salmon in Prince William Sound, Ott also explains in her *Sound Truth and Corporate Myths: The Legacy of the Exxon Valdez Oil Spill* (2005) why it took so long for the truth to come out. A number of scientific studies were conducted in the public interest, but Exxon did everything possible to block or delay them. The corporation funded a flood of its own studies to contradict or obfuscate the others. As Ott shows, Exxon's tactics served not only to cripple the legal proceedings but to corrupt scientific efforts to understand coastal ecology. The only way to calculate the actual damage caused by the spill, she explains, is to include not only the damage done by the spilled oil itself, but by Exxon's initial efforts to remove the oil with steam and powerful solvents. Most important, Ott shows how the prolonged legal and scientific battles have left us still with no effective public policy on how to prevent spills or how to deal with them when they do happen.

All through April, May, and early June that year, I kept telling myself that things might work out for us in Cook Inlet. I talked with fishing friends from Kenai and Homer and, though we were all worried, we knew that very little oil was showing up in the Inlet so far, only a small amount from well below Anchor Point, the southern boundary of the Inlet's gill-net fishery. Also, time seemed to be on our side, because the sockeye wouldn't begin to enter the Inlet in any numbers until late June. I bought my ticket to Kenai and kept thinking about *Ishmael*'s new helm pumps and the new aluminum rails. I finished the long article on Darwin in Kate Chopin's *The*

Awakening by early June, then flew into Kenai on the 15th, a little earlier than usual, and still confident that we would have a season.

The real nightmare was playing out in Prince William Sound, where the massive, chaotic cleanup was still under way, and where they'd already lost the herring and pink salmon seasons. Still, it was good to be back in Kenai, where I could lose myself in work on the boat, the nets, and the old pickup. Going ahead with all that, I didn't make my first entry in *Ishmael's* log until June 22: "So far, nothing but bad rumors and confusion about the fishing season because of the oil spill. Test boats are finding oil in the Inlet—in the southerly part. Will we fish at all? Will Exxon settle in a fair way? What about the market? The price for west-side set-netters opened at $1.75 a pound for reds but is falling. Is the low price due to a damaged market because of the spill? The price seems worse than the yen-dollar ratio would indicate. Lots of boats not yet in the water–waiting to see what's going on."

The first fishing period had been scheduled for the 26th, but on the 24th Fish and Game announced a closure until further notice. On the same day fishermen came out in record numbers for a meeting in Kenai. Our fishermen's organization, UCIDA (United Cook Inlet Drift Association), had called the meeting and invited speakers representing Fish and Game, the Alaska Department of Environmental Conservation, and Exxon. I described the tense meeting in my log: "Lots of questions and few answers. How much oil is there in the Inlet? How much will it take to shut us down? The State has a policy of 'zero tolerance,' but what *is* 'zero tolerance'? Fish and Game thinks we will fish, finally, if only in the northern Inlet, and they promise not to squeeze the fleet into a little area if that's the only clean place. Exxon's preliminary proposal for possible settlements distributed. Many questions. Most people are skeptical and depressed."

Since there was nothing to do now but fret and wait for further news, I decided to go ahead and launch the boat. You had to be ready to go if there was an unexpected opening. Even if we weren't allowed to fish this season, it would be better to get the boat in the water and run it, rather than leave it in winter storage for another year. So we scheduled the boat lift for high water on the evening of the 28th and went ahead with it, even though we'd heard early that afternoon that Fish and Game had closed

Inlet fishing until at least July 7. It was good to be in the water, at least, to hear the engine come to life and purr along in our trial run. But even at that twilight hour the whole community along the river seemed in a state of suspended gloom.

We were feeling a little like injured players missing their big chance to play in the Rose Bowl, but forget the roses—there was no game at all. We tried not to think about it and decided to use the week to play around. One of the best things that summer was that my Uncle Frank had come up to fish with us for a second year. In his late sixties, he had been an unpaid deck hand on our big season the previous year and had the time of his life. He was brilliant at fixing things and doing projects on the boat, and nothing could suppress his sense of play or his determination to keep our spirits up. Part of what drew him to Alaska, of course, was the lingering absence he felt after his big brother's death in the Gulf of Alaska thirteen years before. That subject remained just below the surface, as did the spill itself when my brother visited us for a few days. Charles had come to Alaska to work on the spill because the mega-law firm he headed in Los Angeles was representing Exxon. We talked about it just enough for me to gather that Exxon knew it had a colossal public relations problem on its hands and wanted badly to appear to be doing everything possible to clean up the mess and make amends. Still, the three of us and my deck hand, Mike, made a kind of family reunion of it, avoiding much talk about the spill, and ran the boat across the Inlet to Kalgin Island. On the way we kept an eye out for oil, but didn't see a drop. We anchored off the northeast corner of Kalgin, caught a few halibut, and had a fine dinner back in Kenai that night.

Charles went back to work on the spill, and when Judith and Todd flew in from Phoenix, we decided to make the most of our time in limbo by taking the boat to Homer. We could visit some fellow fishermen and play around in Kachemak Bay while waiting for further word from Fish and Game. Anyhow, if Fish and Game did open the season, we'd be better off fishing out of Homer this early in the season than out of Kenai. Again, running from three to five miles off the beach all the way to Homer, we kept a close watch but saw no sign of oil, not even an oily piece of driftwood in the debris along the east rip. We pulled into Homer with lifted spirits that night, but it didn't take long for us to sense the gloomy tension that lay over the harbor like a fog. The real mess was in the Sound, but as the Alaska Coastal Current swept some of the oil to the southwest, the stuff began to appear inside of Kodiak Island, fouling beaches on the Alaska Peninsula. And, passing that way, below the tip of the Kenai Peninsula, some of the oil had begun to flow up into the lower Inlet.

The spill had also begun to create a social mess in Homer and the surrounding communities. Among fishermen, old friendships were strained over whether or not to sign on with Exxon for charter work on the cleanup. Some of my friends did and some were adamantly opposed to being involved with Exxon in any way. I could understand both sides of the question and, having arrived in Kenai two and a half months after the spill, after the cleanup charters were arranged, I never had to decide. If you fished for a living and were now looking at no fishing income for the year, or even if you just wanted to help in some way, it might make sense to sign on and get some of the cleanup money that Exxon was throwing around. You could say, "Screw the bastards! I'll take anything I can get from them." Or you could think, "Screw the bastards! Damned if I'm gonna help them win the PR game. Let's see what kind of settlement they offer, and I'll see 'em in court."

I don't know what kind of money people made chartering their boats in the cleanup effort that was based in Homer, but it was clear to them and everyone else that there was little actual cleanup to be done in the lower Inlet. When the oil was mixed with water it made a gray mass the consistency of mousse, and was called that. But when cleanup workers fished little globs of it out of the lower Inlet, they called them moose turds. You could spend a day looking around in the rips and fish out only a few moose turds, which you then took back to Homer in plastic bags. The cleanup workers themslves were overwhelmed with supplies such as packaged pastries, distributed by VECO, the company that Exxon contracted for the cleanup effort. Even at the time, people referred to it all as part of the second spill, "the money spill" Exxon dispersed in order to appear to be doing everything possible to make things right.

We thought it was a good idea to leave the Homer gloom and try to have some fun at the Fourth of July celebration in Seldovia. It's hard

Exxon Valdez: Death in Prince William Sound

not to enjoy hanging out in Seldovia, especially with its funky lawn-chair parade, log-rolling contest, fireworks, and all the food and drink. Besides, no one expected further announcements from Fish and Game for a few more days, in time for the next scheduled fishing period on Friday, the 7th. We tried to keep busy on the 5th but there were only a few maintenance chores and a few of last year's holes in the net for Judith to mend. Fish and Game broadcast the next announcement on the 6th, as expected, but gave us the bad news that fishing would be closed on both Friday *and* Monday.

On Friday the 7th Exxon opened an office in Homer to take preliminary claims. They also distributed initial checks intended to get people through the next week or so, until a more complicated formula could be worked out for further compensation. It takes a fair amount of money to get a fishing operation going for the season and, as usual, most of us were buying supplies with our credit cards until we could catch some fish and go to the bank. I picked up a check for ten thousand dollars and was happy to have it. I immediately wrote a check for 15 percent of it for my deck hand, Mike, who was also running on empty. The Exxon officials at the claims office were friendly and efficient, but everyone connected with the fishing industry was getting more and more angry with the corporation. Like the other fishermen, we were nervous, but also determined to have some fun while waiting it out. One day we took the boat across Kachemak Bay to Sadie Cove and Tutka Bay, which Fish and Game had opened to seiners. Apparently Fish and Game felt there was no threat from oil in these bays, but there were no fish, either. We hung around to watch one boat make a couple of sets, hoping we could get a fish from them to barbecue on the beach, but all they got was water. Another day a party of friends came aboard *Ishmael* for a trip to Halibut Cove and then a hike to Grewingk Glacier. After the hike we picked up the anchor and as I ran the boat from the bridge back toward Homer, my friend Jon diffused some of the tension we were all feeling by tossing the buoy over and stringing out about fifty fathoms of my net before I looked back to see what was going on. All I needed was a run-in with Fish and Game, but luckily no one saw us. We picked it up in a hurry—a waterhaul—and all got a good laugh out of it.

Waiting around in Homer, we visited the museum's exhibition on the spill and got even more frustrated and angry. All the photographs of oiled otters and seabirds, the huge stretches of fouled beaches in the Sound, and the tanker stuck on the rocks. What the hell was going on with this Captain Hazelwood the night he ran *Exxon Valdez* onto Bligh Reef? And how could Exxon have been so unprepared to deal with a spill right there where the tanker traffic was so heavy? Outside the museum we heard more rumors of oil found further up the Inlet, in the worst possible place, between the Kasilof and Kenai rivers. So we were more or less prepared for the announcement that came on the 12th: there would be no fishing through the 17th, and we shouldn't expect further announcements before July 19th. We'd about lost our season. The run was beginning to peak, but there was still a slim chance that we could have some heavy fishing if they opened it on the 20th. We knew that Fish and Game was trying to make the most of the bleak situation, but it was a tough call. If they decided to enforce the "zero tolerance" policy, thus protecting the good name of Alaska salmon from reports of oil-contaminated fish in the market, they risked creating another kind of problem. If the commercial fishery didn't intercept its normal share of this large run of sockeye, the spawning grounds upstream could be overwhelmed. Over-escapement could be just as bad as under-escapement.

After hearing the announcement on the 12th, we decided it was time to get back to Kenai. If there were openings after the 19th, we'd be fishing up there, anyhow; and if they closed it for the rest of the season, we wanted to be ready to get the hell out of there. It took a lot of money to keep the operation going, and the whole situation would be much worse, emotionally, if we just hung around after the closure to lick our wounds and bitch about Exxon. Again, on the run up to Kenai we kept a close lookout but didn't see a single moose turd all the way. And when we began to see quite a few jumpers, from Ninilchik all the way to the mouth of the Kenai, our frustration grew more intense and confused, and we cursed not just Exxon but Fish and Game's "zero tolerance."

The canneries along the river were just marking time, leaving fishermen and cannery workers to watch nervously as more fish entered the river on each tide. UCIDA conducted more meetings in town, providing the latest word from Fish and Game on escapements in the Kasilof and Kenai and on the oil their test boats were finding in the rips. And the UCIDA officers filled us in on Exxon's developing thoughts about how to compensate us. There was a lot of talk about lawsuits, and about the local firm that had represented fishermen after the *Glacier Bay* spill in '87. Fishermen gathered in small groups to commiserate, question Fish and Game's approach to it all, and vent our shared anger.

Again, we tried to keep ourselves busy by making another trip across the Inlet to Kalgin Island, looking for oil and hoping to get another halibut. We were encouraged by not finding any oil on the way, and by catching a twenty-pound halibut in the hole off the north end of the island. It helped to catch something. But when we went ashore and hiked to Packer's Lake we were both encouraged and frustrated to see so many spawning sockeye. From what we saw there and in the mouth of the Kenai, it seemed clear that our fish had escaped damage from the spill. Here they were, already thick—maybe too thick—in the spawning grounds, and we hadn't made a single drift. Later that night, after we ran back to Kenai, again seeing no oil, I drove over to the bluff above the mouth. It was about the end of the flood, and from the bluff we could see all kinds of jumpers streaming into the river. A number of other fishermen had come to check things out, standing with their hands in their pockets and shaking their heads. We were drawn together like refugees. One of them was Harold Wik, who was born and raised in Kenai and had fished the Inlet for over thirty years. A lot had happened to Kenai since he was a kid, he said. He pointed over to a place on the bluff above the first bend just a few hundred yards inside the mouth and told us how he had watched it slowly slough away over the years. The family home he lived in as a kid had a great, windy view from up there near the edge of the bluff and he couldn't remember just how many years ago it was exactly that they had to move out before the bluff wore away right up to their house and it finally began to fall.

When Fish and Game opened the river to the general public for dip-netting salmon, we knew it was probably all over. But you couldn't really hang it up until they gave the final word. For one thing, we didn't know how our eventual settlement with Exxon would be affected if Fish and Game finally gave the drift fleet a shot at the fish and we weren't there to take advantage of it. So, in between fishermen's meetings we did our best to help Fish and Game keep too many fish from making it to the spawning grounds. The river was full of jumpers and anyone with a skiff to drift along the banks could dip-net as many as you could want. We got all we could eat and all we could handle in our little smoke house, and we just hoped that the thousands that were being netted in the river wouldn't go to waste. It's not hard to catch more fish than you can deal with finally, and we all saw people who seemed more excited in catching them than they probably would be in the work of freezing or canning them. The beaches at the mouth were strewn with rotting fishheads and backbones.

No one was really surprised when Fish and Game finally gave us the word on the 19th. The drift gill-net fishery was closed through August the 5th, at least, because oil from *Exxon Valdez* was still being found along the tide rips. According to a "Memorandum of Understanding" between Fish and Game and the Alaska Department of Environmental Conservation, any area would be closed if there was "an appreciable likelihood that gear will be fouled or fish harvest adulterated." In fact, the expected bad news came as a kind of relief, a little like what you might feel when a loved one's protracted suffering finally ends. Later that day I made my last entry in *Ishmael*'s log for 1989: " July 19th. The expected announcement. Main task now, begin claim work. Boat scheduled for lift out tomorrow 6 p.m." Depressed as I was in writing that, it was nothing compared to what I felt three and a half years later when I wrote the last entry I ever made in *Ishmael*'s log:

> *March 22, 1993. After much hesitation, many doubts and questions, considerable soul-searching, and many periods of depression, I agreed to sell Ishmael and my permit. This is hard even to write. What will I do with myself in the summer months after thirty years on Cook Inlet? I'll miss that life and those friends. But the future of Cook Inlet looks very dim for at least the next four years, because of aftereffects of the 1989 Exxon spill and the consequent over-escapement.*

It took a few years before I could see it coming. Even the biologists were slow to realize what had happened. It was clear that Exxon's spilled oil itself had not damaged the Kenai River sockeye. God knows we had *nothing* like the enormous ecological damage the spill caused in Prince William Sound. Rather, Exxon's damage in Cook Inlet was indirect—from Fish and Game's understandable response to the spill, their decision to close the fishery because of the likelihood that harvested fish would be contaminated by oil. Without the usual commercial harvest in '89, too many spawning sockeye produced too many fry for the lake to sustain. The sockeye have evolved an excellent strategy to protect themselves from a disastrous year, some fry spending one year in the parent lake, then returning as four-year-old fish; and the others spending two years in the lake and returning as five-year-old fish. But Fish and Game found only very small numbers of outmigrating smolts for both years and could therefore project only very weak returns in 1993 and 1994. They were also worried that it would take many years for this cycle to renew itself.

As this picture began to emerge in late 1991, and as people began to calculate the risk of further oil spills in the Inlet, after the successive spills of 1987 and 1989, the prices for Cook Inlet drift boats and limited-entry permits began to fall. And now there was a further complication. The production of farm-raised salmon around the world increased dramatically and was beginning to drive down the price of wild salmon. I wanted to continue fishing until 1998, when I would be sixty years old, but now I had to think about protecting my investment in the boat and permit. Todd was about ready to go to college and I was getting closer to retirement from my other career in the university. So, even though I had good seasons during the three years after the spill, despite depressed prices due to the increased market competition from farm-raised fish, I decided to bail out before the poor seasons that were forecast to begin in 1993.

My first season away from the Inlet was hard. As predicted, 1993 was a poor season on the Inlet, justifying my decision to sell out in advance, but I had never spent a summer in the Phoenix heat. Worse, I now found myself in the position of many other university colleagues who tried to make ends meet by teaching summer school. The long classes five days a week left little time for the research and writing I had also planned for the summer months. Most of the students who took these classes were also trying to make ends meet, many by working full time, and I wondered how they could possibly find time to read the assigned material or to write the required papers. It seemed that the university, the students, and I were all pretending that you could cover a normal semester's work in these short summer sessions, and the university and I had decided to take the money and run. As I spent the necessary hours it took to read the too-hastily-written papers, I couldn't help thinking how often I had enjoyed not only the adventure of a good day's fishing on the Inlet but enough income from a single day's catch to equal what I would earn from teaching a whole semester of summer school.

In the meantime, litigation over the spill moved at glacial speed. The *Exxon Valdez* trial did not begin until five years after the spill, in the spring of 1994. The trial itself did not take that long. Jury selection began on May 2, 1994, and on June 13 the jury delivered its verdict that Captain Hazelwood's and Exxon's recklessness had caused the spill. After another month the jury awarded the plaintiffs (thousands of fishermen, cannery workers, and others whose income depended on the affected fisheries) $286,700,000 in compensation, three times what Exxon had offered but only one third of what the plaintiffs had asked for. In reaching this figure the jurors determined that the decline in fish prices had been due not only to the spill but to the growing market competition from farm-raised salmon. Finally, on September 16 the jury awarded the plaintiffs five billion dollars in punitive damages. These were the highest punitive damages ever awarded, but at that time they were roughly equal to only one year's net profit for Exxon. The presiding judge, Russel Holland, upheld the jury's awards, writing that the *Exxon Valdez* spill was the "greatest environmental disaster in United States history and disrupted the lives of tens of thousands of people."

In the course of Exxon's repeated appeals, many plaintiffs have died. The original judgment included a provision charging the corporation a little less than 6 percent interest, but, as the *Anchorage Daily News* wrote on August 4, 1998, "Delay pays. Exxon is earning $90,000 an hour, about $2 million a day or nearly $800 million a year, on the same $5 billion [judgment for punitive damages] as long as the case drags on and the money stays in its coffers. As it stands now, if the appeals linger a couple of more years, Exxon will have earned enough interest alone to pay the $5 billion plus the accrued interest." Good business practices such as this helped lead Exxon to its enviable position in October of 2005, when the company now known as ExxonMobil announced earnings for a single quarter amounting to $9.9 billion, the largest ever recorded by any entity in the history of the world. Over the same period the corporation has played a major role in preventing the USA from joining the Kyoto treaty on climate change.

As part of the "money spill," Exxon was quick to compensate Cook Inlet drift fishermen for the lost season. We all needed it and were all happy to get it quickly, but, like other fishermen, I suppose, I found that my compensation from Exxon, before and after the trial, was about 60 percent of what I had earned in each of the two previous seasons. They still owe me a lot of money, and this doesn't begin to measure the intangible value of my lost way of life in 1989, or the years that I'd planned continue in that way of life. I feel fortunate that I'm not hard pressed for the money they owe me, but many of the plaintiffs are less fortunate. Among those who most need their share of compensation are the cleanup workers who were exposed to several lethal chemicals Exxon used in the clean-up. As Riki Ott explains, the corporation has fought these plaintiffs all the way, easily defeating them in the costly legal arena. Similarly, the corporation has fought every effort by the state and others to reveal the actual volume of oil it spilled in 1989. Even now, most discussions of the spill rely on Exxon's own estimate that it spilled eleven million gallons, but both the State of Alaska and Ott provide data showing that the spill was actually three times that, their conservative estimate being thirty million gallons.

The most infuriating of Exxon's legal tactics is its determination to corrupt scientific studies of the spill—studies seeking to measure the long-term and continuing damage to the marine life of Prince William Sound—and thus minimize its own liability. This is nothing new in corporate America, of course, as Robert F. Kennedy Jr. has shown in his work to restore the Hudson River. With nearly unlimited resources, corporations such as Exxon can easily "buy scientists, university professors and others," as Ott puts it, "to spin counter stories, create public confusion, and stall unfavorable policy changes." One example she cites is Exxon's use of the Freedom of Information Act to disrupt scientific studies that posed a threat to the corporation, by repeatedly demanding "data from the NOAA Auke Bay Lab [in Prince William Sound] on studies still in progress." These studies helped produce what Ott calls a "scientific revolution in our understanding of oil toxicity," showing that, contrary to Exxon's claims, the spilled oil in Prince William Sound continues to cause persistent, long-term damage to marine life.

The long law case over the spill began drawing to a close in February 2008, when the Supreme Court heard the last of Exxon's many appeals. Over the fourteen years since the jury had awarded the plaintiffs $5 billion in punitive damages, that sum was challenged, affirmed, refigured, and finally cut in half by the Ninth Circuit Court of Appeals. And remarks from a number of Supreme Court justices at the final hearing suggested that they were inclined to cut the punitive damages once again. This was no surprise to legal experts such as Jeffrey Rosen, who showed in an article ("Supreme Court, Inc." in *The New York Times Magazine*, March 16, 2008) that the Court has long exhibited a strikingly "pro-business outlook" that seems unlikely to change "anytime soon." Indeed, one of the justices, Samuel Alito, recused himself from participating in the appeal because he owns something like a quarter of a million dollars in Exxon stock. Although this left us plaintiffs with hopes that a four-to-four decision would leave the Ninth Circuit's $2.5 billion judgment intact, we were not quite prepared to hear Chief Justice Roberts' remarks from the bench: pointing out that Exxon's policy had prohibited its captains from drinking on duty, Roberts asked, "What if there is a breach of the corporate policy? *What more can a corporation do*?" (My italics.) The Chief Justice flatly ignored the jury's main point: because Exxon had long known of Joseph Hazelwood's continuing problems as a relapsed alcoholic, the corporation was reckless in waiting until *after* the spill to fire him. Thus, on June 25, 2008, the Court ruled in a five-to-three decision that the punitive damages be cut to $500 million, 10 percent of the original award. The Court took this opportunity, in this unprecedented environmental disaster, to establish a new principle that a ratio of no more than one-to-one between compensatory and punitive damages is appropriate. The day the decision was announced, an e-mail message circulated among Alaskan fishermen with a subject line reading, "SUPREME COURT, INC. KISSES EXXON'S A$$."

Viewing Exxon not as just a personal enemy because of the spill, but as a chief aggressor in corporate America's war to dominate the world economy, I will often drive miles out of my way to avoid pulling into an ExxonMobil station. Of course I know that I am part of the American consumerism that is tied to Exxon and the oil industry in general. Most of our fertilizer is made of oil. It's in the comfortable high-tech gear I wear to hike and in every plastic thing that we don't really need. I burned a lot of diesel in *Ishmael's* big 671, though that is a fairly economical engine. And I'm afraid to look closely at my own retirement investments, mutual funds that probably hold shares in ExxonMobil. Still, I think it is not only possible but necessary to resist Exxon's grip on our culture and the world's environment. I like Ott's advice on how we can all resist Exxon by being more informed and demanding consumers and by being socially responsible in all kinds of ways. One thing I can do is to convey my admiration for the work of writer/activists such as Kennedy, Ott, and Diane Wilson, the one-time shrimp fisherman in Texas whose book *An Unreasonable Woman* tells how she fought the plastics industry and others that polluted her fishing grounds near Matagorda Bay on the Gulf of Mexico.

In my own emotional life it helps me contend with the way I feel about Exxon's vast web of power to focus my thoughts on poor Captain Hazelwood. I do this even as I recognize the romantic futility of it. The fool drove his ship aground on Bligh Reef, but he is less than a pawn in Exxon's wider effort to steer the national course. Even if you could corner Exxon's CEO, hoping to strangle the beast, the oily mass would slip through your fingers and finally taint us all.

So, I'll drive on with my four-cylinder engine, using as little gas as possible and avoiding Exxon or Mobil stations at all cost, suspecting all the while that the gas I do buy is Exxon's anyhow. And I can imagine having a talk with Joe, himself. I have the first word in this conversation.

"Look, can I call you Joe, or do you want to be Captain Hazelwood?"

"Joe's better."

"Good. Well, you know, I've been wanting to talk with you for a long time, ever since it happened. I know you've been through some shit and you must be sick and tired of it. The thing is, I was a fisherman in Cook Inlet, and I went through some shit, too, nothing like what they had in the Sound, but bad enough."

"Hey, think I don't know about all that?"

"I'm sure you do, and I bet you wish you could replay it all, starting about 11:30 that night. I think that's about when Murphy the pilot left the ship after he got you through the Narrows, right?"

"Yeah."

"You know, I've got a lot of respect for your experience as captain on that kind of ship, a thousand feet long, right?" He nods yes. "And ten years as captain. Good record, too, despite the drinking problem. So, what's the deal? *Were* you drunk?"

He looks at me with one eyebrow cocked in disdain and says, "Hey, you know about the trial, OK? That's part of the bullshit. I had some drinks but I wasn't drunk. You know that wasn't the deal, right? But tell me, you never had a drink when you were running that boat of yours?"

"Well, a beer after the last set, and sometimes maybe another one on the run in."

"Right."

"But, what the hell, man, it was your gig. You steered out of the lane to miss the ice and headed it toward Bligh Reef. Then you ordered the turn back into the lane, and then you left the bridge before the helmsman even *began* to make the turn. You're responsible for that god-awful mess."

Gnawing at his lower lip and looking down, "Tell me about it."

"But what do you think? Did the guy you gave it to, the third mate Cousins, did he fuck up? Or the guy at the wheel, Kagan? The guy that didn't make the turn? From what I hear, he wasn't very swift. Was it his fault?"

"I was captain. It's about me, OK?"

I think of the *Titanic* thing, and Joseph Conrad. And I think of Captain Raib in *Far Tortuga*, when his mate Will tells the crew about another old-time captain who lost his ship. Raib laughs, with tears in his eyes, as he tries to ease Will's conscience–"Nemmine, Will. (*in a different voice*) Yah, mon! (*laughs*) Copm Steadman told de men dat mornin dat he had fifty-four years of sea experience. And by noon he had had a sea experience dat were not much use to him, cause he were dead." Hazelwood sits silent, staring off at nothing. His beard is much more neatly trimmed than mine and doesn't hide the clinched jaw.

In a minute he clears his throat and looks back at me. "So. You had, what? something like thirty years running a boat? Thirty-eight footer? Perfect score, right?"

"Yeah, thirty years, and my last boat was a thirty-eight footer," I said, instantly awash with some things I'd rather forget.

Like one time on the grounds when I spotted Jon on a drift and figured I'd run over to see how he was doing. Coming in upwind of him, I saw a hit in his net and decided to make a set off the end of his net. I saw another hit and didn't want to waste any time pulling along side to talk with him, or running around his boat and then on past the other end of his net. I thought I was going slow enough but when I made the turn I couldn't get off the breeze and even when I punched the throttle as hard as I could I ended up bumping the side of his boat with the corner of mine. It was a good thump, no crunching sound or anything, but I still barely cleared his net. In the adrenalin rush I saw Jon run to the side of his boat to see if there was any damage. There wasn't. And in a minute, when Mike gave him a call on the radio to see how he was doing on that drift, Jon said that we'd just had a close call when I came by to check his net. Mike was very kind and asked only, "Did you touch?" There were some other things my deck hands could probably tell you about.

"Well," I finally add, "maybe not a perfect score, but no major mishaps."

"Pretty lucky, huh?"

I'm about to nod in assent . . . but he's gone, and I'm a little relieved. Oddly, I end up wishing he could make a comeback and be captain of ExxonMobil itself, the whole vast gray mass of it. They loved it when he was around to take the heat during the trial. I like to think that he, or any real captain, would put the whole F-ing corporation on the rocks, with every last shareholder–before he'd try to ram the Kyoto Protocol or continue to rip off the sick workers from the cleanup and to deny what really happened in Prince William Sound.

Captain and Crew

WELL, BY "CREW" I MEAN only John, my deck hand at the time. And I admit it's a bit of a stretch to refer to myself as "captain." I remember being uneasily amused when someone first called me that, sometime in the sixties. During those years the whole drift fleet monitored one main frequency on the old marine-band radios, and you could assume that everyone followed the talk. If you called one of your own cannery's tenders, the skipper would call you by your first name. "*Beaver*, this is *Sounion*. Pick me up, Bill?" And Bill would answer, "*Beaver* back. How's it going, Bert?" But if you called another tender, maybe to see about buying fuel or getting a tow, or if you called a tug that was towing a barge and headed your way, the skipper would probably respond to you as "Cap." It seemed odd. There you were, alone on a little thirty-foot boat. What? You're the "captain" instead of the grubby, not very experienced and slightly insecure guy who's running this little operation by the seat of his pants? Years later, after I'd bought a good many marine supplies and attended the Fish Expo, I received advertisements that arrived in impressive envelopes addressed to me as "captain."

Even under different circumstances, when I wielded the full, official authority vested in me by the U.S. Army Reserve, "captain" didn't fit all that easily. Once, serving my annual two weeks' active duty at Fort Ord, I was actually injured in the line of duty as an infantry captain. This was during the years of the Viet Nam War, but I didn't report the injury and have no Purple Heart to show for it. I was simply out of shape and unprepared for the rigors of official duty. Fort Ord was filled with recruits in basic training, and this made it tough on officers. Just walking around the base, or driving onto base, your silver bars were in plain view and every enlisted man would give you a sharp salute. Recruits would often *whip* you a salute, out of a passionate belief in the hierarchy or perhaps only out of fear. You had to salute in return, and, not wanting to show any disrespect to the passionate recruits, I snapped my return salutes with so much force that I tore the rotator cuff in my right shoulder. I had to avoid being seen in uniform.

In my first three years of fishing, Dick and I were partners on *Margaret*, and neither one of us felt like a captain. After that I fished alone for several years and twice took on members of the family as unofficial deck hands, a younger cousin and a stepson. It wasn't until my fourteenth year of fishing, in 1976, that I hired a regular deck hand. John was just thirteen years old then, a skinny little kid whose dad was a fellow professor at the university where I taught. John could barely carry five gallons of water, but it was good to have him aboard. He could take the wheel when I needed to do something else and he was a big help in all kinds of situations where two hands weren't enough. He could hand me a wrench if I was trying to tighten a fitting in an awkward place. He was brave and game and he learned fast. He got seasick the first year, and lacked the strength and experience to be of much help picking fish. But he pitched them into the hold and cleaned the boat after we delivered. He earned the 3 percent share I paid him that first season, and within a few years he learned how to pick fish and hang net. We kept each other company as something like a nephew and uncle. Sometimes, at the end of the season during those first years, I'd take him to the airport for his return flight home, and his eyes would glisten when I thanked him for his work and hugged him goodbye.

John worked with me for ten years, during which time he went on to high school and college. During his high school years he turned out for football and I attended a few games where he saw action as second team quarterback. He used his summer earnings to finance most of his education at Middlebury College, which his dad appreciated, and he pleased me very much by writing a story about our fishing for one of his English classes. I couldn't have had a better deck hand, and my fishing friends envied my good fortune; some of my friends went through a number of different deck hands over the years, sometimes during a single year. But after he graduated and took a full-time job, John could no longer get away for the six to eight weeks' work on the Inlet. John and I are still good friends, but as he grew into manhood, slight tensions sometimes developed between us—mostly the sort of things that might arise between any two people confined with each other on a small boat. But some grew out of the normal interactions between a skipper and deck hand in the gill-net fishery, and only once that I remember did our conflict rise to the level of potential mutiny.

Two people working together on a little boat can get on each other's nerves in any number of ways, even if they're the best of friends. Close quarters in a small cabin, after long hours of hard work. Tense periods of waiting for a break in the weather or for announcements from Fish and Game. Frayed nerves over personal idiosyncrasies. I never had anything to complain about in John's behavior or the way he did his job, but I was a stickler on a few stupid little things and sometimes must have seemed like a real jerk. I would show a *little* impatience or irritation over the way we used paper towels, for example. Paper towels are indispensable on a boat, and we used them for all sorts of things, from cleaning the windows to drying our hands or cleaning up messes. You hate to run out of them. Also, I hated to waste them, partly because the used ones filled our limited space to carry garbage, partly because I didn't want to run out of them, and partly because I just didn't like to waste the trees. At first, if I was in the engine room and asked John to hand me a paper towel to wipe up some oil, he might hand me a wad of them—two or three. He'd see the mess I was dealing with and want to help as much as he could. But I probably didn't hide the impatience in my voice when I'd respond, "I only asked for one!" And I'm sure I must have seemed a little weird whenever I would tear off just part of a paper towel. I hated to use a whole piece when all I needed was just a half or a third of a towel. And unless you tear the towel lengthways, as the roll unwinds, you get an odd-shaped piece that isn't much good for anything. It wasn't the money, but I know I must have seemed like a terrible tightwad. John put up with it.

There were a few other things that probably drove him nuts over the years. I used to show a little irritation if he left the jar of mayonnaise sit out too long, or if he didn't rinse the dishes in hot water. I'd heard in the Army that a whole company or platoon could come down with diarrhea from eating off dishes that hadn't been properly rinsed. I was also a stickler about economizing on our limited fresh water, which made it very hard to rinse the dishes. I was particularly concerned that John should fill our ice chest to the very top before we headed out for a fishing period, because I didn't want our food to spoil. And I remember that John himself helped us safely navigate one potential problem that might have bothered us—how to divide our food. When you're both tired and hungry and there's only one main dish of moderate proportions, it's not easy to divide things fairly. John recommended the method he and his two brothers used in such situations: one person divides and someone else gets first choice. (This excellent method might work in much larger and more important social disagreements, as when Congress is about to pass out tax cuts to the haves and have nots.) In addition to such momentary irritations involving paper towels or fresh water, there were undoubtedly the usual things having to do with personal hygiene or privacy that will test any two people's patience with each other. But aside from this kind of friction in our domestic arrangements, we got along just fine.

In the actual work of fishing, though, the "captain" has to run the show, make the decisions, and give some orders. Even on a little boat with only two people, there's no escaping the old problem of how to wield authority. I was sensitive to this problem from my background of sympathizing with the working man, such as my dad, the union welder, instead of management. And in my study of sea fiction I also appreciated the way that nearly all American writers after Richard Henry Dana favored the common seaman, as opposed to the captain. I affirm the democratic values that Melville celebrated in his characters Ishmael, Jack Chase, and Billy Budd. "When I go to sea," Ishmael tells us, "I go as a simple sailor, right before the mast, plumb down into the forecastle, aloft there to the royal masthead." No matter that the officers "order me about some, and make me jump from spar to spar, like a grasshopper in a May meadow." Of course deck hands on modern gill-netters don't have to go aloft, but they're often ordered about in ways that can easily offend.

So, favoring Ishmael and knowing the many stories of mad or abusive sea captains in American literature, such as Ahab, Vere, or Wolf Larsen, not to mention the dreadful history of mistreated seamen according to *The Red Record*, published by the National Seamen's Union of America in 1895, I was especially intent on treating John with respect. There are no instances of deck hands being flogged in the Cook Inlet fishery, as far as I know, or of being held in chains. The most common offense is for the skipper to yell out orders. But, from the deck hand's point of view, it can be infuriating to have some one bark out orders and verbal abuse. I remember cringing sometimes to hear men yell at deck hands who were their own sons. I don't like remembering doing that once myself, even in circumstances that probably justified it. But skippers in the gill-net fishery are most likely to yell at their deck hands when setting out the net. Running *Ishmael*, I was usually at the wheel on the flying bridge, looking and maneuvering for a place to make a set. Sometimes I'd be in a tight situation, on the edge of a rip, for example, or in competition with other boats to get the net out first and lay claim to a drift. John would stand in the stern, waiting for my signal to throw out the buoy and peel out the net.

With the engine noise and often the waterproof deck speakers blaring fishing reports from other boats, you can't always hear. John stood facing me, waiting for my signal and knowing how to judge when it might come. We kept eye contact and I could signal when to throw it out by jerking up my fist and extended thumb, and everything was cool. But there were hitches. I might be in a close race to a drift and need to get our net in the water *now*! Or, trying to throw the buoy over, John might skip a beat. Or maybe we'd be running in sloppy weather and he'd lose his balance for a second, just enough to slow us down. I'd yell, "Get it overboard!!" Or maybe he'd get the buoy over, but as the net began to unwind off the reel, we'd get a backlash and he couldn't clear it before we started tearing the web. He'd yell out and wave one hand for me to slow down, and I'd back off the throttle and kick it out of gear, waiting for him to get enough slack so he could untangle it and, if it was taking too long, I'd yell at him, "Come on!!" Maybe we already had a little piece of net out and it was getting good hits. I wanted to get the whole thing out, right away, but John was still fighting with the backlash, and I'd yell, "What's the matter?!!"

Being on the bridge, next to the noisy stack, I could never hear what John probably threw back at me at such times, like, "Fuck you, for Christ's sake. I'm doing the best I can!" Some years after I quit fishing, I got a clearer idea from John about what he felt at such times. We were having drinks

at a party about five years after I'd stopped fishing, and John's younger
brother, Mike, was there as well. When John resigned as my deck hand, he
recommended Mike. I followed up on that, and Mike was willing. I hired
him in 1986 and he stayed with me through my last year, in 1992. He
too was an exceptional deck hand and he too used his earnings to finance
most of his college career at Middlebury. Over drinks the two brothers
joked about my having yelled at them from the bridge as they tried to put
out the net. They told of mumbling things to themselves like, "*You* try
putting it out for Christ's sake!" All I could say was, "Yeah, I was probably
an asshole, but I wish you guys could run a boat some time and see if
you could keep your cool." I found myself edging too close for comfort
to Melville's ironic defense of Captain Vere's brash action in *Billy Budd*.
He quotes "a writer whom few know" as apologizing for beleaguered
captains in nautical crises. In sympathy with "the sleepless man on the
bridge," though, this unnamed author remarks that "the greater the fog
the more it imperils the steamer, and speed is put on though at the hazard
of running somebody down." Vere arranges and manipulates an unusually
speedy trial for Billy and then hangs him with equal speed.

John and Mike talked about other situations, and I had to admit that I
must have been a pain in the butt at such times. Early in the morning just
before the fishing period opened, especially as the minutes ticked down
toward the opening, I'd be really keyed up looking for jumpers, hoping
to find them and stay with them, jockeying for position with other boats.
Sometimes we'd hear radio reports of people spotting lots of jumpers,
and we hadn't seen any. If it was raining or if we were taking spray on the
bridge, I couldn't keep my glasses clean enough to see anything and ran
the boat from inside the cabin while Mike stayed on the bridge to look
for jumpers. We had a hatch that opened above the wheel through the
cabin ceiling to the bridge, and we could yell to each other through it, or,
at other times, pass something such as a tide book or maybe a sandwich
up from the cabin to the guy on the bridge. At the party Mike told how
exasperated he got before we made our first set on those mornings. The
minutes were ticking down to opening time, nearby friends were seeing
lots of jumpers, but we hadn't seen a one. I'd yell up through the hatch
to Mike, "Haven't you seen anything? Come on! Keep looking!" At the

party Mike told how he felt the pressure at such times, and, still not seeing any jumpers, got me off his back by yelling out, "There's one over there!" He'd point vaguely to the blank water and yell again, "Over there!" I'd slow down, point the boat in that direction, and waste our time looking for nothing. I was a little surprised to find myself feeling that John would never have done that. It seemed to betray what we had between us, being in the same boat and sharing the catch. Maybe Mike was just ribbing me. He was a terrific deck hand and always gave me the kind of support that skippers need most: the lift of his emotional energy and readiness to do whatever we had to do. You never had to prod Mike or pull him along. I'd been lucky to have him, too, but his story reveals something of the inevitable conflict between skippers and deck hands.

Only one serious disagreement between John and me about how I ran the boat rose to the level of potential mutiny and, given our long record of working together so well, even *potential* mutiny sounds a little melodramatic. The incident developed late one season when we weren't catching much and I was feeling a little pressure to end the poor season with some kind of a flourish. The fish had already hit the beach, and the fleet was scratching for whatever we could find. Some boats always did well at that time of year by fishing the beach above the mouth of the Kenai, but I was never very good at it, or comfortable trying. *Ishmael* drew a foot more water than the boats that did well by getting closer in and, besides, fishing the beach could get a little crowded and combative. The problem was not only how to work around the rocks at low water, but to keep as close as you could to the beach while also keeping the legal distance between your drift net and the beach fishermen's outside set nets. The fish run right along the beach. If you set too far out you won't catch a thing and yet see all kinds of hits in the set nets. The real pros, like the Columbia River fisherman Eddie Hankin were famous for scoring big catches along the beach late in the season. But Eddie was something of an outlaw and could dash close into the beach at slack water, in between the set nets and way inside their outside buoys. He'd make a quick set, wait until the tide began to run hard, and then round haul it and run outside to pick. "Fast Eddie" brought in lots of fish, but he got a few tickets over the years, along with some blasts from a set-netter's shotgun.

I moved in as close as I could that day, right up to what I thought was the legal distance between us and a set-netter's outside net, and we began our drift. I knew how much set-netters hated drifters when they came in close to the beach, but the same thing applies to the competition between drift boats in open water. You're pissed if someone sets too close to you and especially if he sets his net right along yours, "corking" you and intercepting the fish that seem headed to your own net. I was close to this guy's outside net, but definitely not corking him. He was working alone in his aluminum skiff, checking and picking his inside nets. We were seeing very little in our net, no splashing hits and only a few bobbing corks that could have been fish hitting along the lead line, or just the lead line dragging along the bottom. And as he worked away along his net we saw him pick only a few. Getting so few, he was probably pissed to think that we might be intercepting some that were coming toward his net from outside. Before long we started picking up, finding only very few deep fish and trying to figure out where to go next. By then he had finished picking one of his inside nets and, running past his outset net, began to run alongside the far end of our net, about two hundred yards from the boat. He must have seen a low spot in our gear and pulled close to it. And damned if he didn't pick out a nice king that had rolled and tangled in the web, one that looked to be about twenty-five pounds. He cleared it and lifted it into the air for us to see, then dropped it into his skiff, raised and shook a fist at us and then ran on back to his own nets.

"Goddamnit! That's our fish!" I shouted at him, but he was on his way. He knew that we were picking our net and couldn't let go of it to chase after him, and he took his chances that we didn't have a gun aboard. Shots are sometimes fired in such situations. It's a good thing I never carried a gun, because I was pissed at being robbed and might have fired a shot, not at him but in his direction. But as we continued to pick the rest of the net, getting hardly anything at all, I got more and more pissed. I thought about running the boat in to his inside net, where he was picking fish, to give him hell and demand that he give back our king. But even in my angry state I knew how dumb that would have been. He could run circles around us in his skiff. And what could I do? Ding up the wheel and maybe get stuck until the tide came in? But I was determined to do something to get even and stomped around the boat in impotent rage. Finally I decided to run over to his outside net and cut the lines. He'd lose some gear and have a little repair job on his hands. John was pissed, too, but when I yelled at him to grab the butcher knife, I was going to cut the guy's net, he said, "No way!"

"Whataya mean, no way? For Christ's sake! The son of a bitch ripped us off! Come on!"

It looked like John was shaking a little, but he was resolute and said again, steadily, "No way. Not me."

I was now pissed at John, too, but I managed to cool off enough to keep my mouth shut and stormed up to the wheel. I looked back at the guy in the skiff, yelled something that he probably couldn't hear, and gave him the finger—then I threw the boat in gear and pulled away. John and I didn't say much to each other the rest of the day. We made lots of disappointing sets and ended up with very few fish. We might have done better if I hadn't been so bound up in anger, thinking how I could get even with the guy. Maybe I could drive up the beach and find his place, give him hell, maybe even let it come to blows if he didn't back off. When the adrenalin and rage are flowing, you can't just step outside of it all and smile at your temporary insanity. It took a few days before I was cool enough to realize how much I owed John for keeping his wits about him and for daring to resist me when I was in a rage.

Nothing like that had ever come up between us before, and nothing like it ever did again. Before long, John could laugh about it, softly and in a friendly way, and finally I could too. We had two more years together before he took a full-time job and had to quit as deck hand. In his last years we continued to make a hell of a team, and when he resigned we and some other fishermen in our group had a party for him. We baked a salmon on the beach, and someone went into town and bought him an ugly green polyester suit at the Salvation Army, to poke fun at his new identity as a banker. I'm sure he missed the fishing life as he proceeded with his career—the excitement, the relatively big bucks he could earn in so short a time. And maybe the bonds we had forged in our relationship. In the last years he worked for me, he was beginning to stake out his career in business and academia. His senior thesis at Middlebury was titled,

"Japanese Investment in the Alaskan Salmon Industry," and he is now a tenured associate professor of finance at the University of Oregon.

During his last years with me, our talks on the boat sometimes touched on political and economic matters, and we occasionally got into questions that defined our different points of view, I being more liberal than he. If subjects involving social justice came up or, say, the question of raising the minimum wage, I'd sometimes express my views more passionately than might have been appropriate. From a loftier economic point of view, John would politely disagree and in other ways avoid getting into too heated a debate with his boss. With just the two of us on the boat, maybe sitting at the table after dinner, it must have been close quarters for him. But if he ever felt that I came a little too close to bullying him in these discussions, he was very adept at holding his own ground. He would sometimes exasperate me by politely responding, "uh-hunh" to a point I had made, seeming to assent though clearly sticking by his guns.

When I was preparing to sell *Ishmael* and my permit in 1992, John hoped to buy me out. He knew about the grim biological outlook that followed the *Exxon Valdez* spill, but he believed that the Inlet would come back. The trouble was, he was just beginning work on his Ph.D. and, newly married, was looking forward to having kids. He also knew that after three hard years of completing his degree, he would face the uncertainty of finding an academic position and, if he were lucky, fighting the long battle to earn tenure. He couldn't imagine having much free time in his summers to set aside the academic work and run the fishing operation. I understood. But I loved it that he wanted the boat and the opportunity to introduce his kids to that way of life. It would have almost been like keeping it in the family. He wanted it badly enough to spend a lot of time drawing up a complicated offer whereby he would buy me out, and I would continue to fish on a percentage for a few years. But the plan offered me nothing up front and only the prospect of being paid over a period of several years, depending on seasonal earnings. The first three of those years were already clouded by the biologists' projected weak runs. It was a very technical and business-like offer, but it was one I could easily refuse. I would have had to bear all the risk and miss my opportunity to salvage as much as possible from my already depleted thirty-years' investment.

The change of ownership might have made a fitting end to the story of one captain and deck hand. But it would have strained and possibly sunk a relationship that had risen on the good fortunes of the Cook Inlet fishery before the Exxon disaster and before the farmed-fish industry crushed the market for wild salmon.

The Cutting Web

 IT WAS THE BEST THING we'd seen all day—a big splash in the net out toward the end. We both jumped to our feet and John yelled, "Yeah! Big one out by the buoy!" We were on a drift out near the middle rip, off the north end of Chisik Island, and I was wondering whether to pick it up and try someplace else. We'd been drawing blanks all day, and nobody else in our group had found much, either. It had been a cool overcast day, a little sloppy at first, and although I seldom tired of watching the net and the water around us for any sign of life, I was losing my edge. If we moved a little north we'd at least have a shorter run to Kenai that night. I didn't want to be too late getting back to Kenai because Todd was flying out in the morning. It was the end of my time with him for that summer. Our usual practice was that he could spend about half the summer on the boat with me and then return to be with his mom in Phoenix. He had to be back by late July for his mom's birthday, and it was time to get ready for school. He liked being with me in Alaska, but he missed his mom and looked forward to starting the sixth grade. Besides, after a cool gray day like this, and especially after the slop we'd had on the way out and for most of the day, he'd be happy to get off the boat. He'd gotten a little woozy and was still sleeping it off in the bunk.

"Must be a king!" I said to John. "Maybe forty pounds. Let's pick it up and get him before he falls out of the net. I was thinking we ought to make a move anyhow."

"Sounds good," he said, putting on his gloves.

I flicked on the hydraulic switch and moved back to the stern with him. I put my foot on the treadle to start the reel and put on my gloves while John guided in the first few fathoms of net. We weren't expecting to find anything in the first part of the net, and didn't, so we just kept reeling it in, hoping for at least a single or two along the way, but wanting mostly to get the king before he dropped out. It's kind of a big deal to catch a king.

They usually pass through our area earlier in the year and travel along the beach. Our only king so far this year had been a little one of about fifteen pounds. Their heads are too big to go through the red gear's five-and-an-eighth-inch mesh, so they usually just bounce off or break a few meshes and go right on through. Sometimes as you're bringing in the net you'll come to one that's barely caught and when you pull on the net it'll just drop out or break free. If you're lucky and if the net's hanging loose, a king might catch a mesh with its snout or a fin for long enough to get balled up in the web and then you've got it.

The biggest king I ever caught was an eighty-eight pounder, and I hadn't seen it hit. The net was slack and the fish had hit deep, getting itself all wound up in the web near the lead line. When I stepped on the treadle and it came tumbling up over the roller and into the boat, I almost jumped out of my rain gear. Seeing the thing still alive but all wrapped up in the web, like a big cocoon, I wondered about the advice an old timer gave me

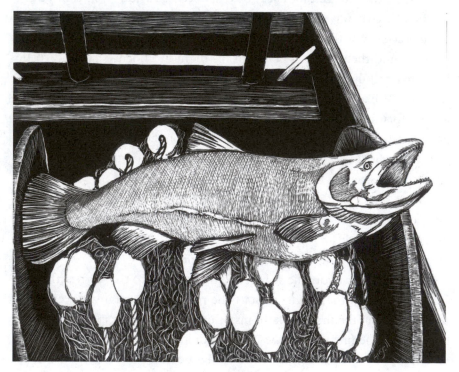

Battle-scarred King Salmon

a long time ago: "If you fall overboard when you're on a drift, swim to your net and hold on to the cork line." I could imagine the web catching on a button or even your nose and knew it wouldn't take much thrashing and rolling around to get yourself as tangled up as that king was. After I got him out of his cocoon I noticed that the magnificent old thing had a big scar along its belly, a long ragged mass of gray tissue that was probably from a close call with an orca or a sea lion.

Picking the first half of the gear, John and I found only a single chum about half way through the net, but we could see some floats jerking up and down out at the end and knew that we still had the king. It only took a few minutes to bring in the remaining bit of net and then we could get glimpses of it at the surface, a good-sized one . . . but then, what? That dorsal fin and the tail! "What is that, a little shark?" John shouted.

"Might be," I said, but I was worried it might be something else. I caught a glimpse that made me think it could be a dolphin or a porpoise. I'd never caught one before and had never heard of anyone who did. Some of our friends had caught big salmon sharks that played hell with their nets, but the only thing I had ever caught besides salmon were a few flounder and some little sharks, spiny dogfish, when we drifted in the shallows along Karluk Reef.

When we got a little closer I saw what it was. I half turned and pounded my fist on the taut cork line. "Oh, no! God*damn*it, John, we caught a little porpoise! We gotta get him out." John didn't say anything, but I glanced at him and saw him wince.

We pulled in some more net until we were as close to it at we could get. It was partly rolled up in the web, but it could still keep itself upright. It was about four feet long, gray on top and grayish white underneath, with a rounded head and nose. It looked tired and frightened, the large eye watching us as we drew nearer, the blowhole puckering and gasping. We began talking to it–"It's OK, it's OK, little guy. We don't want to hurt you. Hold on there. Hold on! We'll get you out!" But we didn't know how to do it. It's a big stretch leaning over between the fairleads and trying to reach down to the water. If we'd been in a skiff we could have pulled close enough to stroke and pat it, anything to reassure it and keep it as calm as possible. Finally edging closer to it, all the time with the

Harbor Porpoise and the Cutting Web

boat moving up and down on the small waves, we reached as far down as possible and could barely touch it. We didn't want to frighten it even more. If it struggled to get away it'd make a worse tangle, and we could already see that it was bleeding around the nose and mouth where the web had cut it. I had my gloves off now and its skin was soft as a child's. We had to get closer but when we pulled on the cork line the web went taut and cut even more. I didn't know if a porpoise could go into shock, but the look in its eyes and the expression on its face scared us. We tried letting go of the cork line, but the web floated around it in wispy swaths and that seemed even worse. If it lurched at all the web would tighten around it. The tips of the tail and the dorsal fin were loosely caught in the mesh.

We didn't know whether it could hear us and tell that we were being as gentle as possible, but at least it wasn't panicking and thrashing about. It actually seemed resigned or patient. When we touched and patted it, it didn't flinch or try to nip at us the way an injured dog might. I hoped it wasn't giving up. The cuts from the web oozed bright red blood that clouded the water, but it looked like they were shallow wounds from when it had hit the net. It just lay in the water, breathing now and then through the puckered hole and letting us do our work. When I touched its belly and sides they felt just like the belly of a dog lying on its back and asking to be petted. Slowly, we managed to push the web aside till it was caught only by a few meshes around its nose and tail. While I leaned over to nudge the web away from its nose, John used the pike pole to loosen the web from the tail. It was almost free and probably could have swum away, but it wasn't struggling at all and seemed almost at ease with what we were doing. But when I pushed the web further from its nose, it sensed that it was time, ducked its head, turned away from the net, swam slowly ahead and then dived down and out of sight in a burst of speed that amazed us.

"Yes!" John and I both shouted at once. I got to my feet on deck and we both stood, shaking, and looking into the water where it had disappeared. We turned and hugged each other, but neither of us could say anything. Finally, I moved to the controls, engaged the reel, and we pulled in the last few fathoms of gear. Normally, with the net aboard after a drift, I'd take the controls at the stern station, steering on toward our next set, but I just stood there. I took off my rain jacket and headed toward the wheel inside the cabin. Before I put it in gear to turn the boat and move on, I stepped down and forward into the bunk area to check on Todd. I wanted to tell him what happened. We'd caught a little porpoise. It was cut by the web, but we got him out and he swam away. Todd was asleep, though, with a peaceful look on his face, as if he was having a pleasant dream, and I didn't want to wake him up.

When he got up later, I tried to tell him what had happened, but I knew there was no way to convey what we'd felt. He was interested and asked a few questions, and then it was time for him to get us something to eat. That had come to be his main job on the boat—cabin boy, getting our food and keeping the galley clean, helping a bit when John cleaned up the boat after we delivered. He had been just eight the first year his mom had let him come to Alaska for two weeks. Before that, when I left for Alaska each summer, I would ask for one of his old socks, to carry in my pocket for good luck. I still have them and the oldest one is a tiny, thin cotton anklet, frayed and stained after all these years. The first year he was on the boat he loved helping to pitch the fish. But a couple of years later he got sick from wading knee-deep in the bloodied, flopping fish, and after that refused to work as a deck hand. I was disappointed at first but soon came not only to accept it but to realize that it was probably best that way. He was only ten years old. I knew of a few cases where boys his age seemed to work well and happily as their fathers' deck hands, but there were many more examples where the strain and sometimes even the bruises showed. I had never worked for my own dad, never had to go with him into his working life as a welder, to clothe myself in the hood or the sooty leather garments he wore, didn't have to endure the long hours of heavy work with the cutting torch and grimy steel plate. Sometimes he asked me to help him work on the car, and I'd lie under it with him to hold a flashlight or hand him a tool. That was mainly just boring, but I remember the tension that arose when he was in a tight spot, needing a certain size wrench, and I couldn't find it quickly enough.

The year after Todd walked away from the mess of bleeding fish, John and I were working in the stern, picking fish as fast as we could. We were getting sucked into a dirty rip and needed someone to pitch fish into the hold while the two of us picked. I yelled back toward the cabin to get Todd's attention, but he didn't respond. I called out a few more times and then ran back into the cabin to get him. "Todd, come on out here. We're in a tight spot and really need your help. Come on, get your rain gear on." Then I rushed back to the net. We were in a little trouble, nothing that posed an immediate danger, but if we got sucked into the rip we'd be picking trash out of the net for hours. Todd didn't appear, and I shouted, "Get out here, damn it! We need your help!" We hustled on and he still didn't come out of the cabin. In a few minutes I stomped back to the cabin and he hadn't budged, and I let out a stream of curses that even now seem justified, under the circumstances—we really needed his help— but he held his ground and refused. I probably said some awful things and must have been a frightful sight. Face and beard flecked with fish scales, shouting in my bloody rain gear. No way. I didn't threaten him but stomped back to continue our work with the net, muttering angrily, while John had the good sense not to say anything. I knew he and others felt that I was spoiling Todd, that he could get away with anything on his dad's boat. He was only eleven then, but I was furious and more exasperated than the lawyer in "Bartleby the Scrivener." Todd hadn't resisted me with Bartleby's meek, "I prefer not to," but he had stopped me in my tracks. Even though I had long been one of the interpreters who believe that Melville condemns the congenial lawyer for muffling his own conscience, it was a few years before I could realize how much courage it took for Todd to face me down that day.

Todd never did develop an interest in working as a deck hand. He was just sixteen the year I sold *Ishmael* and my permit, but even if I'd continued fishing I doubt that he would have ever embraced that life. It's not for everyone—the grime, the blood, rough seas, the exhausting labor. I know how sons chafe—how they *must* chafe—at living within the sphere of any father, much less an especially energetic father, whether he be a corporate lawyer or a minister, a colonel, a fisherman, or a professor. And it was probably fortunate for our relationship that I stopped fishing just before he reached the age when sons most need to assert their independence. I couldn't possibly love him any more as the person he might have become had I pulled him into the fishing life than I do as the person he is now in his thirties.

Though I understand these natural conflicts between fathers and sons, I can't deny my disappointment when Todd entered his teens and asserted his independence, rejecting the thought of being deck hand on *Ishmael*. I loved the idea of our working together as a team, he responding to the same excitement of the hunt and spurred on by his own self-interest, his share of the catch. And it would have been better to keep fishing income within the family, to enlarge the fund for his college education. Sometimes, forgetting my own inclination to identify with my mother more than my father, I foolishly blamed Todd's lack of interest in the fishing life on his mother. She limited the time he could spend with me in Alaska, and I thought she was overly protective. There's more to it than that, of course, extending to the inherent conflicts within our nature as descendants of the primal horde, and to the mysteries of personality formation or the differences between one person's taste in music and another's.

Somehow, though, I had learned enough about the conflicts between fathers and sons to help me accept our differences. Having studied fathers and sons in literature, I knew of Hemingway's trouble with his father and with his own sons, and I saw the tensions in Roethke's "My Papa's Waltz" or Sherwood Anderson's *Windy McPherson's Son*. I remembered that when Henry James, Senior, died, the son quickly and officially removed the "Jr." from his name. I was aware of such conflicts, but I was also caught by the guilt I felt as a divorced father. You might compensate by giving your son too much or, in the limited time you have with him, you might err by intensifying your efforts to influence his life and end by driving him further from you. At the ages of fifteen and sixteen, during our last two years with *Ishmael*, Todd was certainly old enough to be a deck hand, but I was happy that he at least wanted to be cook and cabin boy. At times that too seemed in question, as he began to think of working independently, not in the fish-processing operation, but perhaps as a cook in the cannery's snack shack. Even so, I'm sure that he loved spending his three or four weeks with me in Alaska, partly to escape the Arizona heat and partly because he enjoyed a freer life around the cannery.

He hasn't been back to Alaska since 1992, but I know that that world and our friends and way of life there still affect him. Although he didn't take to the fishing itself, his exposure to that life helped shape his identity. He loves the ocean of tide pools and subsurface life that we've seen together when snorkeling in the Sea of Cortez and the Caribbean. Catching sight of sea turtles below us and swimming into clouds of schooled fish. He was with me, collecting sea shells along the beach with Judith, when I swam with the tiny black fish in the Sea of Cortez, and he kept an aquarium for years. In one of my favorite pictures, he is about nine and stands leaning on an old piling near the Kenai River. Dressed in jeans and fisherman's boots, he has just climbed back up the bank after tumbling down to the river's edge. Behind him *Ishmael* and other boats swing on their anchors in the river below. It is a brilliant day and in the distance Mt. Iliamna rises above Snug Harbor while, to the north, Mt. Redoubt draws the eye past the mouth into the Inlet beyond. I am lost in his smile.

In an earlier photograph, he is only two. We are on the waterfront in Seattle, waiting at the terminal for a ferry to Port Townsend, where I was building *Ishmael*. He's wearing my old Greek fisherman's cap and it covers most of his blond hair. He can hardly wait for the trip to begin. I can't help thinking of our phone conversation years later, when he was twenty-five years older than the boy in the picture. He told me of a bad dream he'd had the night before, when he awoke in distress from my having hounded him about something. He wasn't angry or hurt, only baffled about why it had been so vivid. I think about the day I stormed into the cabin in my own distress, angrily demanding that he put on his rain gear and come help us pitch fish. The web of my fishing life cutting into his. But then a year or so later he told me of another dream, a lovely and mysterious one in which he was swimming in the muddy Kenai River, while spawning salmon—kings, reds, silvers, and pinks—swirled in the water nearby.

Ninety-Two

ARRIVING IN KENAI late that June I expected a hard year. My deck hand Mike had a cast on his broken wrist, and we were worried that he wouldn't be able to pick fish, his most important job. Mt. Spurr was threatening to erupt and we knew that if it popped during the peak of the season we might take a serious hit. There were bad rumors about the shaky market for wild salmon. And this was the year I'd have to decide. Should I sell *Ishmael* and my limited-entry permit or hang in there and risk losing much of my thirty years' investment in the fishery? In the wake of the Exxon spill, Fish and Game biologists were projecting a series of poor runs, beginning in 1993. That prospect had already caused the prices for boats and permits to fall by over 30 percent. I wasn't the only Cook Inlet gill-netter heading into this season with a little anxiety. It would be a good year to remember my motto from *To Have and Have Not*, "You got to have confidence steering."

It was also a year that proved the ambiguous truth, "It ain't over till it's over." Mike's wrist held up during the first two fishing periods, and we knew it would be OK. He could pick fish almost as fast as ever. But we caught only twenty fish on our first day and twenty-five on our second. By the third period we were over the worry about Mt. Spurr, which hadn't spouted any steam for a number of days, and fishing picked up. We caught about two hundred twenty-five reds that day, and when we pulled into Homer that night, we saw Judith waving to us from the beach at Land's End. She had just flown in from Phoenix and we were planning July Fourth get-togethers with friends in Seldovia and Halibut Cove. Two days of play kept our momentum going. We caught about six hundred the next time out and were encouraged to learn that the fleet in general had had a very good day for so early in the season.

After the next fishing period we ran into Kenai for what would be a normal four-day closure, and over that time we busied ourselves with maintenance on the boat and net. We expected the fish to continue moving up the Inlet, and we were keyed up for what should be the biggest week of the season. The night before the next opening I wanted to sharpen our edge with a kind of pre-battle celebration, a trip into Kenai for dinner at Pizza Paradisos. It's got to be the best pizza on the peninsula, and if you go there before or after a fishing period in July, you'll have to share the place with fishermen who might not have found a chance to clean up and put on their best jeans. Our party included Judith, Todd, my nephew Chris, and Mike. Finding the place jammed as usual, we felt lucky to get a table just inside the plate-glass window that opened onto the street.

We were enjoying our drinks and salads, looking forward to the pizza and also a big fishing day in the morning, when we heard some balloons popping somewhere toward the back of the place. Somebody must be having a birthday party, but in place of the expected "Happy Birthday" came screams and shouts to "Get down!" Then absolute silence, some sounds of chairs and tables being moved around, a few more pops and more screams. The five of us ducked down and squeezed together under our small table. A man in the back of the room broke the silence, saying in an oddly calm voice, "I'm going to die tonight." Then a few more shots and screams, and then we heard someone walking toward the front of the restaurant. We relaxed when he walked on out the front door and into the street, but now he had a clear view of us squeezed together underneath our table. We and the others in that part of the restaurant would have been easy targets if he'd wanted to do further harm, but he walked a short distance along the street, and in a minute we heard two shots from a larger gun. The police had arrived and, when he didn't respond to their warnings, took him out with a shotgun. Beyond scaring us half to death, the guy hadn't hurt anyone in the restaurant. He had come to confront a girlfriend who worked there, and she had escaped into a rest room. He died later that night.

The incident left us all shaken and hardly in the frame of mind I hoped we'd be in for the next day's fishing period. When we left the anchorage that morning at 4, I noted in the log that we had "a terrifying experience last night at Pizza Paradisos." Had we gone on to have a bad day, I might have attributed it to our psychological upset, but the whole sequence of events now seems to suggest only that there are no such patterns. You might be in a good or bad frame of mind, or see any number of good or bad omens before a period, but circumstances unfold on the fishing grounds as they will, and you can't always control them. As it turned out, that was our best day of the season. The fish were there, we found them, and through luck and hard work we caught nearly two thousand. We were high boat in our group, but we'd all done well, and it was on our run back into river that evening that one member of the group came on the radio and sang an old Norse whaling song, an eerie and rousing strain. He sang for a couple of minutes and struck a note deep within us all. We were like a pack of wolves after a successful hunt, and the old song reminded me of the moment in *To Have and Have Not* when Harry Morgan felt "what he always felt . . . coming home from a trip": "Above the roar of the motors and the high, slapping rush of the boat through the water he felt a strange, hollow singing in his heart."

We and the rest of the fleet continued to do very well over the next several days. Fish and Game were now convinced that it would be a large run and gave us increased fishing time in order to prevent an over-escapement of reds in the Kenai system. We picked so many fish that I was afraid my hands wouldn't hold up. The hard nylon web tears at your hands, and years of this kind of work leaves gill-netters with not only powerful grips but the telltale thick, gnarled fingers that you can see among fishermen anywhere from Kenai to Corfu. When my hands had given out earlier in the season, I'd hired another deck hand for a couple of periods, but now we were expecting another big day on July 20th.

We were just getting out of the mouth of the river at about 4 a.m. when the engine alarm started blasting its unbearable noise inside the cabin. As usual, I was running the boat while Mike got his sleep. I immediately slowed down, took it out of gear, and then began checking the gauges. Earlier that year I had installed a new water-temperature gauge that was wired to sensors for both the oil pressure and water temperature—just one alarm for both possible problems. But the oil pressure showed normal and the new gauge showed that we were running just a little on the warm side, but at about 190 degrees it was well within the acceptable range.

Sometimes the alarms go off for no discernible reason, so, after checking and finding nothing to be concerned about, I yanked the wire off the alarm horn. I couldn't have stayed inside the cabin with the blaring alarm, and Mike couldn't have slept. We had a long run ahead of us and had to keep going. You can't afford to miss the first set. Mike went back to sleep and I put the boat in gear and headed on south, taking care to keep an eye on the oil pressure and water temperature. I'd have to rewire the alarm horn or buy a new one when we had a day off.

We pressed on and finally made our opening set, but after an hour or so we had only about three hundred reds. That was a disappointing start for what everyone had expected to be a much bigger day. But, as is often the case, we just had to wait it out until the tide began to turn. Not long after slack water everyone in the group began to see a few hits. I checked our oil pressure and water temperature, and both remained unchanged. And on our last drift of the day we had about twelve hundred, which amounted to enough fish-picking to mess up my hands again but also make me not give a damn.

We ended the day not far below Kasilof, and I decided to run into the river there instead of making the longer run to Kenai. There were rumors that Fish and Game would let us fish again tomorrow, and the problem now was how to maneuver with the other boats. Every one had a good load, and we all wanted to deliver our fish as soon as possible. If you're slow getting in line you might not get unloaded til three or four in the morning, and if there's another opening the next day you won't get much rest. In the Cook Inlet fishery and most others there's a race to market at the end of the fishing period, even when there are only average-size catches. Running in, you don't want another boat to pass you and get ahead of you to deliver, and you like to edge ahead of others that seem in direct competition with you–especially if it's one of your fishing friends from the same group. You not only want to catch more fish than your friend, but beat him in to the harbor. This reflects a kind of adolescent competitive spirit among fishermen, but on the other hand, the stakes can run into thousands of dollars if you're too slow to deliver. In fact, the need for speed on the run to deliver is sometimes as important as the need for speed in getting to a school of fish, and for these reasons Cook Inlet gill-netters have become faster and faster in recent years, some being propelled by twin engines of three or four hundred horse power each.

For some reason, I've never been comfortable running a boat at full throttle. With *Margaret*'s little four-cylinder Willys, it didn't make much difference. Her maximum hull speed was a little over six knots, so it didn't make sense to beat the poor engine to death. Running *Sounion*, though, with its big Chrysler V-8, I had good reason to throttle back. The boat would really move out, but I couldn't pack enough fuel to keep it going, and I wasn't a good enough mechanic to take care of it if I pushed it too hard and damaged something. But I think my tendency to hold back has some deeper source, because I still have a recurrent dream where I'm driving a wonderful old car; it's something like a Model T, and was passed on to me from my Grandpa Bender. The old car chugs along well enough in the dream, even on modern freeways, and I keep checking the oil and wondering how long it can hold up. But the dream gets sweaty when I either find that I'm going too fast and can't take my foot off the pedal—there's a kind of paralysis—or find that I can't get the brakes to work. When I try to put on the brakes, the pedal goes clear to the floor and I can barely get it to stop. I keep telling myself that I've got to get a brake job.

I should have had the dream that day when we were approaching the mouth of the Kasilof, because I was a little high, still revved up from our big set just before the closing, and feeling lucky to be among the first boats to make it back in. I was at the wheel on the flying bridge, and just about the time we caught sight of the channel markers we saw our friend Jon coming in just a little to the south of us and angling in at a speed that would make it a close race. As was often the case, we were neck and neck in what we'd caught for the year, and now we were going to have this little race to the outside marker. I could see from Jon's exhaust that he was pushing it as hard as he could. We were both having fun with this, and I punched the throttle to let him know that we still had more to go and that we could easily take him. The boat responded at once and I think Mike and I were even laughing on the bridge, imagining Jon's irritation at seeing us nudge forward with such ease. But then there was an awful spasm, like having the wind knocked out of you, and our exhaust stack suddenly belched out a sickening gray-yellow cloud that soon turned black, and the boat fell back into the water with a kind of sigh. I ran down into the cabin, found it full of smoke, held my breath, threw open the windows, and then stumbled back out on deck, where I cursed myself in a string of insults that did little to clear the air. I'd blown the goddamned engine and we still had about a third of the season to go!

Jon saw the blast of smoke from our exhaust and immediately called on the radio to see if we were OK. We weren't in any trouble, weren't taking on water and didn't have a fire in the engine room, but we were out of business, and before I could ask if he'd swing by to give us a tow in, he'd already turned our way.

You can try to console yourself after such mishaps. You know, "It could've been worse." "Nobody was hurt. It's only an engine." "You're lucky it happened right in the mouth of the river and you had a friend nearby to tow you in." Or, "Hey, man, it's no big deal to burn up an engine. Happens all the time." Right, it's not all that unusual in the fishing business–blowing an engine, or maybe a transmission. You lose some fishing time but do your best to get things fixed up and try to get back on the grounds as soon as you can. But to have done it out of sheer stupidity and have done this to your own boat, the boat that you think of as alive and even part of yourself. It's as though I'd caused an old friend's heart attack or made him have a stroke. The boat all smoked up and helpless, dead in the water. I still cringe to think how I abused *Ishmael,* even though it wasn't a fatal blow, and even though I know of far worse losses. I didn't have to step off *Ishmael* and just leave it there to sink, as Peter Nichols did when he had to abandon his doomed sail boat *Toad* in the Atlantic Ocean. Before he was taken aboard a passing ship, knowing he couldn't leave *Toad* half afloat in the open ocean, he cut an intake hose to send it down.

It took a while for me to figure out just what I had done, and it came down to the new alarm switch on the water-temperature gauge. When I installed it I hadn't known, and the directions hadn't explained, that when you set the gauge for the temperature you want to activate the alarm, the indicator arrow won't go beyond that point even if the engine overheats. I had set the gauge at 190 degrees, the alarm had gone off, and then the arrow stayed there all day, indicating that the engine was running a little hot, but well below the boiling point. A pinhole leak in the heat exchanger had drained too much coolant, and I had burned up the engine. As soon as Jon left us tied to the dock, I called a diesel mechanic, but even before he arrived the next morning to see what could be done, I knew we'd need a complete overhaul. The trouble was, a job like that would take more time than we had left in the season. I'd have to get the boat back to Kenai, where we had facilities to cut through the hold and lift out the engine. I'd then have to truck it to the shop in Anchorage, where the rebuild job would take at least three weeks. The shop would truck it back to Kenai, and their mechanics would have to go there to reinstall it and supervise a trial run. After that, I'd need a fiberglass job to repair the bulkhead between the engine room and the hold. The boat wouldn't be ready to fish till *next* season, and I was now even more uncertain about whether to sell out before the coming slump.

But the problem was what to do *now*. The season had shaped up to be a good one, but it was only the 21st of July and there were maybe two weeks to go. If I quit now, I'd end up with a fair season, even after paying the fifteen to twenty thousand dollars I thought it would take to rebuild the engine. But there was an outside chance that I could find another boat to lease for the rest of the season and catch enough fish to at least pay for the engine. The trouble was, everyone who had a boat was fishing it, and there wasn't any time to put an ad in the paper to try to find one. I heard about one that was in storage nearby, in Kasilof, but it took only a quick trip to see that it wouldn't do. It might have been a workable rig, but it was on blocks in someone's field and hadn't been run for years. I didn't have time to mess with it. The word of my mishap had got around, though, and someone told me of a little boat that a local family already had in the water at Kenai, where they kept it ready as a backup in case their main boat broke down. When I found it and went aboard to check it out, it didn't look very promising. It was a poorly arranged little bowpicker, twenty-eight feet long and powered by a gas-guzzling outdrive. The owner, George, said it would move out, but that you couldn't run it very hard without running out of gas. It could pack about a thousand fish, at most. There was a tiny, uncomfortable little cabin in the stern, but it had a new radar set, a depthfinder, and two radios, one CB and one VHF. Its name was *Inlet Lady*, and the deal was that I could fish it for 20 percent of whatever I caught.

Mike wasn't enthusiastic about going out on the little thing, but I remembered *Margaret*, and although this one was smaller than *Margaret* and not as good a sea boat, it was much faster. Besides, it had a reel and all those electronics, so I could easily get in touch with the owner if something went wrong. It helped that I had thirty years' experience on the Inlet and a good enough reputation as a fisherman to make it worth while for George. We didn't fuss with anything like insurance—George and I just shook hands on the deal, and by late that afternoon Mike and I were aboard *Inlet Lady* headed out the mouth of the Kenai for Kasilof. We'd load our net from *Ishmael* and have time to make it out for an opening the next morning. As we loaded the net and transferred some other gear, boats began coming into the river after the fishing period we had missed, and they had catches of five to eight hundred reds.

When we left the Kasilof at 3:30 the next morning I had reason to believe that our luck might have turned. Fish and Game had given us a seventeen-hour opening, but in a limited area close to shore called the corridor. Normally, I wouldn't have liked being stuck in the corridor, but now I thought that it might keep us from running out of fuel. Also, it was a clear calm day. But we were apprehensive about the new boat. You had to crawl on hands and knees to get into or out of the cabin, and we were expecting some initial confusion in setting the net. The only other bowpicker I had fished was arranged so that you could lay out the net while running forward, using a slotted guide along the rail, but on *Inlet Lady* we had to set the net in reverse. We just needed practice and soon got the knack of it, though we caught very few fish. Then, just after we'd finally found some fish late in the afternoon, we blew a line on the hydraulic steering. We couldn't find a single tool on the boat and so just lay there with our net out, unable to move and creating our own little oil spill. We dispersed it with liquid detergent and scrubbed the deck clean enough that we wouldn't slip off our feet. We tried for two hours to raise

George on a CB channel that he had agreed to monitor. When we finally reached him he was only about five miles away, and while he made his way to us, we started getting hits in the net.

George had the right tools, repaired the hydraulic hose in only a few minutes, and then got back to his own fishing. We picked up our net and were happily surprised to find that we had close to eight hundred fish, mostly reds. We set it again and picked up another two hundred, leaving us with over a thousand for the day. We'd done as well as most of the others in our group. Our fishing from *Inlet Lady* continued in this way until we quit for the season nine days later. We had three more days with catches of a thousand fish, and three with about five hundred. Although the *Lady* held together, we blew another hydraulic line, ran out of fuel three times, and had to be towed in once. Each time, George was standing by on the CB and came to our rescue, happy to do so because we were catching more fish than he was and his 20 percent was adding up to a tidy sum. We missed another day because I'd begun pissing blood from a kidney infection, and had to see a doctor. But when we made it back into the Kenai on the evening of July 31, I noted in the log that the continued fine weather helped us bring in another four hundred reds, which was very good for so late in the season. And I also wrote, "Was this the last day of my career?"

Having quit fishing for the season, I was buoyed as always with the thought of getting back home, even though that meant returning to Phoenix at the height of the muggy monsoon, and the usual disorienting quick change from fisherman to professor, with classes scheduled to begin in three weeks. But, after cleaning up *Inlet Lady* and settling up with George, I was left with the immediate and depressing problem of what to do with *Ishmael*. I arranged for it to be trucked from Kasilof to Kenai, where we blocked it up near the tide flats at the edge of the cannery. Even if I hadn't been confronting the disturbing prospect of letting go of the boat and the fishing life I loved, it would've been hard to deal with the crude surgery that was necessary to remove the engine and send it to Anchorage to be rebuilt. As I cut through the hold with a skill saw, opening it up to the smoked-out oily mess in the engine room, and then disconnected the wires, hoses, shaft, and engine mounts, it all seemed too much like an autopsy. When it was done and the crane lifted out the engine and set it on the truck for Anchorage, the sight of the chaotic empty space where the heart had been left me in one of the most depressed moods I'd ever experienced. Standing on deck above the dangling wires and hoses in the gaping oil-stained space, it didn't help to look up and see the grassy tide flat with Mt. Redoubt rising from across the Inlet in all its old allure.

Call Me

I wish I was a fisherman
Tumbling on the sea
Far away from dry land
And its bitter memories
　　　"Fisherman's Blues," The Waterboys

 BETWEEN AUGUST OF 1992 and March of 1993 I agonized over whether to sell *Ishmael* and my limited-entry permit. I wanted to fish for six more years, until 1998, when I would be sixty years old and Todd would finish college, but Fish and Game's biologists were very pessimistic about projected runs for the next four years. The bad projections sent the prices for Cook Inlet drift boats into free fall, and by the end of March I'd seen enough. I agreed to sell the boat and permit to a fisherman from Homer who knew of the dim biological forecast but still wanted to take the gamble. It helped to know that he owned a small business in Homer that might help him wait out the Exxon slump. We agreed that I would fly up to Kenai and meet him at the boat. I wanted to help acquaint him with *Ishmael*, assure both of us that the newly rebuilt engine was properly installed, and then accompany him on a first run from Kenai to Homer.

Tim, the new owner and now a good friend, helped ease my pain by showing his appreciation of *Ishmael*. Still, after thirty springs of gearing up for the seasons ahead, sustained by the surge of physical and emotional energy from anticipating the season's hunt, I wasn't prepared for the dismal process of cutting loose. Packing my things off the boat, preparing to leave our trailer and summer camp on the bank of the Kenai, and holding a "garage" sale from the back of the pickup, I felt enough self-pity to imagine that I actually knew what it was like to be a homeless person pushing a shopping cart in an urban slum.

Some of my fishing friends tried to keep me on track by telling me how smart I was to sell out before things got worse. Then they'd rush off to finish hanging a net or replace a cutlass bearing before launching their boat on the next high tide. But one old friend gave me the only real help I found that spring. Dreading to let go of the boat, I imagined how much better I'd feel if I only had a model of it. I had seen the very impressive models of fishing boats on display in the Pratt Museum at Homer and even contacted the man who built them. Although he had given up work on such models, the blues note of my appeal seemed to touch him enough to make him at least consider building a model of *Ishmael*. He didn't want to commit to it. Just give him a month or so to think it over.

In the meantime, I walked over to the old Columbia Wards cannery to talk with Thor and say goodbye. He still fished for Wards Cove, as it was now called, and I found him at work on *Cheryl Lynn*, *Ishmael*'s sister. He knew I was selling out and wanted to buy a few tools I was trying to get rid of. When I told him about my talk with the model-builder in Homer, he lit up. That man had been Thor's shop teacher in high school, and in fact had helped inspire Thor to make a model of his own former boat, *Mabel E*. I had seen and admired that model, and then it occurred to me that, of all people, Thor should build the model of *Ishmael*. A practicing architect, he had played a major role in designing our boats. No one else could possibly know *Ishmael* more intimately than he. The idea excited him. He'd been thinking about building a model of *Cheryl Lynn* for himself and for his son Taylor, and, besides, he was anticipating a few years of poor income from fishing. The best part of it was that we made a deal then and there that avoided the exchange of money. I told him that I was trying to sell our trailer, and he happily took the trailer in exchange for the model. Oddly, I had priced the trailer at fifteen hundred dollars, which was exactly the price I'd paid him several years earlier for another, much smaller trailer he wanted to get rid of. Now, needing a place for him and Taylor to live during the fishing seasons, he wanted the trailer, and we shook hands on the deal.

Just the idea of having a model *Ishmael* helped me step off the boat for what I thought would be the last time. It buoyed my spirits when I walked away from the river and helped me get on the plane and off it in Phoenix. That was the first and most difficult of ten long summers. I had learned to love the Sonoran Desert's oceanic expanse, where you can lose yourself—but only in the cooler months. So, for the rest of that summer I remained clinched to my desk, like the landsmen Ishmael describes in *Moby-Dick*. Yet I did find relief in thinking of Darwin and a number of American writers who had turned to his theories in their own efforts to know themselves. I'd have preferred being on the water, swept up in the tidal rhythm of the fishing life, but the Darwin project offered its own excitement, of a drier kind. I soon realized that I was embarked on a kind of long strange trip. It wasn't anything like what Ken Kesey or the Grateful Dead had in mind, but my own trip gave me the pleasure of prodding the academic dead. It was almost amusing to realize how the godlings of literary theory refused to consider Darwinian evolution, especially the theory of sexual selection. Many scholars in the humanities still resemble the Victorians whom F. Scott Fitzgerald chided for shuddering "when they found out what Mr. Darwin was about." Their persistent distaste for evolutionary biology obscures the remarkable fact that many American writers, especially women and African Americans of both sexes, have revered Darwin as a great liberator, comparable to Abraham Lincoln (who was born on the same day as Darwin).

It is not so amusing, However, to contemplate how our culture's fear of Darwin prevents us from embracing the ecological world view that he founded. Pretending that there is no such thing as human nature or "Man's Place in Nature," as T. H. Huxley put it, we cannot know ourselves or understand the ecological crises that threaten our existence. I began to value the American writers who first explored the Darwinian foundations of ecology: Jack London and then John Steinbeck and Aldo Leopold. Their subject brought them into conflict with the same old America that still clear-cuts forests, paves over wetlands, worships the oil-burning internal-combustion engine even as it chokes us to death, and dines on pesticides and farm-raised salmon.

In addition to the rewards I found in academic work on Darwin, there was sustenance in the other academic work of teaching. It could never substitute for the fishing life, not even when friends tried to convince me that I was now mainly a fisher of men, but I never doubted my great fortune in having found that kind of work. I emphasize the work of it, particularly the English teacher's endless labor of reading student papers, yet I always knew that it was a rare privilege to help students discover and appreciate their cultural forbears. Not all students can be coaxed into pushing aside the commercial blare and emptiness of Hollywood and television land, the demeaning show business of the nightly news, or the imperial America of preemptive wars. But many are open-minded and hungry for the companionship to be found in authors who take our humanity seriously. Nothing is so deeply satisfying, even in the fishing life, as acquainting students with their true American "relatives"—those such as Melville, Whitman, Emily Dickinson, or Sherwood Anderson, who address the eternal problems of loneliness and death, sustain our belief in an enduring American spirit, and show us the way. "This is what you shall do," Whitman tells us. "Love the earth and sun and the animals, despise riches, give alms to every one that asks, stand up for the stupid and crazy, devote your income and labor to others, hate tyrants, argue not concerning God, have patience and indulgence toward the people, take off your hat to nothing known or unknown or to any man or number of people. . . ."

Still, cut off from the fishing life, I felt incomplete or troubled by something like the vague itch or irritation that made Poopdeck scratch at his missing fingers. I'd lost the balance that fishing gave to my cerebral existence—the simpler life of staying afloat and finding fish, the excitement and flush of physical strain. Wanting the companionship of old fishing friends, I met up with some on sport-fishing trips to the Sea of Cortez. And feeling the need to have my own boat and be on the water, I bought a twelve-foot fold-up boat, named it "Pip" after Ahab's cabin boy, and spent nights alone fishing for flathead catfish on Arizona's desert lakes. Judith and I twice joined other friends to charter sailboats in the Caribbean, and I sailed with a friend on Lake Huron and from Baltimore to Bermuda. But, whether in the Sea of Cortez, the Aegean, or the Caribbean, I watched the fishing boats. Once, near St. Vincent in the Windward Islands, Miron Griffith, a beautiful young fisherman with impressive dreadlocks sensed my longing and invited me to join him for half a day's fishing from his dugout canoe. My job was to tend the bait fish that swam in the bottom of the dugout. I used a gourd to dip old water from the boat and then removed a plug to let fresh seawater in. We didn't catch anything that day, but Miron shared a ganja dream and told me that his uncle had carved the dugout and sold it to him for the equivalent of four hundred and fifty dollars. His new independence as a fisherman freed him from demeaning work in the tourist trade.

Over the years I maintained my subscription to *Alaska Fisherman's Journal* and checked each issue to track the price of boats and limited-entry permits. I toyed with the idea of buying back into the fishery. Even as I grew old enough to know that it was a younger man's work, I told myself, "Hell, Poopdeck fished till he was eighty," or I imagined hiring two deck hands and running the boat as a "slipper skipper." I could run the operation as others did, more or less from the wheel house, figuring out where to make the next set, talking on the radio, and emerging on deck once in a while in fisherman's slippers to watch the deck hands pick fish. Even if there wasn't enough money in it anymore, I could at least be on the water with old friends and see fish hit the net. I'd think, maybe I *will* do it if Exxon ever stops its endless appeals and coughs up the punitive damages they owe us.

A few trips back to the Inlet over the last several years helped me keep things straight. I had a great time in July of 2000 being on the water again and deckhanding for a day at a time on three old friends' boats. In 2002 a short season's work as Tim's deck hand on *Ishmael* showed me both how much I still loved the fishing life but also how foolish I'd be to attempt an actual comeback. It was another poor season, the price for reds had dropped to fifty cents a pound, and there were plenty of stories about local fishermen falling behind in payments on their boats and permits. Tim told me about some who'd lost their homes and even their marriages from the economic stress. He was sweating the year's payment on his own loan. Still, from my point of view, being free of such economic pressure, it was exciting to be back on *Ishmael*, to get revved up in anticipating the chase, to see hits in the net, and even to feel the physical strain of the work—the long hours, tired back and sore hands, cuts and scrapes. It was good to be working together with Tim for our shared single purpose, to be reconnected in a network of old friends in their own boats, all of us working cooperatively as a group, drawn together on the water in our effort to find the fish even as the individual boats within the group pushed to out-fish the others.

I also found how good it was to make our last drift of the season and head in. Even when I owned *Ishmael* I had celebrated our last drift of the year by throwing back a live fish, a ritual that looked ahead to future seasons. Now I could appreciate how my deck hands John and Mike must have felt at the end of a season. Enthusiasm will wane a bit when it isn't *your* boat and *your* identity. Packing my things off the boat that season I knew that my enthusiasm for the fishing life had waned somewhat because I no longer felt the edge of economic need. Also, feeling the slight strain in knee and back as I stepped from *Ishmael*'s rail down into the skiff, I was quite happy to leave the remaining work to Tim.

Unexpectedly, I also realized that being only the deck hand that season and not having the responsibility to run the operation, I was a bit freer to appreciate the *place* than I had always been. This was particularly so on days between fishing periods. Tim anchored the boat in the Kasilof River, where he sold his fish, and then drove the fifty miles to Homer to be with his family and look after his small business. I stayed on the boat, partly to keep an eye on things but mostly because it was a rare pleasure to do so. My being on the boat gave Tim a little peace of mind because of the Kasilof's high tides. Boats often drag anchor there and one night when Tim was in Homer I helped protect the boat when three gill-netters that were tied together upriver from us dragged down on the ebb. Tim worried that I'd be bored living alone on the boat for two or three days at a time, but I might have been in heaven. Twenty-four years after I built *Ishmael*, and nine years since I last lived and fished on it, the chance simply to be aboard, intimately and alone, with no need to busy myself repairing or maintaining it, was like embracing an old friend you'd thought was lost in the war. And I blinked my eyes in realizing how many times I had anchored in the Kasilof over the years since 1963 and still hadn't taken it in. I would pull into the river, deliver my fish, have dinner, go to bed, and leave on the next day's tide, my attention fixed on the season and its work.

Once, sitting in the cabin, I caught a reflection of my former self. Fish and Game had announced a limited opening that caught most of the

Sandhill Cranes along the Kasilof

drifters by surprise, but a few boats had scrambled to take advantage of it and were heading down river, hoping to cross the bar before low water. Tim was still in Homer, so, like most of the other fishermen, we would be sitting this one out. But my friend John had decided to give it a try. I saw him coming down the river in *Buckwheat*, and when he got close enough I stepped out on deck to wave at him. He didn't see me. It was getting close to low water, he was running fast with the current, keeping an eye on the channel. I saw the tension in his face and shoulders as he stood at the wheel. When he reached for his microphone I knew that he was in touch with the group and that they were caught up in the chase.

But this season I watched from the bridge as the boat fell with the ebb to below the grassy banks and then rose until the mountains on the west side of the Inlet, Mt. Redoubt and Mt. Iliamna, came into view and slowly regained their dominating height. From the bridge at high water I looked over and down on the tide flats, watched sandhill cranes feeding while a coyote eyed them from nearby, and looked into the mud banks below the grassy flats at low water, watching nesting gulls nurture their chicks. During my three weeks here I'd watched the chicks grow. At first the parents sent the nearly helpless hatchlings scurrying to safety beneath the banks, or flew squawking in alarm when the chicks ventured into the current for their first short swims. They soon began to stretch and flap their wings, and take instruction from the adults. As though learning their ABCs of probing for food, they'd follow their parents in mechanical drills back and forth along the silt banks, their heads bent forward in earnest. On each flood a few more sockeye nosed upstream, sometimes jumping two, three, four times. Western sandpipers foraged in the silty mud. Arctic terns hovered over the river or gathered alongshore in groups, keeping their distance from the gulls. One landed on the exhaust stack seven or eight feet from where I sat. I admired its forked tail, delicate orange legs and slender orange beak, black head and masked eyes. It would soon begin its migration, but how could it fly those ten thousand miles?

I went ashore each day to stretch my legs, walking through stands of black spruce that were barely holding on against the infestation of bark beetles. People all over the peninsula were alarmed at how the landscape was being transformed by the beetle kill, some claiming that the spruce forests would die out completely and never return, while others speculated that the infestation was a cyclical phenomenon. The spruce would regenerate, though none of us would live to see it. But one little grove seemed to be doing quite well, just off the road leading to the beach on the north side of the river. A dark, peaceful little grove, it shelters a tiny cemetery that I had never seen. One of the markers reads

> *In Memory of Alex Benson*
> *Native of Sweden, aged 38 years*
> *Died May 6, 1907*

Another reads

> *Harry Mason of Norway*
> *Aged 67 years*
> *Died June 4, 1915*

The writing on others is too dim to read. I wondered what but the salmon could have drawn these men to Kasilof, and where were the much older Native graves?

At the museum in Homer I've seen stone weights and other implements that Cook Inlet Natives used to fish. The Natives, the Scandinavians, and the Nova Scotian, Joshua Slocum, would all recognize our modern gill nets, though they would wonder at their length and especially at the deadly new synthetic materials—the clear nylon web and even less visible monofilament web. If Benson and Mason were gill-netters, they probably fished from boats like those that Joshua Slocum introduced to the area. But what would they make of the modern boats, especially the sleek, forty-foot, high-speed aluminum boats, or the ugly box-like boats that have moved here recently from Bristol Bay, the high-sided ones that are only thirty-two feet long but fourteen to fifteen feet wide, and powered by twin diesels of four hundred horse power each?

Seeing the new boats even from our point of view in 1963, aboard the converted sailboat *Margaret*, Dick and I would have rubbed our eyes. But I wonder whether we and others knew the Inlet more intimately then. I'm sure that the powerful new boats make Cook Inlet seem a much smaller and tamer body of water than it did to us. You can cross it much more quickly now or buck the tide with relative ease—in good weather and if you have the fuel. Nearly all the present-day gill-netters navigate the Inlet with a new kind of electronic certainty, rarely consulting the old paper charts. *Ishmael* still carries the charts I used in the early seventies aboard *Sounion*, but they're rolled up and stored, gathering mildew, beneath one of the bunks. In their place is a new GPS chartplotter, whose small computerized screen shows your position on a scrolling chart, gives your exact coordinates, indicates your ground speed, and shows the course to your destination.

I wouldn't want to do without one of the chartplotters if I were fishing again, any more than I would reject the word processor in favor of my old Underwood portable typewriter. Fishermen today give their precise positions in latitude and longitude, but in the sixties and seventies you'd radio your location to a friend: "I'm about five miles off the island, and Redoubt's right over the high spot on the south end." Before long, your friend might appear on the horizon. Of course that system didn't work at night or in the fog. I remember hearing some pathetic, almost mournful calls, such as, "The white boat to the east of us. This is the boat to the west of you. Can you see us over here?" But one of the most reliable ways to give your position was to spot a boat with a distinctive silhouette, maybe *Bernice M* or *Saint Christina*. If you heard another fisherman say he was catching fish and that *Saint Christina* was about a mile to the west of him, you might be able to stand on top of your cabin and see your way. The most distinctive boat was a stately-looking old sailboat named *Altair*, and if you could spot her silhouette you always felt that you knew where you were, as you might in seeing the north star at night. *Altair* now sits with a number of other old boats on the Kachemak Bay side of the Homer spit. Some of the aging boats display faded signs in their cabin windows, indicating that the owners are possibly still alive and hoping to sell the old vessels. But *Altair* is beyond that. Several of her grey, weathered planks have sprung loose and fallen away, letting the light pass through.

I can't watch *Altair* slowly falling apart on the Spit without feeling that the fishery itself is in decline, even though I know that hundreds of gill-netters still make a go of it. I've given up tracking the prices of boats and permits with an eye toward getting back into it. The fishing life as I knew it is gone. But even today the Cook Inlet gill-net fishery is still good enough to excite a number of old friends as they look forward to each new season. They worry mainly that the farm-raised salmon industry will drive them out of business, but hope that the public will learn about the real costs of aquaculture and the value of wild salmon. The ecological risks of aquaculture comprise only a small part of the larger problem we humans have created for ourselves. Still refusing to think seriously about "Man's Place in Nature," most of us ignore the old problem of overpopulation, and even many with scientific credentials absolutely deny that it threatens our existence. We too easily forget that the sea cradles all life on earth. The most powerful country in the world refuses to acknowledge the threat of global warming, and many nations join in degrading the ocean environment through industrial overfishing and chemical or biological pollution. Maybe we'll become smart enough to develop and practice only sustainable forms of aquaculture, but those of us in "developed" countries must learn to curb our appetites for carnivorous species such as shrimp and salmon, in favor of herbivorous fish or filter-feeding oysters. Among the many problems associated with shrimp and salmon farming—

environmental degradation, the use of antibiotics and other drugs, and the corruption of wild genetic stocks—the most serious is that it takes about three pounds of wild ocean fish (in the form of fish meal and fish oil) to produce one pound of farmed shrimp or salmon.

Although some Cook Inlet gill-netters, as well as others in Bristol Bay or the Copper River, are being driven out of business by farm-raised salmon, the wild fish themselves seem in good shape for the foreseeable future. According to Mark Willette, now serving as Fish and Game's area research biologist for upper Cook Inlet salmon and herring, biologists acknowledge that escaped farm-raised salmon might eventually infect the genetic stocks of wild salmon. Aside from that, they are fairly optimistic that both the resource and the fishery can be sustained. Their main concern is the growing human population in that part of Alaska. This complicates the agency's efforts to manage the resource, particularly as they must balance the conflicting political interests of the commercial fishery and the sport-fishing industry for shares of harvestable fish. The biologists also worry about habitat damage by the increasing number of sport fishermen who trample the banks of the spawning streams, and by increasing amounts of hydrocarbon pollution from outboard motors.

Beyond that, they are concerned about a second and more ominous threat to the Cook Inlet sockeye—global warming. The two main rearing lakes on the Kenai River, Kenai Lake and Skilak Lake, are fed by glacial streams. As the glaciers melt more rapidly, pouring greater volumes of silt into the lakes, the water is becoming more turbid. The increased turbidity prevents sunlight from penetrating to the depths that it did when biologists began measuring turbidity in the 1980s, and this (the reduced euphotic zone) has brought an alarming decrease in the growth of microscopic plant life that supports the copepods that feed the fry. Fish and Game has recorded marked reductions in the biomass of copepods in these lakes and, consequently, in the weights of fry. Biologists also worry about other threats to salmon that might be related to global warming, such as the fungus, *Ichthyophonus hoferi*, that has inflicted serious damage to the Yukon River chinook run in recent years.

In view of the political, economic, and ecological problems that cloud the Inlet's future, the question arises whether we should allow the commercial fishery to continue at all. With the depressing record of so many fish stocks now threatened or already driven to near extinction around the world, it is tempting to say enough! Over the last one hundred and fifty years we have come a long way in our thinking about the human role in the extinction of species. When Melville wondered whether nineteenth-century whalers would drive the sperm whale to extinction, he acknowledged that the "wondrous extermination" of the buffalo was caused by "the spear of man," but he believed that the whale was a special case. Repeatedly singing its praise as the greatest of God's creations, he believed that it would take refuge in polar seas, where it would remain "in a charmed circle of everlasting December" and evade "all pursuit from man." And writing in 1883, even T. H. Huxley (author of "Man's Place in Nature") thought that the cod were not threatened by extinction because "any tendency to over-fishing will meet with its natural check in the diminution of supply." But by 1975 Peter Matthiessen offered a much darker view of ocean life in *Far Tortuga*, his remarkable novel about the green turtle fishery in the fouled Caribbean. We do finally know, don't we? that we humans can wipe out almost any species. The North American bison, the passenger pigeon, old-growth forests around the world, the green turtle, the Atlantic cod, the Atlantic salmon—and the sockeye?

Had we not been so slow to discover and finally acknowledge the field of ecology and our key role in promoting biodiversity and protecting the environment, we might have found ways to manage resources such as the Atlantic cod and salmon in sustainable ways. Although we are a little smarter now and know that we must manage such resources for sustainability, the commercial-fishing industry in general will probably continue to protect its own interests and resist efforts to manage it. According to its cover, the leading industry journal, *National Fisherman*, promotes "Informed Fisherman. Profitable Fisheries. Sustainable Fish," but its central purpose is made clear in a featured column by Nils Stolpe, whom it identifies as "a longtime consultant to the commercial fishing industry." In the April 2006 number, for example, Stolpe complains about "all the fisheries management inflicted on fishermen" and asks, "Are we on the verge of 'managing' our commercial and recreational fishermen right off the water . . . ?" His point here is that the spiny dogfish and many protected species such as dolphin and harbor seals consume large quantities of fish stocks that we are trying to manage. "It's time we realized it's not all about fishing," he argues. "With so much emphasis on ecosystem management," we should address these other factors as well.

For my own part, I applaud the Alaska Department of Fish and Game's impressive record in managing its various sockeye and other salmon populations for sustainability. The problem is how to keep it going. Fish and Game can't manage the larger issues such as the threat of global warming, or even the large political problems regarding habitat preservation. But with a little luck it can assure that we do not destroy the Alaskan salmon runs by overfishing. As long as the gill-net fishery on Cook Inlet is prevented from harvesting more sockeye than are needed to sustain the resource, we should embrace it as a way of life. It is an invigorating way of life and a true way of life. It acknowledges our place in nature as direct participants in the bloody reality that we must kill to eat. I do not know how present-day Americans such as myself can ever make amends for our nation's history of destroying the Native American cultures that were based on the Pacific salmon. My only response to this haunting question is to suggest that our first national priority should be to preserve the salmon runs; the next should be to assure that Native Americans seeking to perpetuate their cultural identity as fishermen be the last to be barred from that way of life. I celebrate the fisherman who knows that he can despoil his part of the earth, and who welcomes the social restraints that can protect it. The fisherman who joins in and relishes the life hunt, knowing what it is to be alive in this elemental sense and, above all, who honors the life that is in him and that he takes.

The sea that began to emerge in my imagination when I heard the radio call to "all the ships at sea" eventually drew me to Cook Inlet and helped me appreciate the ocean world of *Moby-Dick*. I became one of the "mortal men fixed in ocean reveries" that Ishmael imagined and I understood his belief that "meditation and water are wedded for ever." By the time Melville published his last sea book (*John Marr and Other Sailors*), he had taken a devastating spiritual blow from the Darwinian revolution and lost his earlier passion for natural theology and "the ungraspable phantom of life." Still, he paid tribute to "the sea, and the blue water of it." Only once in my life—sailing across the Gulf Stream to Bermuda—have I felt the astonishing truth and pull of the blue water. I knew nothing of it in my years on Cook Inlet, and nothing that resembled the high-seas adventures of men like Dana or Joshua Slocum. But even on that silty finger of the Pacific Ocean many men and women are still drawn to the fishing life as with the force of tides.

I've been looking at Thor's model of *Ishmael* and, in a dream, remember where I've stored my old marine-band radio—in the back, there, under the boots and the Grundens rain gear. I power it up. The light comes on and there's faint static. I dial in one of the old frequencies, 2638, then key the mike and give it a try: "*Ishmael*, Ishmael. Do you read? . . . Call me."